Optimal Regulation

Optimal Regulation

The Economic Theory of Natural Monopoly

Kenneth E. Train

The MIT Press
Cambridge, Massachusetts
London, England

Second printing, 1992
© 1991 Massachusetts Institute of Technology

This book was set in Palatino by The Maple-Vail Book Manufacturing Group and
printed and bound in the United States of America.

Library of Congress Cataloging-in-Publication Data

Train, Kenneth.
    Optimal regulation : the economic theory of natural monopoly / by
Kenneth E. Train.
        p.   cm.
    Includes bibliographical references and index.
    ISBN 0-262-20084-8
    1. Monopolies.   2. Trade regulation.   I. Title.   II. Title:
Natural monopoly.
    HD2757.2.T73   1991
    338.8'2—dc20   91-4361
                                                                                    CIP

Instructors who assign this book for a course can obtain copies of
problem sets and exams by writing to the author at the Department
of Economics, University of California, Berkeley, CA 94720.

For John

Contents

Preface   xi

Introduction: The Economic Rationale and Task of
Regulation   1
I.1 Motivation   1
I.2 Characteristics of a Natural Monopoly   5
I.3 Welfare Concepts with Natural Monopoly   12

1 The Averch-Johnson Model of Rate-of-Return Regulation   19
1.1 Purpose   19
1.2 Behavior of the Unregulated Firm   22
1.3 Rate-of-Return Regulation   33
1.4 Behavior of the Regulated Firm   35
1.5 Empirical Evidence on the A-J Effect   61

2 Regulatory Mechanisms to Induce Optimal Outcomes for One-
Product Natural Monopolies   69
2.1 Introduction   69
2.2 Return-on-Output Regulation   72
2.3 Return-on-Sales Regulation   80
2.4 Return-on-Cost Regulation   81
2.5 Price Discrimination   88

3 The A-J Model under Uncertainty   95
3.1 Motivation   95
3.2 Behavior of the Unregulated Firm under Uncertainty   98
3.3 Behavior of the Firm Facing Uncertainty under Rate-of-
Return Regulation   101
3.4 Results   104

4 Ramsey Prices   115
4.1 Motivation   115
4.2 Description of the Ramsey Rule   117
4.3 A More Rigorous Derivation of the Ramsey Rule   125
4.4 Finding the Ramsey Prices   135
4.5 Relaxation of Assumptions   138
4.6 An Application of the Ramsey Rule: Transit Pricing   140

5 The Vogelsang-Finsinger Mechanism   147
5.1 Introduction   147
5.2 The V-F Mechanism   149
5.3 Demonstration for a One-Good Firm   152
5.4 Demonstration for a Two-Good Firm   156
5.5 Strategic Issues in V-F Regulation   164

6 Surplus Subsidy Schemes   177
6.1 Introduction   177
6.2 Loeb and Magat   179
6.3 Sappington and Sibley: The Incremental Subsidy Surplus
   (ISS) Scheme   182
6.4 Finsinger and Vogelsang: An Approximate Incremental
   Surplus Subsidy (AISS) Scheme   187

7 Multipart Tariffs   191
7.1 Introduction and Definitions   191
7.2 Access/Usage Tariffs   197
7.3 Block Rates   213

8 Time-of-Use Prices and Riordan's Mechanism   239
8.1 Motivation   239
8.2 First-Best TOU Prices Given Capacity   241
8.3 Riordan's Mechanism for Inducing First-Best TOU Prices
   with Fixed Capacity   247
8.4 Optimal Capacity   252
8.5 Riordan's Mechanism Applied to Capacity Choice   258

9 Self-Selecting Tariffs and Sibley's Mechanism   263
9.1 Introduction   263
9.2 Customer Choice among Tariffs under Traditional
   Assumptions   267

9.3 Equivalence to Multipart Tariffs   270

9.4 Welfare Implications of Self-Selecting Tariffs   273

9.5 An Application of Self-Selecting Tariffs   282

9.6 Sibley's Mechanism   284

9.7 Welfare Implications When Standard Assumptions Are
    Inappropriate   291

10 Optimality without Regulation   297

10.1 Introduction   297

10.2 Auctioning the Monopoly Franchise   299

10.3 Contestability   303

10.4 Sustainable Prices in a Contestable Market   306

10.5 Market Forces versus Regulation for a Natural
     Monopoly   314

Appendix: Price Caps   317

A.1 One-Output Firm in a Fully Static World   319

A.2 Multi-Output Firm in a Fully Static World   323

A.3 Demand, Costs, and the Price-Cap Change over Time   325

References   329

Index   335

Preface

Over the last thirty years, and especially during the last ten, the field of optimal regulation has emerged as a fairly unified body of thought with commonly accepted objectives and approaches. Stated most broadly, the problem that the field addresses is how to induce firms in noncompetitive markets to act in a way that is compatible with social goals. The task is complicated by a basic informational asymmetry: regulators usually have far less information about the costs and demand conditions facing the firms they regulate than do the firms themselves. Regulatory mechanisms must be established, therefore, that induce firms to produce the optimal output with the optimal inputs—but without the regulator knowing what these quantities are beforehand. Prerequisite to this task, of course, is the issue of what exactly constitutes "optimality" in each particular situation.

These questions have spawned an extensive literature. Taken as a whole, this literature tells an interesting and persuasive story. My motivation for writing this book was to tell this story, and to do so in a way that is accessible to a wider audience than the original literature. As an outline of the book, I give a summary of the story here.

Overview

In 1962, Averch and Johnson proposed a powerful method for examining the effects of regulation on the behavior of firms. They showed that the type of regulation most commonly used in the United States—rate-of-return regulation—induces firms to use inputs inefficiently. Baumol and Klevorick (1970), Bailey (1973), Das (1980), and numerous others clarified and extended this analysis, while reinforcing the basic conclusion. Empirical work showed that in many cases the inefficiency induced by rate-of-return regulation can be quite costly to consumers, who bear these costs through their bills.

This finding gave rise to the need for other regulatory procedures that do not provide firms with an incentive to be inefficient. Creative proposals have been numerous. For situations in which a natural monopoly can be subsidized, regulatory procedures have been developed that induce the firm, in equilibrium, to price at marginal cost and use the cost-minimizing input mix. Examples include the "incremental surplus subsidy scheme" of Sappington and Sibley (1988), which requires that the regulator have information on demand but not costs, and a variant on this scheme proposed by Finsinger and Vogelsang (1985) that obtains optimality more slowly but does not require that the regulator have demand information.

When the natural monopoly cannot be subsidized, the question arises of what constitutes optimality, because pricing at marginal cost results in the firm losing money. This issue was resolved by, for example, Baumol and Bradford (1970). The optimality conditions are equivalent to those proposed much earlier by Ramsey (1927) in a different context. Consequently, the term "Ramsey prices" is used to denote optimality for nonsubsidized natural monopolies.

Vogelsang and Finsinger (1979) proposed a regulatory procedure that induces a nonsubsidized firm to charge Ramsey prices and produce efficiently in equilibrium. Under this procedure the regulator uses information on the firm's observed costs and output in one time period (say, a year) to constrain the firm's pricing choices in the following period. Over time, the firm moves to the Ramsey prices. This proposal raises a host of strategic issues for the firm. Sappington (1980) pointed out, for example, that the firm might, under certain circumstances, have an incentive to waste inputs in each period prior to reaching equilibrium as a means of manipulating the regulator into allowing higher prices in the next period. For the same reason, the firm might have an incentive to misreport its costs, reporting higher costs to the regulator than are actually incurred. Baron and Besanko (1984), Townsend (1979), and others developed optimal methods for auditing the costs of the firm to prevent or reduce the extent of misreporting.

A variety of different billing algorithms, called tariffs, have been used by regulated firms for charging their customers. Under time-of-use pricing, for example, the customer is charged a different price at different times of the day, with price being higher, presumably, in the "peak" periods of the day when demand is high and capacity is strained. Multipart tariffs are another example; under these, the customer might be charged one price for consumption up to a certain level and then another price for consumption beyond this level. Some regulated firms in fact offer a variety of tariffs and let the customer choose the tariff under which to be billed. For example, a firm might offer both time-of-use prices and non-time-differentiated prices, with the customer signing up beforehand for one or the other. These tariffs are called self-selecting, because the customer selects among them.

Various authors have shown that each of these types of tariff situations has the potential to increase social welfare, at least under certain circumstances. And regulatory procedures have been developed to exploit this fact. Boiteux (1960), Williamson (1966) and others identified the optimal time-of-use prices. Then Riordan (1984) proposed a method to induce firms to choose these prices without the regulator knowing the firm's demand in each period. Willig (1978) and Panzar (1977) showed that multipart and self-selecting tariffs can be designed that benefit some customers and the firm without hurting any other customers. Sibley (1989) proposed a regulatory procedure, similar to the incremental surplus subsidy scheme mentioned above, that uses self-selecting tariffs in a way that induces the firm to move to optimality in equilibrium without the regulator having information on either costs or demand and without the need for direct subsidy.

Methods of regulation have even been proposed that essentially eliminate the need for regulation. These methods are based on the notion that competition among numerous firms that *could* produce in an industry induces optimality even if, as in a natural monopoly situation, only one firm actually *does* produce. Demsetz (1968) and Posner (1972) suggested that the monopoly franchise (that is, the right to be the monopolist) be auctioned off to the firm that offers to charge the lowest per-unit price. Under certain conditions (such as many noncolluding bidders), this auction results in the lowest possible price for consumers. No regulation is needed beyond the holding of the auction, at least in a static world. Baumol, Panzar, and Willig (1982) formalized and generalized the concept of competition among potential producers. In their theory of contestability, the threat of entry by new, competing firms regulates a monopolist effectively. That is, instead of establishing a regulatory procedure that induces optimality, the regulator can simply allow entry of competing firms into the industry. If certain conditions are met, this entry—or, more exactly, the *threat* of entry—induces the existing monopolist to act optimally. Though allowed, entry does not actually occur as long as the monopolist behaves optimally; therefore the cost advantages of having only one firm are retained.

Purpose of the Book

Stated in this concise fashion, the field emerges as possessing a definite unity. The individual topics are interesting in themselves and as they relate to other topics. For my courses on regulation, I have found a way to present these topics meaningfully in lecture. However, I— and more directly, my students—have been frustrated in my attempt to provide useful and adequate reading material. No textbook covers this material as a whole, and some of the most important and most recent concepts are not included, to my knowledge, in any text. I have been assigning the original articles. However, most undergraduates, and some graduates, lack the technical background necessary to read them and quit trying after a few incursions. Even those students who can read the articles have difficulty connecting the concepts from different papers because terminology and the framework for analysis vary greatly. I wrote this book to provide a textbook for my courses on regulation, both undergraduate and graduate. I imagine, and hope, that other instructors will find the text useful also.

I have attempted to present the material in a form that elucidates the driving forces behind the results while using the minimum technical apparatus. The text is intended to be readable by upper-level undergraduates and graduates with strong, but not necessarily highly mathematical, training in microeconomics. Calculus is used only once,[1] and this one derivation can be skipped or skimmed without substantial loss because the concepts that motivate it are discussed nonmathematically. Algebra and basic logic are used extensively, along with graphical devices.

For graduate students especially, and for any reader wanting more complete rigor, the original articles still serve as the source and should be read. I have found, however, that even students with strong technical training often follow the arguments in the articles more readily, and with greater insight into the economics behind the mathematics, after going through the analyses in this book.

---

1. For result 5 of chapter 3. I have not been able to devise a noncalculus demonstration of this result and would be grateful to readers for suggestions.

Introduction:
The Economic Rationale
and Task of Regulation

I.1 Motivation

Competition, in theory if not always in practice, is nothing short of a miracle. Each firm tries to make as much profit as possible without regard (at least directly) for social welfare. Each consumer maximizes its own utility, ignoring others. Yet the result of all this selfishness is that social welfare, in the Pareto sense, becomes as great as possible. This consistency of private goals with social goals—the existence of this "invisible hand" that molds privately motivated actions into socially desirable outcomes—serves as the basis for much of economics as a field of thought and, to a great extent, provides the rationale for "free" markets.

To work, competition requires certain conditions. Most important, the market must contain many firms with none dominant, allow free entry and exit, and exhibit no externalities.[1] Unfortunately, these conditions cannot always be met. Intervention in the market is often required to ensure that the pursuit of profit does not conflict with social welfare. Natural monopoly is the classic case. Loosely defined, a natural monopoly exists when the costs of production are such that it is less expensive for market demand to be met with one firm than with more than one. In this situation it is optimal, from a cost perspective, to have only one firm. More fundamentally, a condition required for competition (that is, numerous firms) conflicts with the attainment of the benefits of competition (namely, production at lowest possible cost, which requires one firm).

---

1. Contestability theory suggests that having many firms is not necessarily required for optimality, as long as entry and exit are sufficiently "free." This theory and its implications for regulation are discussed in chapter 10.

In such cases, regulation becomes important. The purpose of regulation is to ensure socially desirable outcomes when competition cannot be relied upon to achieve them. Regulation replaces the invisible hand of competition with direct intervention—with a visible hand, so to speak.

The term "visible hand" is actually quite appropriate. The regulator must work *through* the firm, inducing the firm to produce the desired outcome. If the regulator had complete information, it could simply mandate the optimal outcome, ordering the regulated firm to produce a certain amount of output with a particular set of inputs and sell the output at a specified price. Usually, however, the regulator does not have sufficient information to determine these levels. For example, the regulator usually does not know the firm's cost function and hence does not know whether the firm is pricing at marginal cost or producing with the most efficient input combination. Instead, the regulator must establish incentive schemes or other methods of regulation that induce the firm, through its desire to earn profits, to attain the socially optimal outcome. In this sense, the regulator applies a hand that molds the private profit motive into socially optimal outcomes, just as competition does. The hand is visible rather than invisible, but the molding function is the same.

The central issue of regulatory economics is the design of mechanisms that regulators can apply to induce firms to achieve optimal outcomes. In any particular setting, this issue consists of two tasks. First, the optimal outcome must be characterized. In many situations, this characterization is a direct application of concepts from microeconomic theory, such as that price equals marginal cost at the optimal output level. However, optimality is not always so easily identified. For example, when marginal-cost pricing results in the firm losing money, what is optimal? The firm cannot lose money indefinitely and stay in business.

Once the optimal outcome is characterized, the second task is to design a regulatory mechanism that induces the regulated firm to act in a way that results in this outcome. The firm is (usually) assumed to act so as to maximize its own profits.[2] Under an effective regulatory

---

2. Researchers have also examined regulatory mechanisms under the assumption that firms maximize something other than profit, such as revenue, output, rate of return to shareholders' equity, or a composite of variables. Seminal studies include Kafoglis 1969, Bailey and Malone 1970, Zajac 1970, and Bailey 1973. As Baumol and Klevorick (1970) point out, the analysis proceeds exactly as under profit maximization, only with a different maximand.

mechanism, the firm obtains greater profit when it chooses the optimal output, prices, and inputs than at any other level of these variables. That is, effective regulation establishes a situation in which the outcome that is socially optimal also generates the most profit for the firm, such that the firm chooses it voluntarily.[3] Creating this consistency between social welfare maximization and the firm's profit maximization is the crux of regulatory economics.[4]

In this book we concentrate on the regulation of natural monopoly. There are several reasons for this restriction. First, competition is clearly inappropriate in these situations, so that the introduction of a visible hand is warranted.[5] Second, there is only one firm to consider, so that interactions among firms do not complicate the analysis.[6] Third, and perhaps most important, public utilities, which are usually natural monopolies, play an essential role in the nation's economy and constitute one of the most prevalent settings for regulation in the country. Electricity, natural gas, local phone service, waste disposal, cable television, and many other goods and services are provided by public utilities subject to regulation by local or state agencies.

Although the book concentrates on natural monopolies, the prin-

---

3. Profits in the optimal outcome need not be large to induce the firm to choose this outcome: they only must exceed profits at each other outcome. For example, it is possible, as demonstrated in the ensuing chapters, to establish regulatory mechanisms under which the firm just breaks even if it chooses the optimal outcome and loses money at any other outcome. Under these mechanisms, the firm's profits are higher in the optimal outcome than any other (because zero is greater than any negative number), but profits are still as low as possible for the firm to remain solvent.
4. The issue of how to regulate a natural monopoly is one case of a broader class of problems that is referred to generically in the literature as the "principal-agent problem." In problems of this kind, the principal must act through the agent, who has more information than the principal. A mechanism that the principal uses to activate the agent is called "incentive compatible" if the mechanism induces the agent to report information truthfully to the principal. Such a mechanism establishes incentives for the agent that make the goals of the agent consistent with those of the principal—hence the term "incentive compatible." In our context, the development of optimal regulatory procedures is equivalent to the development of incentive compatible mechanisms. If the firm reports all information on costs and demand truthfully, the regulator can determine the optimal prices, output, and inputs and mandate the firm to choose them. In this book we use terms that are descriptive of the specific case of natural monopoly, namely, "the regulator," "the firm," and "optimal regulatory procedures" for "the principal," "the agent," and "incentive compatible mechanisms," respectively.
5. Actually, chapter 10 describes conditions under which a regulator need not intervene directly in order to attain optimality, even with a natural monopoly. However, in these situations, the regulator must still perform some functions to ensure that the conditions are maintained. These functions are in themselves a form of intervention, though indirect.
6. Interactions among firms become relevant if entry is allowed, as in chapter 10.

ciples and lessons are relevant in all regulated settings, that is, in all situations in which people would like to harness the profit drive of firms to produce particular outcomes. The form that this relevance takes is important to recognize. The concepts and, in particular, the regulatory mechanisms that are described in this book are not intended to be applied *directly*. Effective regulation in the real world must consider so many factors—political, psychological, practical—that the application of any particular economic model would be extremely naive. Rather, the economic concepts provide insights into the process and purpose of regulation; they condition the way one thinks about regulation and the approach one takes in handling individual problems that arise in a regulatory setting. In short, they provide what Erik Erikson identifies as the true contribution of any field of thought, namely, "a way of seeing things."

Two further notes are required. Throughout the book we assume that regulators try to benefit society. This need not be the case, of course. Regulators can have their own agendas that include career advancement, self-aggrandizement, political support, and the like. At an extreme, capture theory (as described, for example, in Posner 1974) suggests that over time regulated firms gain control over the process by which they are regulated. Our emphasis on publicly motivated regulators is not intended to reflect an opinion on regulators' true motives. Rather, the emphasis reflects the current state of the field. Differences in regulators' goals (or, more precisely, in the factors that give rise to regulation) have been discussed extensively as a way of explaining the regulation that actually occurs in various settings; however, little has been said about how to design optimal procedures when regulators have these other goals. In theory, of course, the concepts in the book could be applied to regulators themselves, the issue being how to devise procedures that induce consistency between regulators' private goals and the public welfare.

More constraining is the assumption, also maintained throughout, that benefiting the public consists of maximizing total surplus (where total surplus is the sum of consumers' surplus and all firms' profits). Fairness and equity, however defined, are important social criteria that are ignored by this approach. Goals such as technical advancement, continuity with the past, conservation, and so on can also be important in certain settings and yet are not addressed.[7] Although

---

7. Often these goals are actually manifestations of surplus maximization or equity considerations. For example, it might be considered unfair for large changes in prices to

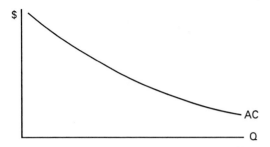

Figure I.1
Average cost curve under economies of scale

equity and other goals are clearly relevant, economists have had relatively little to say about them, certainly in the realm of designing regulatory processes. In defense of the traditional approach, experience has shown that insights obtained from the analysis of surplus maximization are helpful in examining and designing procedures that serve other goals. I hope the reader will discover the same.

The following sections provide some preliminary information. Section 2 characterizes a natural monopoly, identifying economies of scale and scope. Section 3 examines social welfare under natural monopoly, distinguishing the first-best and second-best outcomes.

I.2　Characteristics of a Natural Monopoly

A natural monopoly arises from two sources: economies of scale and economies of scope. Economies of scale exist when the average cost of production decreases as output expands. Figure I.1 illustrates such a situation. The average cost curve slopes downward, indicating that average cost falls as output increases.[8] [9]

---

be instituted abruptly. Continuity with the past becomes, therefore, an expression of equity. However, sometimes these goals are indeed separate concepts. For example, technical advancement can be seen as an aesthetic pursuit that expresses a desirable and basic human drive, or as evidence of preeminence, independent of the surplus it generates and the cost of its development.

8. Economies of scale can be defined equivalently in terms of total cost. Suppose a firm expands its output by a given percentage (say 10%). If the total costs of the firm increase by *less* than this percentage (say, by 8%), economies of scale exist. The two definitions are clearly the same. Average cost is total cost divided by output: TC/Q. If total cost (the numerator) increases by a smaller percentage than output (the denominator), the ratio of these two terms must decrease.

9. A distinction is necessary between "pecuniary" and "nonpecuniary" economies of scale. Often a large firm can negotiate with its suppliers to obtain lower prices for

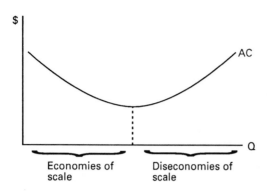

Figure I.2
Economies and diseconomies of scale

The most prevalent source of economies of scale are fixed costs, that is, costs that must be incurred no matter how many units of output are produced. Electricity production is a case in point. A generation plant is required to produce the first kilowatt-hour; yet many kilowatt-hours can be produced in the same plant.[10] When output expands, the fixed costs (in this case, the costs of the plant) are spread over more units, such that average cost declines.

Economies of scale can exist over some ranges of output but not others. For example, at low levels of production, scale economies may be present, while at larger output levels the opposite—diseconomies of scale—may occur.[11] This situation gives rise to the standard U-shaped average cost curve shown in figure I.2.

The existence of natural monopoly depends on the range of economies of scale relative to market demand. In particular, a natural monopoly exists in the production of one good only if economies of scale

inputs than would be charged if the firm were smaller. Average cost therefore declines as the size (i.e., output) of the firm increases. However, the reduction in average cost represents simply a transfer of income from the suppliers to the firm, such that the total cost to society (including both the firm and the suppliers) is unaffected. Reductions in average costs that reflect transfers only are called pecuniary, while those that represent an actual reduction in the resources used per unit of output are called nonpecuniary. From a social perspective, only nonpecuniary economies are relevant. We therefore use the term economies of scale only in reference to nonpecuniary economies. A similar distinction and usage is relevant for economies of scope.

10. Other inputs, such as coal in a coal-burning plant, must be expanded, but the plant itself need not be.

11. At high levels of output, management might not be able to oversee closely all the operations of the firm, giving rise to inefficiencies that can dominate any cost advantages of large-scale operation.

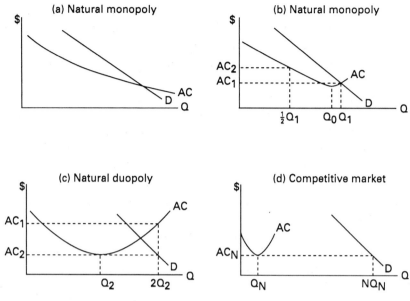

Figure I.3
Relation of average costs to demand

exist over a sufficient range of output relative to demand, where "sufficient" is defined by the situation. Four illustrative cases are shown in figure I.3. Panel (a) depicts the standard situation: average costs decline over all levels of output that would be demanded at any price, that is, over the entire range to the left of the demand curve. A natural monopoly clearly exists in this situation. A natural monopoly can exist, however, with economies of scale existing over a smaller range of output. Panel (b) depicts such a case. Economies of scale continue only to output Q_0, after which diseconomies set in. One firm could supply Q_1 output at an average cost of AC_1. If two firms supplied this output, each firm would incur average costs of $AC_2 > AC_1$ if they shared the market equally. If the two firms split the market unequally, their average costs would differ, but the total cost with two firms would always exceed that with one firm. At any division of output, production with two firms costs more than with one firm, indicating that a natural monopoly exists.

If economies of scale are exhibited over an even smaller range of output relative to demand, then a natural monopoly does not exist. In panel (c), two firms can produce output Q_2 apiece at an average cost of AC_2; one firm producing the same total output, $2Q_2$, would incur much higher average costs. This case constitutes a natural duopoly. Competition occurs when economies of scale are exhausted at a level of output that is small compared to market demand, as in panel (d), such that minimum-cost production is attained with numerous firms.

When more than one good is being produced, natural monopoly can arise from economies of scope as well as economies of scale. With several goods, there are sometimes shared equipment or common facilities that make producing them together less expensive than producing them separately. Economies of scope are said to exist if a given quantity of each of two or more goods can be produced by one firm at a lower total cost than if each good were produced separately by different firms.

This definition can be expressed in terms of the total cost function and illustrated graphically. Let the total cost to a firm of producing two goods in the quantities x and y, respectively, be represented as $f(x,y)$. The cost of producing good x only is, therefore, $f(x,0)$, because the firm produces none of good y. Similarly, the cost of producing good y only is $f(0,y)$. Economies of scope exist if $f(x,y) < f(x,0) + f(0,y)$. That is, the cost of producing both goods together, $f(x,y)$, is less than the combined cost of having one firm produce good x but none of good y, $f(x,0)$, and another firm produce good y but none of x, $f(0,y)$. Figure I.4 illustrates this possibility. The cost function facing any firm in the industry is shown as the shaded surface, which gives the cost of producing any combination of the two goods. Point A represents production of quantities x_A and y_A. The cost function evaluated at point A is $f(x_A, y_A)$, the cost to a firm of producing both goods. This cost is the distance OL on the cost axis. If a firm produced x_A only and no y, then its costs would be $f(x_A,0)$, which is the distance OM. Similarly, a firm producing y_A but no x would incur costs of $f(0,y_A)$, distance ON. The combined costs of the two firms, each producing one of the goods, is $ON + OM$ (or, as given on the graph, the distance from O to $N + M$). Because $N + M$ is higher than L, it is less costly to have one firm produce these quantities of the two goods than to have two firms produce the two goods separately.

As with economies of scale, it is possible for economies of scope to exist at some levels of outputs of the goods and not at others. For example, it may be cheaper to have one firm produce two goods when small quantities of the goods are being produced, but not for large quantities (or vice versa). Whether having one firm is desirable from

Total cost in $

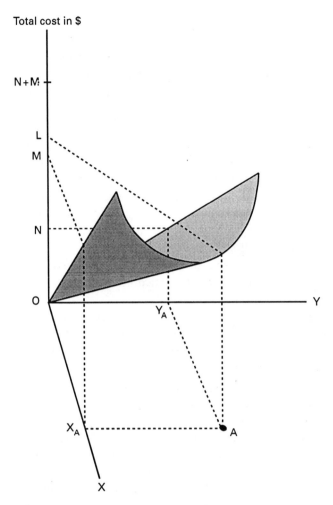

Figure I.4
Economies of scope

a cost perspective depends on how these regions of economies and diseconomies of scope relate to the demand for the two goods.

The existence, or relevance, of economies of scope often depends on how goods are defined. Local and long-distance telecommunication service is a case in point. If local and long-distance service are considered to be the two goods, there are strong grounds for believing that economies of scope exist. The wires that connect the phone to the "local exchange unit" (that is, the switchboard that directs the call to its destination) are used for both local and long-distance calls. Having two companies provide the two services separately entails redundant equipment: two sets of wires going to each phone, one for each company. Under this definition of goods, it would seem preferable to have one company provide both local and long-distance service, so as to obtain the benefits of the economies of scope. This was the rationale for AT&T, prior to the divestiture, being allowed a monopoly franchise for telecommunication service in most areas of the United States.

The relevant goods can be defined differently, however, in which case the argument for economies of scope is not as strong. Consider the provision of a long-distance call from a phone in one city (the origin city) to a phone in another city (the destination city.) The call consists of three parts: first, the call moves along a wire from the originating phone to the local exchange unit in the origin city; it is there combined with other calls and placed on a larger wire to the local exchange unit in the destination city; at that point it is disentangled from the other calls and moved along a wire from the local exchange unit to the phone being called. Three services are being provided in moving the call: service from the phone to the local exchange unit in the origin city, service between local exchange units, and service from the local exchange unit in the destination city to the phone receiving the call. Having three separate firms—a local phone company in the origin city providing service between phones and local exchange units, a long-distance carrier providing service between local exchange units in different cities, and a local phone company in the destination city providing service between phones and local exchange units in that city—is not necessarily more costly than having one firm provide all three services. Only one wire goes to each phone, as provided by the local phone company, such that redundancy in these facilities does not occur; and no other redundancies are immediately obvious. In fact, the concept that economies of scope do not seem to exist in the provision of services defined in this way is the economic justification for the divestiture of AT&T. Today, service between phones and local exchange units is provided by a local phone company in each area, and service between local exchange units is provided by long-distance carriers. Furthermore, since economies of scale in the provision of service between local exchange units is thought to be exhausted at a level of output that is small compared to market demand, competition is permitted and encouraged in the long-distance market (rather than allowing AT&T to hold a mandated monopoly, as would have been appropriate if a natural monopoly existed in long-distance service).

Economies of scope can exist with or without economies of scale, and vice versa. For example, it is possible that joint facilities can be used in the production of two goods and yet expanding production of both raises costs more than proportionately. Whether a natural monopoly exists depends on the overall cost situation, considering both economies or diseconomies of scope and/or scale. Economists use the term "subadditivity" for this purpose. A cost curve is said to exhibit subadditivity at a given level of one or more outputs if the cost of producing these outputs is lower with one firm than with more than one firm, regardless of how the output might be divided among the multiple firms.

Consider, for example, a situation with two goods, labeled A and B, and the possibility of production by two firms, labeled I and II, instead of one. Several different divisions of output between the two firms are possible. Firm I could produce all of good A and firm II all of good B. This arrangement would be appropriate if economies of scale existed, but not economies of scope. Or, each firm could produce both goods, with each supplying half of the total output of each good. This arrangement would be cost-effective if economies of scope existed but diseconomies of scale started to arise at half the market output of each good. Or, firm I could supply one-third of the units of good A and two-thirds of the units of good B, while firm II produced the remaining two-thirds of good A and one-third of good B, and so on, for numerous other possible arrangements. Costs exhibit subadditivity only in the event that one firm producing all of goods A and B is cheaper than any of these, or any other, arrangements with two or more firms. Thus, the concept of subadditivity incorporates considerations of both scope and scale and identifies whether, given all considerations, one firm is cheapest.

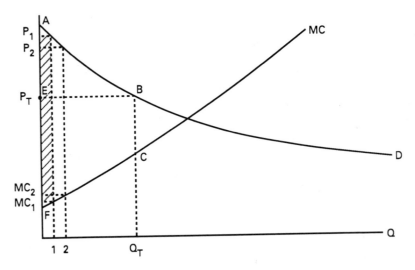

Figure I.5
Total surplus

Just as economies of scope and scale can exist at certain levels of output and not at others, so can subadditivity. A natural monopoly exists when the cost curve exhibits subadditivity in the relevant range of market demand. Because subadditivity essentially means that natural monopoly exists, we simply use the latter term throughout the book.

I.3 Welfare Concepts with Natural Monopoly

Given that a natural monopoly exists, what output, price, and inputs should the regulator try to induce it to choose? That is, what is the optimal outcome?

The definition of optimal outcome relies critically on the concept of total surplus, a term readers will recall from microeconomics. To refresh the memory, a brief discussion of the term is useful. Total surplus is the dollar amount by which the benefits from consumption of a good exceed the cost of producing it. Consider figure I.5, which illustrates typical demand and marginal cost curves for a good. The total surplus that accrues from Q_T units of the good is the area $ABCF$, the area above the marginal cost curve and below the demand curve, up to Q_T units of output. To see this, consider the benefits and costs of producing each unit of output up to Q_T. The first unit is labeled 1 in the graph. Consumers are willing to pay P_1 for this first unit. (At a price P_1 consumers demand one unit, which means that they value that unit at P_1.) The cost of producing this unit is MC_1. The benefits to consumers exceed the cost of this unit by $P_1 - MC_1$, which is the shaded column in the graph. This shaded column is the total surplus from the first unit.

Consider now the second unit. Consumers are willing to pay P_2 for the second unit and the unit costs MC_2 to produce. Total surplus from this second unit is $P_2 - MC_2$, namely, the area below demand and above marginal cost. Continuing for all units up to Q_T, total surplus from all units is the area $ABCF$.

Total surplus consists of both consumer surplus and producer's profit. Suppose price is P_T. Consider only the first unit of production. Consumers benefit by P_1 for this unit of output and must pay P_T for it. Their net benefit, or surplus, is therefore $P_1 - P_T$. The firm obtains revenues of P_T from this first unit and must pay MC_1 to produce it. Its profits are $P_T - MC_1$. Total surplus on this unit $(P_1 - MC_1)$ is the sum of consumer surplus $(P_1 - P_T)$ and profit $(P_T - MC_1)$.

Consider now the total output Q_T. Using the same logic as above for each unit of output, consumer surplus for all Q_T units is the area ABE, the area above price and below the demand curve. Profit is the area $EBCF$, the area above the marginal cost curve and below the demand curve up to Q_T. Total surplus $(ABCF)$ is the sum of consumer surplus (ABE) and profit $(EBCF)$.[12]

Optimality can now be defined. The optimal outcome is that which provides the greatest total surplus, that is, the largest dollar value of benefits in excess of costs.[13]

From microeconomics, we know that total surplus is maximized when the firm prices at marginal cost, sells the output demanded at this price, and uses the least costly input combination to produce the

---

12. No fixed costs are included in this example. If there are fixed costs, total surplus is the area $ABCF$ minus these fixed costs. Consumer surplus is the same as before (ABE), and profit is $EBCF$ minus the fixed costs. Alternatively, fixed costs can be incorporated in the graph as part of the marginal cost of the first unit of production. In this case, the marginal cost curve would be very high for the first unit and lower for the second and subsequent units.

13. Note that this definition ignores the issue of equity, namely, which consumers obtain benefits and the allocation of surplus between consumers and firms. When total surplus is maximized, it is theoretically possible to distribute the surplus in a way that makes every party (each consumer and each firm) better off than under any other possible arrangement. (Essentially, with a larger pie, each person can get a larger slice.) In practice, of course, implementing such a distribution is difficult.

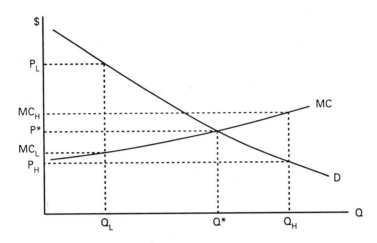

Figure I.6
Optimal outcome: first-best

output. For a one-output firm, the situation is illustrated in figure I.6. The optimal output is Q^*. The logic indicating that this output is optimal can be observed by considering any other output level, say Q_L. At Q_L, consumers are willing to pay P_L for an extra unit of the good. The cost of an extra unit, given that Q_L is produced, is MC_L, which is less then P_L. Because consumers are willing to pay more than it costs the firm to produce one extra unit, surplus increases when the unit is produced. That is, surplus increases as production is expanded from Q_L toward Q^*. A similar argument holds for levels of output above Q^*. At Q_H, the cost of an extra unit (MC_H) is greater than the amount that consumers are willing to pay for the unit (P_H) such that expanding production decreases total surplus. Stated conversely, decreasing output toward Q^* increases surplus. Only at Q^* can surplus not be increased by expanding or contracting output. Given that Q^* is the optimal quantity, the optimal price is P^*. At this price, any consumer who is willing to pay at least the marginal cost of the good obtains it, and those not willing to pay the marginal cost do not.

In the presence of economies of scale, the firm necessarily loses money when pricing at marginal cost. Economies of scale imply that the average cost curve of the firm is downward sloping. Declining average costs mean that marginal cost is below average cost.[14] There-

---

14. If an extra unit costs less to produce than the average of all previous units, then producing an extra unit lowers the average cost. Stated conversely, if average cost is declining, marginal cost is necessarily below it.

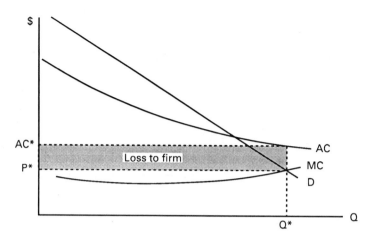

Figure I.7
Firm loses money at first-best price under economies of scale

fore, in the presence of economies of scale, marginal cost is below average cost. When price is set at marginal cost, as required for optimality, the firm loses money on each unit sold. Figure I.7 illustrates the problem. At Q^* and P^*, the firm loses the amount given in the shaded area: the amount by which average cost exceeds price, times the number of units sold.

A firm cannot lose money indefinitely and remain in business. In theory, the firm could be subsidized by the amount of its loss each period. In the United States, however, the tradition has been not to subsidize public utilities directly, under the belief that customers should pay the full costs of production. More important, if the firm is subsidized, the procedure by which the funds are raised (such as taxing income or property) distorts prices elsewhere in the economy away from marginal cost.

Without a subsidy, the only solution is for prices to be raised sufficiently for the firm to break even.[15] In a one-output situation, the requirement is clear: price must be raised to average cost. This price

---

15. Chapters 2 and 7 suggest that if the firm charges a different price for different levels of consumption (e.g., a higher price for consumption up to a certain number of units, and then a lower price for consumption beyond that number), the price for marginal consumption can sometimes, depending on various factors, be retained at marginal cost without causing the firm to lose money. In these cases, the higher price for low levels of consumption provides the needed subsidy: essentially the firm is taxing its customers for the additional funds required to break even. For the present purpose, however, we assume the firm charges one price for each good independent of consumption level.

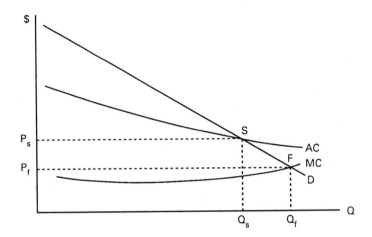

Figure I.8
First- and second-best outcomes

is optimal in the absence of subsidy because any lower price would result in negative profits, which is infeasible, and any higher price would distort price further away from marginal cost than necessary. Figure I.8 illustrates the situation. Production at F provides the greatest total surplus, but results in the firm losing money. S is the closest point that allows the firm to break even.

Points F and S represent two different concepts, or definitions, of optimality. Total welfare is as high as possible at F, where price equals marginal cost. This is called the "first-best" outcome, or first-best pricing, to indicate that no other outcome provides greater surplus. If at all possible, this is the outcome that the regulator would like to achieve. In the case of natural monopoly, the firm obtains revenues under first-best pricing that are insufficient to cover its costs.

At point S, total surplus is greater than at any other outcome that allows the firm to earn at least zero profits. This is called the "second-best" outcome, reflecting the fact that it provides less surplus than the first-best outcome. The regulator would like to achieve the second-best outcome if first-best is infeasible.[16]

16. Stated alternatively, F is the unconstrained maximum of total surplus, while S is the constrained maximum, with the constraint being that profits be at least zero. F provides greater surplus than S even though the firm's profits at F are negative because consumers obtain sufficiently greater surplus at F compared to S to compensate for the loss in profits.

In competition, the distinction between these two concepts of optimality is not re-

If the firm produces two or more goods, the second-best outcome is not immediately obvious. Unlike a one-output firm where zero profit is attained only when price equals average cost, many combinations of prices for a multi-output firm can result in zero profits. For example, an energy utility that provides gas and electricity can make zero profits by pricing electricity at marginal cost but gas far above marginal cost (earning profits on gas to make up for the losses on electricity), or by pricing electricity far above its marginal cost with gas at marginal cost, or by pricing both moderately above their marginal costs. There is, in fact, an infinite number of possible price combinations for the two goods that would result in zero profits. Of these combinations, the one that provides the greatest total surplus is the second-best outcome.

While the definition of second-best pricing is straightforward in a multi-output situation, the identification of which price combination actually constitutes the second-best is not. One of the major accomplishments in the field of regulatory economics has been to determine, or characterize, the second-best prices for multi-output natural monopolies. We address this issue in chapter 4. For the present, distinguishing the concepts of first- and second-best is sufficient.

---

quired. In equilibrium, each firm produces at the minimum of its average-cost curve, where marginal cost equals average cost. Points F and S are therefore the same. These points being different only arises in a natural monopoly situation where the firm does not produce at the minimum of the average-cost curve (because, usually, the minimum is beyond market demand).

1

The Averch-Johnson Model of Rate-of-Return Regulation

1.1 Purpose

Averch and Johnson (1962) initiated one of the earliest and most influential investigations into the effects of regulation on the behavior of a regulated firm. They argue that the most prevalent form of regulation currently applied to public utilities, rate-of-return regulation, induces the firm to engage in inefficiencies. These inefficiencies are the natural result of the regulation, in that a firm that is attempting to maximize profits is given, by the form of the regulation itself, incentives to be inefficient. Furthermore, the aspects of monopoly control that regulation is intended to address, such as high prices, are not necessarily mitigated, and could be made worse, by the regulation.

Averch and Johnson conducted their analysis within a relatively restrictive model that abstracts from many real-world issues. Their model and conclusions have been questioned from a number of perspectives,[1] and, in fact, some errors in their logic have been discovered (though these errors do not affect their essential conclusions).[2] Their work is nevertheless invaluable, not only for its specific conclusions but, more generally, because it introduces a fundamental criterion for evaluating regulatory mechanisms plus a method for applying

---

1. For example, Bailey and Coleman (1971), Davis (1973), Klevorick (1973), Joskow (1974), Bawa and Sibley (1980), and Logan et al. (1989) show that the inefficiencies are mitigated or even eliminated when the analysis is changed to allow for a time lag in the regulatory process. In these models, the firm, during the period between price reviews, takes its price as given and retains whatever profit it earns. The firm therefore has less incentive to produce inefficiently than when, as in Averch-Johnson's model, the firm's profits are constrained continuously. Similarly, various authors (see note 3 to the introduction) show that different results obtain if the firm is assumed to maximize some variable other than profits (such as output or return on shareholder equity).

2. Takayama 1969; Baumol and Klevorick 1970, p. 168.

this criterion. In the case of rate-of-return regulation, their method shows that the regulatory procedure does *not* induce the firm to choose the socially optimal outcome. However, the method can be used to identify other types of regulation that do.

The following sections describe the Averch-Johnson (or A-J) model and its implications for rate-of-return regulation. Section 1.2 describes the behavior of an *unregulated* firm, using a method that facilitates comparison with the firm's behavior when regulation is imposed. Section 1.3 defines rate-of-return regulation, identifying exactly the form of regulation that is imposed on the firm. Section 1.4 determines the behavior of a firm that is subject to this rate-of-return regulation and compares this behavior with that of an unregulated firm and with the behavior the regulator would like to induce. Throughout, the discussion draws on clarifications of the A-J model provided especially by Zajac (1970), Baumol and Klevorick (1970), and Bailey (1973).

Before entering the substance of this and each subsequent chapter, we summarize the major results and conclusions in the chapter introduction. This summary provides both a preview of what is to follow and a concise reference for later review. The statements will not always be completely clear prior to reading the chapter itself. However, on returning after completing the chapter, the reader may find the summary a useful reminder and guide.

The findings of chapter 1 can be summarized as follows. Under rate-of-return (ROR) regulation, the firm is allowed to earn no more than a "fair" rate of return on its capital investment. The firm is free to choose its price, output level, and inputs as long as its profits do not exceed this fair rate. We show that this form of regulation provides perverse incentives that operate against optimality.

Suppose first that the regulator sets the fair rate of return above the cost of capital. In this case:

• The regulated firm will utilize more capital than if it were unregulated.

• The regulated firm will use an inefficiently high capital/labor ratio for its level of output. That is, the firm's output could be produced more cheaply with less capital and more labor.

• It is possible that the firm will produce less output and charge a higher price than if it were not regulated.

• The firm might increase its output above the level it would produce if not regulated. However, the firm will always produce in the elastic portion of demand. That is, ROR regulation will not induce the firm to expand output so far that it moves into the inelastic portion of demand. Insofar as the optimal output is in the inelastic portion of demand, ROR regulation cannot induce the firm to produce the optimal output (and may, as noted in the previous point, induce the firm to reduce output).

· There is one bright spot. Contrary to popular notions, a firm under ROR regulation will not waste capital. The firm will produce as much output as possible given its inputs. The firm will choose an inefficient mix of inputs (this is the second point above), but it will use the inputs that it has chosen efficiently.

In short, ROR regulation with the fair rate of return above the cost of capital induces the regulated firm to use an inefficient input mix and does not necessarily induce it to increase output.

Suppose instead that the regulator sets the fair rate of return equal to the cost of capital. In this case, the regulated firm becomes indifferent between many possible outcomes, and its choice is indeterminant. In particular, the firm would earn the same profit whether it increased or decreased output, used an efficient or inefficient input mix, and wasted inputs or not. In fact, the firm would make the same profit if it closed down and sold off its capital. Because the firm's profits are the same in each of these cases, the firm is as likely to choose one as the other. Consequently, ROR regulation with the fair rate set at the cost of capital cannot be relied upon to induce the firm to act in any particular way.

Suppose finally that the fair rate is set below the cost of capital. In this case, the firm makes more profit by shutting down and selling its capital than by remaining in operation. If it is legally able to do so, the firm will choose this option. Otherwise, it will reduce its capital as much as possible, which could result in less output and a higher price.

The overall picture is quite damaging. The basic problem with ROR regulation is that it provides incentives based on the amount of capital that the firm invests, whereas the goal of the regulator is not to increase capital per se. The regulator's goal is to induce the firm to increase output, decrease price, and produce at minimum cost. Other forms of regulation that match incentives more closely to the regulator's goals are more likely to be successful. Some of these are explored in chapter 2.

To derive our results regarding ROR regulation, we first consider the behavior of an *unregulated* firm. We then examine how behavior changes when the firm is subjected to ROR regulation.

1.2 Behavior of the Unregulated Firm

To describe the behavior of an unregulated firm, a method and some terms are employed that are somewhat different than those used in standard microeconomics textbooks. While the behavior of the firm is the same as in the standard presentation (that is, the firm behaves the same in either case), this alternative representation facilitates analysis of how the firm's behavior changes when regulation is imposed. In fact, part of the value of the A-J model is the development of this alternative way of describing the behavior of the unregulated firm, which generalizes more readily than the standard method to situations with regulation.

Consider a monopolist that produces only one output (such as electricity), the quantity of which is denoted Q. Assume, for convenience, that the firm produces this output with only two inputs, capital K and labor L. The price of capital (interest rate) is r per unit, the price of labor (wage rate) is w, and the firm takes these input prices as given.

The input possibilities of the firm are summarized by the familiar isocost-isoquant mapping, as in figure 1.1. The axes represent the two

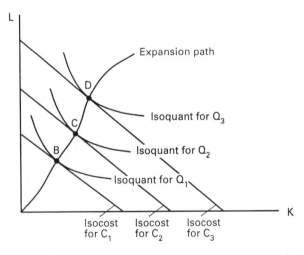

Figure 1.1
Isocost-isoquant mapping

inputs, such that each point in the graph denotes a certain quantity of each input. An isocost line is defined as a set of input combinations that cost the same amount. For example, all of the K and L combinations on the isocost for C_1 cost exactly C_1; that is, the input levels times their prices sum to C_1: $rK + wL = C_1$. Rearranging, we find the equation for the isocost line as $L = (C_1/w) - (r/w)K$, namely, a line with a y-intercept of C_1/w and a slope of $-r/w$. There is an infinite number of isocost lines, one for each possible level of cost. They all have the same slope and differ only in their distance from the origin (i.e., their y-intercepts). Higher isocost lines (that is, those further from the origin) represent higher costs. Three isocost lines are shown in the graph representing three levels of costs: $C_3 > C_2 > C_1$.

An isoquant is defined as the set of input combinations that can be used to produce a given level of output. For example, output level Q_1 can be produced using any of the input combinations on the isoquant for Q_1.[3] The shape of the isoquant depends on the technology available to the firm, as summarized in its production function. The slope of an isoquant at any point is the negative of the marginal rate of technical substitution (*MRTS*), which is the extra quantity of one input that must be used to continue producing the same level of output if one unit of the other input is foregone. For our inputs, *MRTS* is the amount of extra labor required to continue producing the same level of output with one less unit of capital. The isoquants bend away from the origin, such that *MRTS* decreases as more capital and less labor is used to produce a fixed level of output. This shape reflects diminishing marginal product of inputs.

An infinite number of isoquants exist, one for each possible level of output. Because more inputs are required to produce more outputs, "higher" isoquants represent greater levels of output. Three of these isoquants, representing increasing levels of output $Q_3 > Q_2 > Q_1$, are shown in figure 1.1.

Given that the firm is producing a certain level of output, the firm minimizes its costs (and, because revenues are fixed by its output level, maximizes profits) by choosing the input combination at which the isoquant for that level of output is tangent to an isocost line. Sup-

---

3. It is always possible to produce less than maximally possible (that is, to waste inputs). Consequently, output level Q_1 can be produced with any input combination either on or beyond the isoquant, where "beyond" means more of either input than a point on the isoquant. To account for this fact, an isoquant can be more precisely defined as the set of input combinations whose maximal output level is a given quantity.

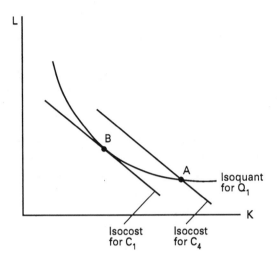

Figure 1.2
Cost-minimization occurs at point of tangency

pose, for example, that the firm is producing output level Q_1 using an input combination at which the isoquant is *not* tangent to the isocost line, say point A in figure 1.2. The firm's costs are C_4, because point A is on the isocost line for input combinations that cost C_4.

The firm can reduce its costs by moving from point A to point B. At point B, output is the same (because A and B are on the same isoquant) but costs are lower: the isocost line through B is closer to the origin than that through A. This same result is obtained whenever the isoquant is not tangent to the isocost line: the firm will be able to reduce costs by moving to the point at which they *are* tangent. When at this point of tangency (point B in our graph), the firm has the lowest possible costs for its level of output.

For each level of output, there is one input combination that is cost minimizing, that is, at which the isoquant is tangent to the isocost line.[4] Because there are numerous possible output levels, there are numerous input combinations that are cost minimizing for *some* level of output. Consider the set of all such input combinations. This set is called the expansion path. For output level Q_1 in figure 1.1, input combination B is cost minimizing; C is cost minimizing for Q_2; and D

---

4. If the isoquant has a linear segment, there can be more than one cost-minimizing point. However, we will ignore this possibility because it does not affect the basic results.

is cost minimizing for Q_3. Connecting these points plus all the other points that are obtained for other levels of output gives the expansion path.

There are numerous ways to view, or define, the expansion path:

1. The expansion path is the set of input combinations that are cost minimizing for some level of output. Production at any point that is *not* on the expansion path is inefficient.

2. The unregulated profit-maximizing firm will necessarily choose an input combination on the expansion path. *Which* combination on this path is chosen depends on what level of output the firm chooses to produce. The term "expansion path" denotes the idea that as the firm expands its output, it moves along the expansion path. For example, when expanding its output from Q_1 to Q_2 and further to Q_3, the firm moves along the expansion path from B to C to D.

3. The slope of each isocost line is $-r/w$ and the slope of the isoquant at any point is the (negative of) MRTS at that point. Because the expansion path consists of input combinations at which the isocost line is tangent to the isoquant, MRTS equals r/w at each point on the expansion path. The expansion path can therefore also be defined as the set of input combinations at which $MRTS = r/w$.

The analysis of isocosts and isoquants provides *some* information about the firm's choice of inputs: it demonstrates that the firm chooses an input combination on the expansion path. However, it does not allow a complete determination of the input choice of the firm. In particular, *which* of the points on the expansion path does the firm choose? This cannot be determined with isocosts and isoquants alone.

The firm's choice among the various input combinations on the expansion path is equivalent to its choice of output. Given an output level, the firm chooses the input combination on the expansion path that corresponds to that output level. For example, in figure 1.1, if the firm chooses output level Q_2, then it also chooses input combination C. Conversely, once the firm chooses an input combination, its output level is determined: if the firm chooses input combination C, then its output is Q_2. Because of this equivalence, the firm's behavior is fully described (that is, its input and output levels are completely determined) by its choice of where to locate along the expansion path.

There is a direct relation, elaborated below, between the input combination the firm chooses and the profits it can earn. This relation

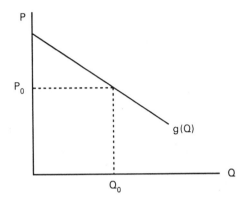

Figure 1.3
Demand curve of firm

provides the information required to locate the firm on the expansion path. The relation between inputs and profit is based on the fact that, once the firm chooses an input level, the maximum profits it can earn are set. To see this, start with inputs. With a given level of inputs, the firm can produce a certain maximum quantity of output. This quantity is given by the firm's production function: $Q = f(K,L)$. The maximum price at which the firm can sell this output depends on the demand for the firm's output. The demand function, denoted $P = g(Q)$, gives the maximum price that the firm can charge and sell quantity Q of output. For example, in figure 1.3, at quantity Q_0 the maximum price the firm can charge is P_0: if it tried to charge a higher price, it would not be able to sell all of its output.[5] Given the output level denoted by the production function and the price denoted by the demand function, the firm's profits are fully determined.

The relation between inputs and profits can be shown functionally. Profits, π, are the difference between revenues and costs:

$$\pi = PQ - rK - wL.$$

Substituting in the demand function for P:

$$\pi = g(Q)Q - rK - wL.$$

---

5. The demand function also can be considered in its inverse form as giving the quantity demanded at each price. Though it is sometimes easier to think of demand in this latter way, it is more fundamental and, in our analysis, more useful to consider price as a function of quantity—that is, the maximum price at which the firm can sell a given quantity.

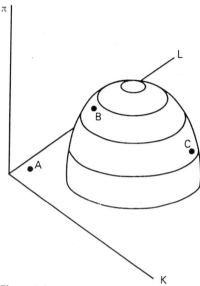

Figure 1.4
Profit hill

Substituting the production function for Q:

$$\pi = g(f(K,L)) \cdot f(K,L) - rK - wL,$$

which is a function of K and L only. Profits depend only on the levels of inputs, such that profits are determined once input levels are determined. (Stated succinctly, the argument is simply: given inputs, output is determined; given output, price is determined; and given inputs, output, and price, profits are determined.)

Because profits are set once input levels are chosen, profits can be expressed directly as a function of inputs only: $\pi = h(K,L)$. This function takes the general shape of a hill, as shown in figure 1.4, reflecting the fact that profits increase at first and then decrease as the use of inputs expands. Consider a low level of inputs, say point A. A firm must usually incur setup costs that are independent of the level of output; that is, it must use some inputs before it is able to produce any output. As a result the firm usually loses money at low levels of inputs, because the revenues that can be obtained from the small amount of output produced are insufficient to cover the setup costs. If more inputs are used, as at point B, output is higher and the firm is able to earn positive profits. Profits increase as the scale of production (the quantity of inputs, and hence, output) expands. However,

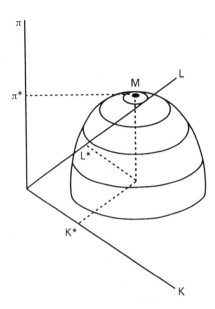

Figure 1.5
Chosen input levels for unregulated firm

this rise in profits does not continue indefinitely. When the firm expands its inputs (and, hence, its output), it must lower its price in order to sell the additional output. Eventually, the firm must lower its price so much that profits drop (the market becomes saturated, in a sense). For example, at point C, with more inputs (and, hence, output) than B, profits are lower. Because profits increase and eventually decrease as input levels increase, the relation between profits and inputs is called the "profit hill."[6]

The behavior of the firm can be visualized with this profit hill. The firm chooses the inputs that give it the highest possible profits. These are the input levels associated with the top of the profit hill, that is, the inputs that provide the greatest profit. In figure 1.5, the firm chooses input levels K^* and L^* and makes profits π^*, which is the top of the profit hill. Given these inputs, the firm produces output $Q^* = f(K^*, L^*)$ and sells it at price $P^* = g(Q^*)$.

We want to combine the information contained in the profit hill with the isocost-isoquant mapping so as to locate the firm's chosen

---

6. This relation is sometimes called the profit function. However, this latter term is more widely used to denote the relation, important in duality theory and econometrics, between profits and the prices of inputs and output. The term "profit hill" avoids confusion, while also signifying the function's shape.

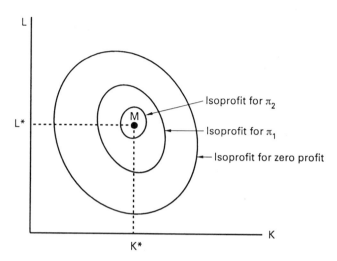

Figure 1.6
Isoprofit contours

point on the expansion path. To do this, we make a topological map of the profit hill. That is, we represent the three-dimensional profit hill in two dimensions, as in figure 1.6. Each contour on this map denotes a given level of profit. Each of these contours is called an "isoprofit contour," defined as the set of input combinations that result in a given level of profits. For example, all of the input combinations on the isoprofit contour for π_1 result in the firm earning π_1 profits. The isoprofit contours are concentric, with inner contours representing higher profits than outer contours. The outermost contour is the base of the profit hill, representing zero profits; it is called the zero-profit contour.[7] The top of the hill is point M. The firm chooses this input combination.

To locate the firm along the expansion path, the isoprofit contours are superimposed on the expansion path, as in figure 1.7. The firm chooses point M,[8] which represents capital level K^*, labor L^*, and

7. The contours could be extended outward to represent various levels of negative profits. Except for a few situations, these negative-profit contours are not relevant.
8. Point M is necessarily on the expansion path. If it were not, then there would be another point at which profits are higher than at M, namely the point on the expansion path where the isoquant through M intersects the expansion path. (At this point, revenues are the same because both points are on the same isoquant, but costs are lower because this point is on the expansion path and M is not.) Because M is defined as the top of the profit hill, there can be no point with higher profits; hence M must be on the expansion path.

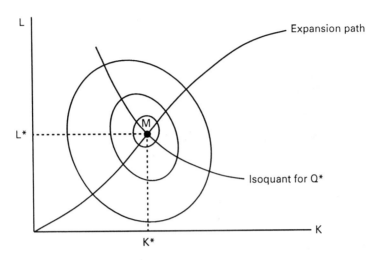

Figure 1.7
Isoprofit contours superimposed on expansion path

resultant output level Q^*. The input and output choices of the firm are now fully determined.

It is important to note, especially in relation to the effects of rate-of-return regulation, that at these chosen input and output levels, marginal revenue is positive. Recall from microeconomics that marginal revenue is the extra revenue the firm obtains from expanding output by one unit. Suppose that marginal revenue is negative. This means that expanding output decreases revenues, or, conversely, that reducing output increases revenues. If marginal revenue is negative, the firm would earn more profit by reducing its output: revenues increase and, because less output is being produced, costs decrease. With higher revenue and lower costs, profits are higher.

Whenever marginal revenue is negative, the firm will decrease its output. Consequently, the firm's final choice of output necessarily occurs at a point where marginal revenue is positive. Generally, marginal revenue is positive for lower levels of output and is negative for sufficiently higher output levels. The reason for this is clear. Marginal revenue consists of two components: (1) the extra revenue that the firm obtains from the sale of one extra unit of output, *minus* (2) the loss in revenue that occurs because the firm has to reduce its price to sell the extra unit. Because the price reduction applies to all goods sold, the size of the second component depends on the output level

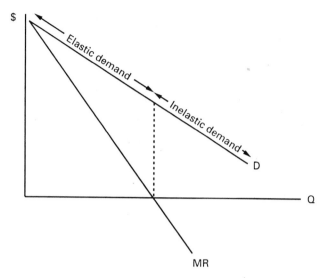

Figure 1.8
Relation of marginal revenue to elasticity of demand

of the firm. For low levels of output, the second component is small, such that the first component (which is positive) exceeds the second (which is negative), for a net effect that is positive. For sufficiently high levels of output, the second component exceeds the first, for a negative net effect.

Figure 1.8 illustrates the situation. Marginal revenue is positive at first, indicating that the firm can increase its revenues by selling additional output. Eventually marginal revenue becomes negative, such that the firm's revenues would decrease if it attempted to sell additional output. The fact that marginal revenue is positive at the firm's chosen output level means that the firm will never expand output beyond the range for which marginal revenue is positive.

We can relate these concepts to the elasticity of demand. Marginal revenue is positive when the elasticity of demand is greater than one (in magnitude). Suppose, for example, that elasticity is two, indicating that a 1% increase in price results in a 2% decrease in quantity demanded. Stated equivalently, a 2% expansion of output requires a 1% decrease in price. Because total revenue is price times quantity, a 2% increase in output coupled with a 1% decrease in price results in an increase in total revenue (the increase in quantity is greater than the decrease in price). Therefore, expanding output increases revenue. Similarly, if elasticity is less than one, marginal revenue is negative.[9]

At low levels of output, the elasticity of demand generally exceeds one, such that marginal revenue is positive. This is called the elastic portion of demand and is labeled as such in figure 1.8. Eventually, at higher levels of output, elasticity falls below one and marginal revenue becomes negative. This is called the inelastic portion of demand.

The fact that marginal revenue is positive at the firm's chosen output level means, equivalently, that the firm will never increase its output beyond the elastic portion of demand. That is, the firm will never choose to operate in the inelastic portion of demand, where marginal revenue is negative.

We can use another method to demonstrate that an unregulated firm will necessarily produce in the elastic portion of demand. This alternative proof ties more readily to analogous statements, made below, about the behavior of a regulated firm. We use proof by contradiction. Suppose the top of the profit hill, which is the firm's chosen point, is in the *inelastic* portion of demand. We can show that this supposition leads to a contradiction and consequently cannot occur. Figure 1.9 illustrates the situation. The isoquant that is shown is for the output level at which marginal revenue is zero. Points on the expansion path below this isoquant represent production in the elastic portion of demand (where elasticity exceeds one and marginal revenue is positive), while points above the isoquant represent production in the inelastic portion of demand. Point M is placed above the isoquant to represent the supposition that the top of the profit hill occurs in the inelastic portion of demand. We will show that this is not possible, that M cannot be above the isoquant for zero marginal revenue.

Consider point J. Profits at M necessarily exceed those at J, because M is the top of the profit hill. However, because marginal revenue is negative along the expansion path past the designated isoquant, revenues are higher at J, which represents less output, than at M. Costs are lower at J than M, because output is lower. Consequently, profits at J exceed profits at M. Because this contradicts the fact that profits at M exceed profits at J, the situation depicted in figure 1.9 is impossible. Point M can only occur in the elastic portion of demand, on the

9. Consider an elasticity of one-half, meaning that a 1% increase in price results in a .5% decrease in quantity demanded. Stated alternatively, a .5% increase in quantity necessitates a 1% decrease in price. Because price drops by more than the rise in quantity, total revenues decrease.

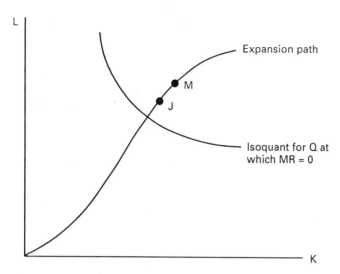

Figure 1.9
Unregulated firm will move to elastic portion of demand

expansion path below the isoquant associated with zero marginal revenue.

1.3   Rate-of-Return Regulation

Under rate-of-return regulation, the regulated firm is allowed to earn a "fair" return on its investment in capital, but is not allowed to make profits in excess of this fair rate of return. The firm can freely choose its levels of inputs, its output level, and its price as long as the chosen levels do not result in profits in excess of the fair return.[10]

The rate of return on capital is defined as revenues minus costs for noncapital inputs, divided by the level of capital investment. With only one noncapital input, L, the rate of return is $(PQ - wL)/K$. This rate must, by the terms of ROR regulation, be no greater than the fair

---

10. In reality, the regulator has oversight control over the firm's choices and can, for example, disallow costs for unneeded inputs. The A-J model's characterization of ROR regulation abstracts from this aspect of real-world regulation. The extent to which the regulator can effectively exercise this oversight function is unclear. (If the regulator could identify precisely efficient input and output levels, there would be no need to have ROR regulation: the regulator could simply mandate the efficient levels.) The A-J model can be viewed as a worst-case situation, in which the regulator is unable to distinguish between efficient and inefficient behavior. The lessons from this model can be expected to hold to a degree when the regulator has some but less than perfectly effective oversight ability.

rate of return, labeled f, that the regulator has previously announced.[11] Therefore, the firm can choose any K, L, Q, and P as long as

$$f \geq (PQ - wL)/K.$$

The firm must operate in a way that satisfies this inequality, that is, that does not result in too high a rate of return.

Economic profits, or what economists call excess profits, are the difference between the firm's revenues and its costs for *all* inputs, including capital: $\pi = PQ - wL - rK$.[12] The maximum return the regulated firm is allowed to earn can be expressed in terms of economic profit. Subtract the price of capital from both sides of the above inequality and rearrange:

$$f - r \geq ((PQ - wL)/K) - r;$$

$$f - r \geq (PQ - wL - rK)/K;$$

$$f - r \geq \pi/K.$$

$$\pi \leq (f - r)K.$$

That is, the maximum (economic) profit that the firm is allowed to earn is $(f - r)K$.

If the fair return is 10% and the price of capital is 8%, then the firm is allowed to earn no more than 2% of its invested capital. For example, if the firm invests $100 million, it is allowed to earn no more than $2 million in profits.[13]

---

11. The regulator establishes the fair rate on the basis of a variety of factors. For the A-J model, the rate is assumed to be established prior to the choices of the firm and not adjusted on the basis of the firm's choices.

12. If the firm borrowed its capital, economic profits are the profits it earns after making the interest payments on the borrowed capital. If the firm uses its own capital, it incurs an opportunity cost per unit of capital, which is the return the firm could obtain by lending out the funds. In this case, economic profits are the profits the firm earns after it subtracts out the profits it could obtain by lending the money.

13. In this example, K is measured in dollars and r in percentages, when it is more customary to measure inputs in physical units and price in dollars per physical unit. While less intuitive, the example can be reworded in terms of the more traditional measuring conventions for inputs. Capital is 100 million units. The fair rate of return is set at 10 cents per unit of capital. The price of capital is 8 cents per unit, meaning that the firm must pay 8 cents in interest for each unit of borrowed capital or can receive 8 cents for each unit of lent capital. The firm is allowed to make economic profits of 2 cents per unit of capital, or a total of $2 million dollars.

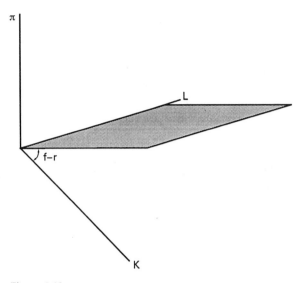

Figure 1.10
Constraint plane

1.4   Behavior of the Regulated Firm

ROR regulation restricts the options of the firm. If unregulated, the firm can choose any K, L, Q, and P. Under ROR regulation, the firm can choose only among those levels that do not result in profits in excess of the allowed amount. That is, there is a constraint on the behavior of the regulated firm. Our goal is to determine the behavior of the firm under this constraint.

Assume for now that the fair rate of return exceeds the price of capital, $f > r$, such that the allowed economic profit is positive for any positive amount of capital. The other possibilities, with f equaling r and r exceeding f, are considered later in the chapter.

The economic profits the firm is allowed to earn are represented graphically in figure 1.10. Recall that the firm is not allowed to make more than $(f - r)K$ profit. This amount is represented by a plane that is hinged on the L-axis and increases linearly with K, with a slope of $(f - r)$. As K increases, the firm is allowed to earn more profits in absolute terms; that is, the plane increases in K. For example, if the fair rate exceeds the price of capital by 2%, the firm is allowed to earn a maximum of $200,000 in economic profits if $10 million in capital is utilized (invested) and $400,000 if $20 million is utilized. (The *rate* of

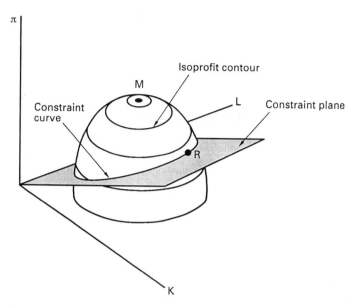

Figure 1.11
Constraint plane and profit hill

return is the same, but the absolute profits are higher.) The amount by which allowed profits increase for each extra unit of capital is $f - r$, such that the slope of the plane is $f - r$. If K is zero, allowed profit is also zero. Furthermore, allowed profits are not affected by the amount of labor that the firm uses; for a given K, the firm is allowed to make the same rate of return on this K no matter how much L it uses. The plane is therefore hinged on the L-axis. (The amount of labor the firm uses affects the profits that the firm is *able* to earn, but does not affect the amount of profits it is *allowed* to earn.)

The firm is not allowed, by the terms of ROR regulation, to make profits in excess of that represented by the plane in figure 1.10. To reflect this fact, the plane is called the "constraint plane," because the firm is constrained to make profits that are on or below this plane.

Given its technology (as embodied in the production function) and the demand for its product, the maximum profits the firm is able to earn at any input combination are given by the profit hill. Figure 1.11 shows both the profit hill and the constraint plane. The profit hill represents the profits the firm is *able* to earn given technology and demand, while the constraint plane depicts the profits that the firm is *allowed* to earn. To distinguish these two concepts of profit, the maximum profit the firm is able to earn given its technology and demand is called the "feasible" profit, while the maximum profit the firm is allowed to earn under its regulation is called the "allowed" profit. Feasible profit is given by the profit hill, and allowed profit is given by the constraint plane.

The constraint plane slices through the profit hill. The parts of the profit hill above the constraint plane correspond to input combinations with which feasible profits exceed allowed profits. The profits that are available to the regulated firm, that is, that are both feasible given technology and demand and allowed by the regulator, are given by the "sliced-off" profit hill: the part of the profit hill that remains after the part above the constraint plane is removed.

The firm maximizes its profits by choosing the highest point on the sliced-off profit hill; or, stated more accurately, by choosing the input combination that provides the greatest profits on the sliced-off profit hill. This is point R in figure 1.11.[14]

The exact location of point R can be visualized more readily when the profit hill and constraint plane are shown in two dimensions, on the K–L graph. Consider the intersection of the profit hill and the constraint plane in figure 1.11. The set of input combinations at which this intersection occurs is called the constraint curve and is mapped on the K–L graph of figure 1.12. The input combinations on the constraint curve are those with which the profits that the firm can feasibly earn given demand and technology are the same as the profits that the firm is allowed to earn. With any input combination inside the constraint curve, the firm can feasibly earn more than it is allowed to earn. If the firm chooses one of these input combinations, it must waste resources in some way (that is, produce less than is maximally possible) in order not to exceed the allowed profit level. With any input combination outside the constraint curve, the maximum profits the firm can feasibly earn given demand and technology is less than the allowed profits. That is, the firm is allowed to earn more profits than it is able to earn at these input combinations.

For each input combination on the constraint curve, the firm earns

14. As stated above, the unregulated firm chooses the input combination associated with the top of the profit hill, point M. If point M is not above the constraint plane (that is, if the constraint plane does not slice off the top of the profit hill), the regulated firm also chooses point M, behaving the same as if it were not regulated. In this case, there is essentially no regulation. We assume that the regulated firm is truly regulated such that the unconstrained profit maximizing point is not allowed under regulation.

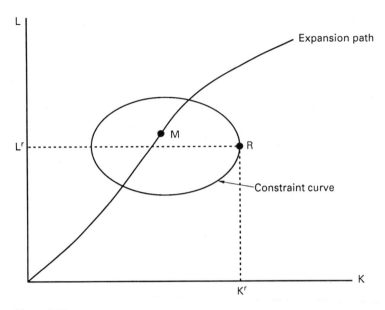

Figure 1.12
Constraint curve

the same rate of return, the fair or allowed rate. However, the absolute level of profits increases as the firm utilizes more capital. That is, points farther to the right on the constraint curve (representing more K) represent greater absolute profits than those farther to the left, though profits as a rate of return is the same. For example, a 2% return on $100 million is $2 million profits, while on $10 million it is only $200,000.

The firm chooses the input combination that results in the greatest absolute profits. This is the point on the constraint curve, labeled R, with the greatest amount of capital, that is, farthest to the right on the K–L graph. Any other point on the constraint curve provides less profit, because any other point represents the same rate of return but on a smaller amount of capital.

Point R also represents more absolute profits than any point inside or outside the constraint curve. At all points inside the constraint curve, the firm is utilizing less capital (all these points are to the left of R). The firm can feasibly earn a higher rate of return at these points than at R; however, the firm is not allowed to earn a higher rate of return. The firm is allowed to earn the same rate of return as at R, but, because the rate is applied to a smaller quantity of capital, absolute profits are lower.

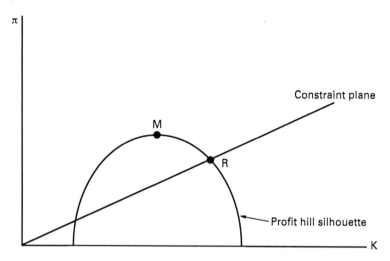

Figure 1.13
Constraint plane and profit hill

For points outside the constraint curve, the firm cannot feasibly earn as high a rate of return as the regulator allows. For points to the left of K_R, the firm earns a lower rate of return on a smaller amount of capital than at R, such that its absolute profits are clearly lower. For points to the right of K_R, the firm earns a lower rate of return but on a larger amount of capital. Recall, however, that point M is the top of the profit hill and that profits drop as the firm moves down the profit hill away from M in any direction. All points to the right of R are farther from M, and hence farther down the profit hill, representing less profit than at R.

Another graph is useful for visualizing the relation of the profit hill to the constraint plane. In figure 1.13, the profit hill and constraint plane are represented in the dimensions of K and π, with the L dimension suppressed. The profit hill in this graph gives the maximum profits that are feasible at each level of capital if labor is adjusted appropriately. That is, it is the silhouette of the profit hill as viewed from the K-π plane. The constraint plane shows the maximum allowed profit for each level of capital. As capital increases, the firm is allowed to make greater absolute profits, though the rate of return is the same. The regulated firm chooses point R, that is, the point on the intersection of the constraint plane and the profit hill where capital is greatest. If the firm were to increase its use of capital beyond this point, it would be allowed to earn more profits, but it would not be able to. That is, the profits that are feasible for the firm to earn

given technology and demand would decrease from using more capital even though its allowed profits increase.

Using the fact that the regulated firm chooses the input combination on the constraint curve that has the most capital, several important results can be shown.

Result 1: The regulated firm uses more capital than the unregulated firm.

This result is essentially definitional at this point. In using the terms
"regulated firm" and "unregulated firm," we refer to two firms that
are exactly the same except that one is subject to ROR regulation and
the other is not. Equivalently, we can think of the same firm when it
is under regulation compared to when it is not. Furthermore, the firm
is considered regulated only if the constraint plane passes below (that
is, cuts off) the top of the profit hill; otherwise the regulation would
not be effective and the firm would behave the same as when unregulated. For a regulated firm, therefore, the constraint curve in figure
1.12 must encircle point M, such that the point on the constraint curve
with the greatest amount of capital, point R, is necessarily to the right
of point M, and therefore represents more capital than M.

The impact of regulation on the firm's use of labor, on the other
hand, is not definite. Depending on the shape on the profit hill, the
regulated firm can use either more, less, or the same amount of labor
as the unregulated firm. The three possibilities are shown in figure
1.14.[15]

*Result 2: The capital/labor ratio of the regulated firm is inefficiently high for
its level of output. That is, the output that the regulated firm produces could
be more cheaply produced with less capital and more labor than the regulated
firm chooses.*

This result is the primary, and most famous, conclusion of the A-J
model. The term "A-J effect" has come to be known as the bias induced by ROR regulation toward using too much capital relative to
labor. To demonstrate the result, we first consider what the result
implies about the position of the firm's chosen input combination relative to the expansion path, and then show why this relative position
is necessary.

Figure 1.15 illustrates a situation that conforms to the result. The

---

15. While the firm might increase its use of labor, as in the first panel of figure 1.14,
there is a limit on this increase. This limit is an implication of result 3 and is discussed
below.

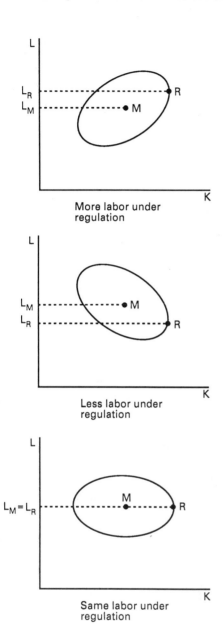

Figure 1.14
Impact of ROR regulation on firm's use of labor

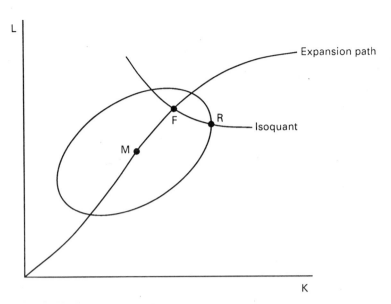

Figure 1.15
Regulated firm's K/L ratio is inefficiently high

regulated firm chooses input combination R. With this input combination, the firm produces the level of output given by the production function. The isoquant through R gives the set of input combinations that can be used to produce the same level of output as is produced at R. This isoquant intersects the expansion path at F. By definition of the expansion path, costs are lower at F than at any other point on the isoquant, including R. Point F represents greater use of labor and less use of capital than at point R. The cost of producing the regulated firm's output could therefore be reduced by using more labor and less capital. Stated another way, the regulated firm's capital/labor ratio is inefficiently high: the firm uses too much capital relative to labor for its level of output.

In figure 1.15, the regulated firm's chosen input combination, R, is "below" the expansion path. Result 2 states that this always occurs. To demonstrate the result, therefore, we must show that the regulated firm will never choose a point above or on the expansion path.

Consider figure 1.16 in which the constraint curve and expansion path are drawn such that the firm chooses a point *above* the expansion path. In this case, the firm would choose an inefficient input mix, but the inefficiency is in the opposite direction than stated in the result:

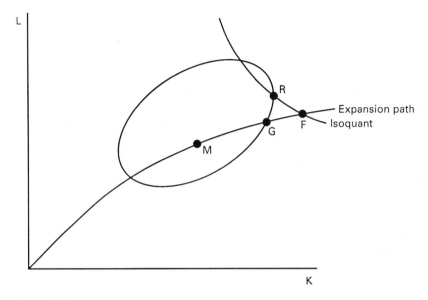

Figure 1.16
Regulated firm's *K/L* ratio is inefficiently low: an impossible situation

the firm uses an inefficiently *low* capital/labor ratio. We can show that this situation is impossible. Consider point *G*, where the expansion path intersects the constraint curve. Absolute profits at *R* are necessarily greater than at *G*: $\pi_R > \pi_G$. This is true because the rate of return is the same at both *R* and *G*, because they are both on the constraint curve representing the allowed rate of return, and yet *R* represents more capital than *G* and hence more absolute profits. Essentially, this comparison is simply a restatement of the fact that the firm chooses the point on the constraint curve that provides the greatest absolute profits, such that π_R exceeds profits at any other point on the constraint curve by definition of R.

It can also be shown, using a different line of logic, that $\pi_R < \pi_G$. Consider point *F*, where the isoquant through *R* intersects the expansion path. As discussed above, $\pi_F > \pi_R$, because costs are lower at F and output (and hence revenues) are the same. Furthermore, $\pi_G > \pi_F$ because *G* is closer to point *M*, which is the top of the profit hill. (Because the profit hill is indeed shaped like a hill with its top at *M*, profits decrease as one moves along the expansion path beyond *M*. F is farther from *M* along the expansion path than *G*, meaning that it is lower on the profit hill.) Because $\pi_G > \pi_F$ and $\pi_F > \pi_R$, it must be the

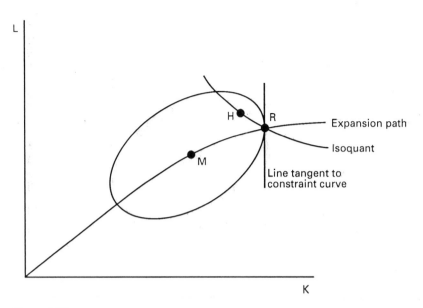

Figure 1.17
Regulated firm's *K/L* ratio is efficient: an impossible situation

case that $\pi_G > \pi_R$. However, this contradicts the fact that $\pi_R > \pi_G$. Because profits at R cannot both exceed and be less than profits at G, the situation depicted in figure 1.16 is impossible.

Now consider the situation depicted in figure 1.17 in which the firm's chosen input combination is on the expansion path, such that the firm is choosing the efficient input combination for its level of output. We can show that this situation is also impossible. Recall that R is the point on the constraint curve with the greatest amount of capital. Because of this, any point on the constraint curve near R is necessarily to the left of R, meaning that the slope of the constraint curve at R is infinite (that is, the line tangent to the constraint curve at R is vertical.) The isoquant through R is downward sloping but not vertical, reflecting the fact that labor can be substituted for capital without affecting output.[16] Therefore, the isoquant cuts and passes inside the constraint curve.

Consider points that are inside the constraint curve and near R.

---

16. If the isoquant is vertical (that is, output depends on capital only and does not increase with labor), then the situation in figure 1.17 is possible. In fact, it is the only situation possible, meaning that the firm necessarily chooses the efficient input combination. This extreme situation is implicitly excluded for the A-J result.

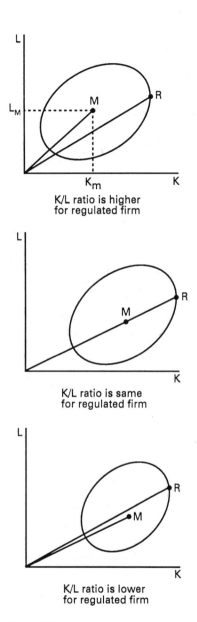

Figure 1.18
K/L ratio of regulated and unregulated firm

Feasible profits at these points are higher than profits at R, because these points represent parts of the profit hill that have been sliced off by the constraint plane (they are higher up the profit hill, closer to M).[17] Now consider a specific point, H, which is inside the constraint curve near R but is also on the isoquant through R. By the above argument, $\pi_H > \pi_R$. However, because R is on the expansion path, $\pi_R > \pi_H$. (Again, costs are lower at R than at H by definition of the expansion path, and yet output and revenues are the same.) Because H cannot obtain profits that are simultaneously greater than and less than the profits at R, the situation depicted in figure 1.17 is impossible.

Result 2 has caused some confusion in the field. The confusion arises from a false syllogism: the capital/labor ratio of the regulated firm is inefficiently high and the capital/labor ratio of the unregulated firm is at the efficient level; "therefore" the capital/labor ratio of the regulated firm is higher than that of the regulated firm. Actually, the capital/labor ratio of the regulated firm can be either greater than, less than, or equal to that of the unregulated firm. In the first panel of figure 1.18, the regulated firm's capital/labor ratio exceeds that of the unregulated firm. To see this, consider the ray from the origin to point M. The slope of this ray is L_M (the "rise") divided by K_M (the "run"). That is, the slope of the ray from the origin to M is the inverse of the capital/labor ratio at M. Similarly, the slope of the ray from the origin to R is the inverse of the capital/labor ratio at R. Because the slope of the ray to R is lower than the slope of the ray to M, the inverse of the capital/labor ratio is lower at R, which is equivalent to saying that the capital/labor ratio is higher.

Contrary to the false syllogism, the capital/labor ratio need not be greater at R than M. The second and third panels depict situations in which the regulated firm has the same and lower capital/labor ratio than the unregulated firm.

The problem with the logic that led to the false syllogism is that it ignores output. Result 2 states that the unregulated firm has an inefficiently high capital/labor ratio *for its level of output*. However, the output of the regulated firm is not generally the same as that of the unregulated firm. It is therefore possible that the regulated firm uses

---

17. Note that the points must be near R for their profits to be higher. The sliced-off part of the profit hill represents points for which the rate of return exceeds the allowed rate. For points sufficiently far from R, absolute profits can be less even though the rate of return is greater.

a capital/labor ratio that is inefficiently high for its *own* output level and yet is nevertheless lower than the efficient ratio for the unregulated firm's output level. Stated graphically, result 2 requires that R be below the expansion path; however, the ray to R can be steeper than the ray to M even though R is below the expansion path. Figure 1.19 depicts this possibility.

For particular types of production processes, it is possible to state definitely the relation between the capital/labor ratios of the regulated and unregulated firms. "Homothetic" production functions, which are widely used in theoretical and econometric work, are an important case. A production function is defined as homothetic if the expansion path associated with the function is a ray. That is, under homothetic production, the cost-minimizing capital/labor ratio is the same for all levels of output.[18]

If the production function is homothetic, then the capital/labor ratio of the regulated firm is necessarily higher than that of the unregulated firm. Figure 1.20 illustrates this situation. The expansion path passes though M and, by homotheticity, is a ray from the origin. By

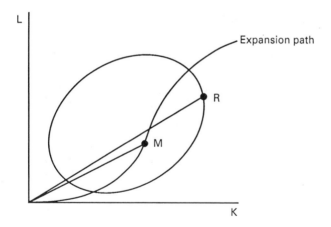

Figure 1.19
K/L ratio of regulated firm lower than for unregulated firm

---

18. A homothetic production function can, but need not, exhibit constant returns to scale. Constant returns to scale exist when output expands proportionately to inputs (e.g., doubling all inputs results in a doubling of output). Homotheticity requires that, when output expands, the cost-minimizing level of each input expands by the same proportion as that of each other input, but not necessarily by the proportion by which output expands. For example, if output doubles, homotheticity is met if the cost-minimizing levels of capital and labor each increase by, say, half.

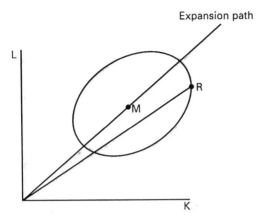

Figure 1.20
Homothetic production function

result 2, point R is necessarily below the expansion path. The slope of the ray from the origin to R is therefore less than the slope of the ray from the origin to M, because the latter is the expansion path that passes above R. Since the slope of the ray is the inverse of the capital/labor ratio, this ratio is higher at R than M.

Consider now the output level of the regulated firm. One of the basic results of economic theory is that an unregulated monopolist produces too little output by setting price above marginal cost. A purpose of regulation is to induce public utilities to increase output and lower price. Unfortunately, ROR regulation does not necessarily achieve this objective. The regulated firm might, depending on the shape of its profit hill, produce more, the same, or less output than the unregulated firm. Figure 1.21 illustrates the three possibilities.

Result 1 states that the regulated firm uses more capital than the unregulated firm. With more capital, one might expect that the regulated firm would produce more output. However, this expectation ignores labor. Recall that the firm might increase or decrease its use of labor. If it uses less labor, output could decrease even though capital increases. This is the situation depicted in the third panel of figure 1.21. Furthermore, because demand is downward sloping, the firm in this situation would raise price to be consistent with its lower level of output, such that the price charged by a regulated firm might be higher than if unregulated.

The firm might raise output, as shown in the first panel. However,

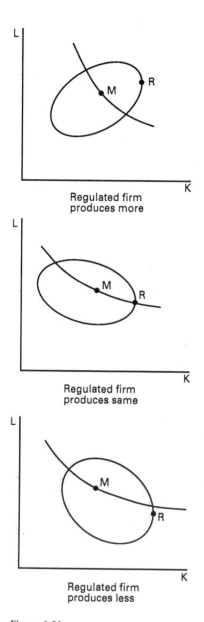

Figure 1.21
Effect of ROR regulation on output level

as shown in the next result, there is a limit on how far output can expand under ROR regulation.

Result 3: The regulated firm necessarily operates in the elastic portion of demand, where marginal revenue is positive. That is, the regulated firm never increases its output beyond the point at which marginal revenue is zero.

Suppose the contrary, that the regulated firm chooses an output level at which marginal revenue is negative. This supposition leads to a contradiction. Figure 1.22 illustrates the situation. As discussed in section 1.2, marginal revenue is generally positive for low levels of output and eventually becomes negative at higher levels of output. The isoquant in the graph is for the output level at which marginal revenue is zero. Consequently, points below this isoquant represent output levels at which marginal revenue is positive, and points above it correspond to output levels at which marginal revenue is negative. Point R is placed above the isoquant, reflecting the supposition that marginal revenue is negative at the firm's chosen output level.[19]

Consider point H, which represents the same capital as R but less labor. With less labor, output is lower at H than at R.[20] Because marginal revenue is negative over these levels of output, revenue is therefore higher a H than at R. Because less labor is used at H than at R (without a change in capital), costs are lower at H than R. Because revenues are higher and costs are lower, $\pi_H > \pi_R$. However, R is on the constraint curve while H is outside of it. This means that the rate of return at R is the allowed rate, while that at H is below the allowed rate. Because both R and H represent the same amount of capital, the lower rate of return at H means that $\pi_H < \pi_R$, contradicting the first comparison.

The reason the regulated firm produces in the elastic portion of demand, where marginal revenue is positive, is intuitively meaningful. At any level of capital, if the firm finds that its marginal revenue is negative, then it can increase its profits by decreasing its use of labor. With less labor, its costs are lower, and it produces less such that its revenues are higher. Because the level of capital is not changed, the firm's allowed profits are the same and yet its feasible profits are

---

19. As shown in section 1.2, marginal revenue is necessarily positive at point M, the top of the profit hill. Therefore, the graph represents a situation in which the firm increases output from the elastic into the inelastic portion of demand when subjected to regulation.

20. Given, as usual, that the marginal product of labor is positive.

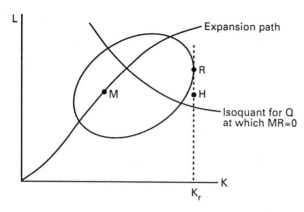

Figure 1.22
Regulated firm operates in inelastic portion of demand: impossible

higher. If feasible profits are less than allowed profits, then increasing feasible profits clearly helps the firm. If feasible profits exceed allowed profits after labor has been reduced, capital can be expanded to increase allowed profits. This expansion of capital decreases feasible profits, but because feasible profits exceed allowed profits, the firm is not able to keep all of its feasible profits anyway. With higher allowed profits, the firm is better off. In either case, the firm will continue to decrease its use of labor until it enters the elastic portion of demand, where marginal revenue is positive.

Result 2 states that the regulated firm will choose a point below the expansion path. Result 3 states that the firm's chosen point will also be below the isoquant for output at which marginal revenue is zero. The complete picture is shown in figure 1.23.

Compare now the firm's chosen point with the socially optimal outcome. As discussed in section I.3, pricing at marginal cost provides the first-best output. However, with a natural monopoly facing continuously declining average cost, pricing at marginal costs results in the firm losing money. If the regulator cannot subsidize the firm, then the second-best outcome becomes the goal. The second-best outcome consists of the firm's pricing at average cost (such that profits are zero) and using the cost-minimizing inputs for the level of output demanded at that price. The expansion path represents points that are cost minimizing, and the zero-profit contour represents points that result in zero profit. The second-best outcome occurs, therefore, at the intersection of the expansion path and the zero-profit contour,

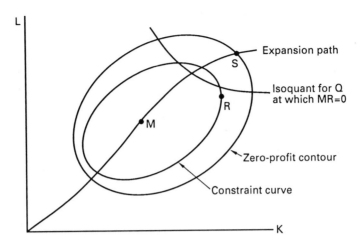

Figure 1.23
Regulated firm chooses input combination below expansion path and the isoquant for $MR = 0$

where profits are zero (such that price equals average cost) and costs are minimized. This intersection is point S in the graph.

Ideally, the regulator would like to establish a form of regulation that induces the firm to move out the expansion path from M to (or at least toward) S, using inputs efficiently and increasing output and reducing price. Result 2 shows that under ROR regulation, the firm will not move out the expansion path but rather will produce with an inefficient input combination. In fact, the firm need not increase output and may even decrease it. If the firm increases output, result 3 shows that there is a limit to how far the firm would possibly increase its output; in particular, it would never move into the inelastic portion of demand. The A-J critique of ROR regulation is therefore quite damaging: ROR regulation induces the firm to be inefficient and yet does not necessarily induce it to increase output and decrease price.

The problems with ROR regulation essentially arise from the fact that it gives the firm incentives based on capital while capital per se is not what the regulator is wanting the firm to increase. We investigate below whether the situation is improved by reducing the allowed rate of return, thereby reducing the profits the firm earns on capital. But first we consider a result that shows that ROR regulation does not induce one type of inefficiency, despite a widely held myth to the contrary.

Result 4: The regulated firm produces as much output as possible given its capital and labor.

This result states that the regulated firm will not indulge in pure waste in the sense of producing less than is maximally possible given its inputs. With respect to capital, the result means that the firm will not acquire nonproductive capital, that is, capital that does not serve a productive function. The result contradicts a commonly held belief that firms under ROR regulation have an incentive to purchase capital that is not used. The result is demonstrated as follows. At any input levels K_0 and L_0, the maximum amount of output the firm can produce is given by its production function evaluated at these input levels: $f(K_0, L_0)$. The firm can choose to waste inputs and produce a lower level of output: $Q_0 < f(K_0, L_0)$. By result 3, the firm necessarily chooses to operate in a region of demand where marginal revenue is positive. The firm therefore earns less revenue if it produces less output. Because the cost of K_0 and L_0 is the same whether or not the firm uses the inputs productively, feasible profits decrease if the firm produces less than is maximally possible with these inputs.

Figure 1.24 depicts the situation in the graph of profits and capital. If the firm uses its capital to produce as much output as possible, then it chooses point R_0 and earns profits π_0. If the firm wastes capital, its profit hill is lower: at any level of capital it earns less profit than if the capital were used productively. With waste, the best the firm can do is operate at point R_1 and earn profits π_1. Because $\pi_0 > \pi_1$, the firm chooses not to waste.

This result does not contradict result 2, which states that the firm chooses an inefficiently large amount of capital. Two different kinds of inefficiency are being considered. The firm chooses an input combination that is inefficient for its level of output (result 2), but *given its inputs* it produces as much output as possible (result 4). Stated in terms of isoquants: the firm will choose the wrong point on the isoquant (costs would be lower if it moved to the expansion path), but it nevertheless produces the full amount of output designated by that isoquant.

The use of nonproductive capital is often called "goldplating," referring to the idea that a firm might plate its building and fixtures in gold simply because gold is more costly than other materials. It is widely thought that the A-J effect means that a firm under ROR reg-

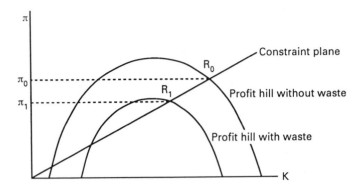

Figure 1.24
Effect of wasting inputs

ulation will goldplate. This conception is incorrect. The A-J effect (result 2) states that the firm will use too much capital relative to labor but does not state that the firm will waste capital. In fact, result 4 implies that the regulated firm will not purchase capital that does not serve a productive purpose, nor will it purchase a less productive type of capital when it could purchase a more productive type instead.

The concept that a firm under ROR regulation will not purchase nonproductive capital is somewhat subtle. If, for example, the firm is allowed to earn 10% profits on any extra capital it purchases and the cost of extra capital is 8%, why would the firm not buy extra capital, even if the capital were unproductive?

The answer depends on a careful differentiation of *allowed* profits and *feasible* profits. Consider figure 1.25. Suppose the firm starts with K_L amount of capital. At this level of capital, the firm is able to earn π_{L1} but is only allowed to earn π_{L2}. If the firm were to stay at that capital level, then it would need to waste inputs to reduce its profits by $\pi_{L1} - \pi_{L2}$, so that its actual profits do not exceed the allowed amount. However, instead of wasting and earning profits of π_{L2}, the firm would earn more profits by increasing its amount of capital toward K_R. With K_R, the profits the firm is able to earn are exactly the same as the profits it is allowed to earn; that is, by using its inputs as productively as possible, the firm with K_R is just able to earn the maximum profits that it is allowed to earn. Now, consider an increase in capital beyond K_R to K_H. The amount of profit the firm is allowed to earn increases, because the firm has more capital. However, the amount that the firm is able to earn decreases, even if the extra capital is used

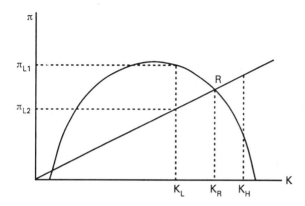

Figure 1.25
Allowed versus feasible profits

as productively as possible. If nonproductive capital is purchased, or the extra capital is not used as productively as possible, the profits the firm is able to earn decrease even more.

To repeat: At levels of capital lower than K_R, the firm must waste so as to reduce profits to the allowed level. However, rather than wasting, the firm is better off by purchasing more capital, such that its allowed profits rise. Once the firm has reached K_R, the maximum profits it is able to earn equal the profits it is allowed to earn. If the firm wasted at this point, it would earn less than the allowed amount. Also, if the firm increased its capital beyond K_R, it would be allowed to make extra profits but would not be able to, whether the extra capital were productive or nonproductive.

Return now to the question about the firm that faces a 10% allowed rate and yet can purchase capital at 8%. At the firm's chosen capital level, the firm would be allowed to earn more profit if it purchased more capital, but it would not be able to, even if it used the capital productively. If the firm cannot earn extra profits with productive capital, it will certainly not purchase *nonproductive* capital.[21]

---

21. In the extreme case of fixed-proportions production (i.e., no substitution between labor and capital), the distinction fades between wasting capital and using an inefficiently high capital/labor ratio. Isoquants are L-shaped under fixed-proportions production, with the cost-minimizing input combination being at the kink. Under regulation, the firm will choose a point on the leg of the isoquant representing more capital than is needed for that output. Result 4 is still correct: the firm produces as much output as designated by the isoquant. However, the same output could be produced with less capital and no extra labor. In that sense, the excess capital is indistinguishable from pure waste.

As stated in relation to results 2 and 3, the basic problem with ROR regulation is that the firm makes profit on capital, whereas the goal of regulation is not to increase capital per se. Let us examine therefore whether the distortions from ROR regulation can be alleviated if the firm is not allowed to make as much, or even any, profits on capital. We obtain two more results.

Result 5: When the fair rate of return is reduced toward the cost of capital (that is, when the allowed rate of economic profit is lowered toward zero), the regulated firm increases its use of capital.

Figure 1.26 illustrates this result. The slope of the constraint plane is $f - r$, that is, the allowed rate of economic profit. As f drops toward r, this slope becomes less positive. More of the profit hill is sliced off with the lower f. The firm chooses the profit-maximizing point on the more severely sliced-off profit hill, increasing capital from K_0 to K_1. Figure 1.27 illustrates the same ideas in a somewhat more discernible fashion, by collapsing figure 1.26 to only the K-π dimensions.

The firm still uses an inefficiently high capital/labor ratio, because result 2 holds whenever f exceeds r. Furthermore, no matter how close f is to r, the firm still does not produce in the inelastic region of demand. If necessary, the firm reduces its labor sufficiently such that the increase in capital does not move it into this inelastic region.

Clearly, reducing the amount of profit that the firm is allowed to earn on capital does not solve the basic problems. Consider, however, not allowing the firm to make *any* economic return on capital.

Result 6: If the fair rate of return is set equal to the cost of capital (that is, if the allowed rate of economic profit is zero), then the firm is indifferent among many levels of output and many input combinations, including the option of closing down.

If f is set equal to r, then the slope of the constraint plane is zero such that it is flat at the base of the profit hill, as shown in the first panel of figure 1.28. The constraint curve in the K-L dimensions is therefore the set of input combinations that result in exactly zero profits. That is, the constraint curve is the same as the isoprofit contour for zero profits, as given in the second panel.

The firm is not allowed to make more than zero profits and is indifferent among the various options available to it for making zero profits. The firm could choose input combinations on the constraint curve, produce as much output as possible with these inputs, and earn zero

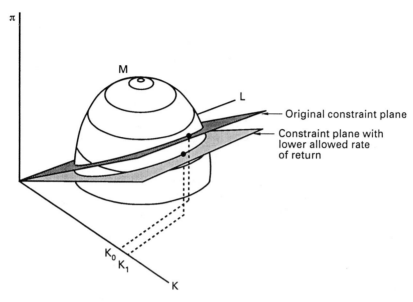

Figure 1.26
Effect of lowering the fair rate of return

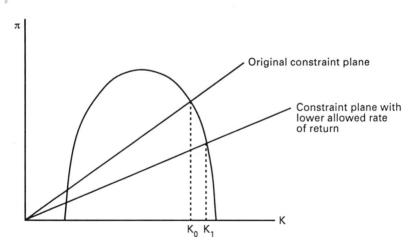

Figure 1.27
Effect of lowering the fair rate of return

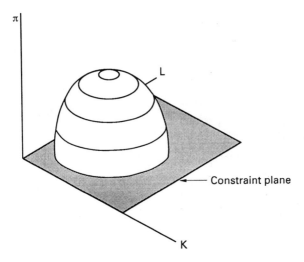

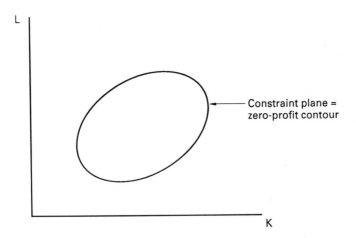

Figure 1.28
Fair rate of return set equal to cost of capital

profits. Alternatively, the firm could choose an input combination in-side the constraint curve. Even though it would be able to earn posi-tive profits with these inputs, it would not be allowed to earn more than zero profits. Consequently, it would waste inputs until its prof-its fell to zero. As a third alternative, the firm could earn zero profits by choosing no inputs and halting production. The firm is indifferent, therefore, among producing without waste at any input combination on the constraint curve, producing with waste at any input combina-tion inside the constraint curve, and not producing at all.

Result 6 contains an important lesson that generalizes beyond ROR regulation. The problem with ROR regulation is that it establishes a mechanism under which the firm earns profits on capital when the regulator is not interested in increasing the use of capital per se. How-ever, the solution is not simply to prevent the firm from earning any profits. If the firm earns zero profit no matter what it does (at least within a range), the firm becomes indifferent in its choice of input, outputs, and whether to waste. In that case, there is no reason to expect the firm to make choices that satisfy the regulator's goals. The solution is rather to establish a situation in which the firm earns *more* profit at the socially optimal outcome than at any other. Profits might be zero at this outcome, but, for the firm to choose it, profits must then be negative at all other outcomes.

Consider now the possibility of lowering the allowed rate of return *below* the cost of capital. An important result obtains.

Result 7: If the fair rate of return is set below the cost of capital, then the regulated firm will choose to utilize no inputs and produce no output.

If r exceeds f, the constraint plane is downward sloping, as shown in figure 1.29. Allowed economic profits are negative for any positive amount of capital. If the firm continues to produce, it minimizes its losses at K_0. At higher levels of capital, the firm is able to earn greater profits, but its allowed profits are lower; while with less capital (but still a positive amount), the firm is allowed to earn more profits but is not able to.

Rather than produce at a loss, the firm will choose to go out of business, that is, use no inputs and produce no outputs. Profits are zero under this option, and because zero profits are greater than the negative profits the firm earns at K_0, the firm exercises this option.

In reality, the firm might not legally be able to go out of business. For example, it is doubtful that the electric utility for an area would

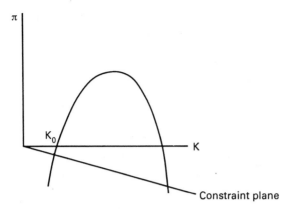

Figure 1.29
Fair rate of return set below the cost of capital

be allowed to stop production. Furthermore, the concept embedded in the A-J model that capital can be bought and sold at a fixed rate r does not reflect the fact that the utility's capital (e.g., a hydroelectric plant) is highly specialized such that markets for it do not exist. The utility might not be able to dispose of its capital, in which case it might make more profits (smaller losses) by producing output than by shutting down. It is probably even more realistic to expect that the price the utility can obtain for its capital depends on the rate of return that the regulator sets as "fair." That is, the most that capitalists would be willing to pay for the utility's capital, which can only be used for the production of the utility's output, is the return the capitalists expect they would be able to earn with the capital. Once the regulator sets a fair rate of return, the capitalists would be willing to pay at most this fair return. Thus, if the regulator attempts to set f below r, r will simply drop until it is below or equal to f.[22]

The point of result 7 is simply that the firm has an incentive to reduce its capital if it is allowed to make more profits (smaller losses) with less capital. The same types of distortions occur as when the firm is allowed to make more profits by using more capital, only in reverse. As discussed in relation to result 6, the solution is to develop an alternative form of regulation under which the firm faces incentives that are consistent with the regulator's goals.

---

22. If there are a sufficient number of capitalists, r would not drop below f, because if r were below f, it would be bid up to f. However, it is doubtful that the number of capitalists who are willing and able to purchase a utility's specialized capital is sufficiently large for the market for this capital to be efficient in this sense.

1.5   Empirical Evidence on the A-J Effect

The A-J model abstracts from many important aspects of real-world regulation. The regulated firm is assumed to be prohibited from earning more than the allowed profits in each time period, even though in reality regulated firms' profits are allowed to fluctuate above and below the allowed level as long as the average profit over a number of periods is within the allowed amount. The firm is assumed to face a capital cost independent of the fair rate of return that the regulator sets, whereas in reality the cost of borrowing funds depends on the fair rate, and the regulator sets the fair rate based, in part, on the cost of capital to the firm. The firm is assumed to know its demand and costs exactly, when usually a firm has only partial information. Strategic considerations, by which the firm might make choices in one period in order to affect the regulator's decisions in later periods, are also omitted.

The A-J model has value, even if its results do not generalize to the more complex situation of the real world. Its value lies in focusing the concept that any particular form of regulation induces the firm to act in a particular way that may be consistent or inconsistent with the regulator's goals.

It is useful, however, to recognize that the A-J model can be tested, because the procedure for such testing further elucidates the model. A study by Courville (1974), one of the first empirical tests of the A-J model, is particularly well suited to elucidating the method and difficulties of such testing.[23]

The main proposition of the A-J model is that the regulated firm employs too much capital relative to labor given its level of output. This proposition can be stated in terms of a hypothesis that is empirically testable. Consider figure 1.30. According to the A-J model, the regulated firm chooses point R while the cost-minimizing input combination for this level of output is F. At F, the isocost line is tangent to the isoquant, as required for cost minimization. At R, the isocost is not tangent to the isoquant. All isocost lines have a slope equal to the negative of the ratio of input prices: $-r/w$. The slope of the isoquant at any point is the negative of the marginal rate of technical substitution $(MRTS)$ at that point. Recall that $MRTS$ is the amount of extra labor that must be employed to keep output constant if capital is re-

---

23. Other empirical studies have been conducted by Spann (1974) and Peterson (1975).

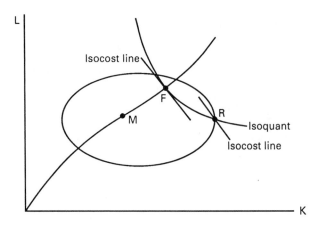

Figure 1.30
Observable consequence of the A-J effect

duced by one unit. By definition, *MRTS* is the ratio of the marginal products of capital and labor; that is, $MRTS = MPK/MPL$.[24] Because marginal products change as the firm uses more or less of an input, *MRTS* is different at different points on the isoquant. At the cost-minimizing input combination, *F*, *MRTS* equals the ratio of input prices because the isocost line and isoquant are tangent. However, at *R*, more capital and less labor is used, such that *MRTS* is lower than at *F* and, in particular, is less than the ratio of prices. Stated succinctly, because the isocost line is steeper than the isoquant at *R*, $r/w > MRTS$. Equivalently, because *MRTS* equals the ratio of marginal products, $r/w > MPK/MPL$.

This fact constitutes a testable hypothesis. The A-J model states that the regulated firm will choose point R, where the ratio of input prices exceeds the ratio of marginal products. By observing the input

24. This equality can be easily demonstrated. If the firm uses one less unit of capital, its output decreases by *MPK*. To keep output constant, the firm must increase its use of labor enough to boost output to its original level, that is, to increase output by *MPK*, which is the amount lost with the reduction in capital. Each unit of labor increases output by *MPL*. Therefore, the amount of extra labor the firm must use is the amount of extra output required (*MPK*) divided by the amount of output obtained with each extra unit of labor (*MPL*). For example, suppose the marginal product of capital is six and that of labor is three. If capital is reduced by one unit, output decreases by six units. To regain those six units of output, the firm must employ two extra units of labor, because each unit of labor boosts output by three units. Hence, *MRTS* (that is, the amount of labor required to keep output constant when capital is reduced by one unit) equals $MPK/MPL = 6/3 = 2$.

prices and marginal products for a regulated firm, the validity of this hypothesis for that firm can be assessed.

The difficulty, of course, is that marginal products are not directly observable. Rather, marginal products are approximated by estimating the firm's production function and deriving marginal products. The ratio of these estimated marginal products are then compared with the ratio of input prices, and statistical tests are performed to determine whether the two ratios are significantly different.

Courville performs this test using data on electric generation plants. He considers three inputs: capital, labor, and fuel (labeled F, with price v). Because fuel costs are treated like labor costs under ROR regulation, the A-J model implies that $r/v > MPK/MPF$, just as $r/w > MPK/MPL$. To derive marginal products, Courville assumes that the production function for electric generation is Cobb-Douglas, which takes the form:

$$\log Q = \alpha + \beta \log K + \mu \log F + \psi \log L + \epsilon,$$

where ϵ is an error term. Under this specification, the marginal products are:[25]

$$MPK = \beta(Q/K);$$

$$MPF = \mu(Q/F);$$

$$MPL = \psi(Q/L).$$

By estimating the parameters β, μ, and ψ, and observing the firm's levels of Q, K, F, and L, the marginal products are calculated.

To reflect differences in the production technologies among plants, two terms are added to the production function. (1) Different-sized plants generally use different technologies and have different levels of efficiency. To reflect this fact, Courville includes the capacity of the plant, denoted C, as an explanatory variable in the production function. Capacity is defined as the maximum output the plant is capable of producing. (2) Output Q is measured as total kilowatt-hours produced in the year. However, each plant's output at any point in time varies over times of day and season (for example, output is often greater in the peak afternoon period, when customers use their air conditioners, than in the morning or evening). This variation affects the estimation of the production function because the efficiency with which

---

25. $MPK = \Delta Q/\Delta K = (\Delta \log Q/\Delta \log K)(Q/K) = \beta(Q/K)$. Similarly for MPF and MPL.

a plant operates depends on the degree of variability in its output. To reflect this fact, Courville includes a variable that partially captures the variation in output: capacity utilization, denoted U, which is the annual output of the plant expressed as a percentage of the plant's capacity.[26]

With these additions, the equation to be estimated is

$$\log Q = \alpha + \beta \log K + \mu \log F + \psi \log L + \zeta C + \theta U + \epsilon.$$

The equation is estimated with annual data on the inputs, outputs, and other characteristics of 134 electricity-generation plants. To reflect the fact that technology changes over time, the 134 plants are grouped into four categories on the basis of when they were built (1948–50, 1951–55, 1956–59, and 1960–66), and the production function is estimated separately for each group.

In preliminary estimation, the variable for labor consistently entered with the wrong sign and without statistical significance. Courville therefore eliminates labor from the equation for final estimation. As a result, he is able to test whether $r/v > MPK/MPF$, but not whether $r/w > MPK/MPL$.

The estimation results for plants built in the period 1960–66 are the following:

$$\log Q = 0.73 + 0.10 \log K + 0.97 \log F + 0.00012C + 0.34U,$$
$$\quad (3.4) \quad (3.1) \quad\quad (17.4) \quad\quad (0.13) \quad\quad (3.0)$$

with the t-statistic for each estimated parameter given in parentheses.[27] Results for plants built in other periods are qualitatively similar, except for those built in 1955–59, for which the coefficient of capital is estimated to be implausibly negative. Eliminating the plants built in 1955–59 left 110 plants for which to compare ratios of capital and fuel prices with ratios of marginal products.

For each plant, the ratio of marginal products is calculated:

$$MPK/MPF = \beta(Q/K) \,/\, \mu(Q/F)$$
$$\qquad\qquad = (\beta/\mu)\,(F/K).$$

---

26. The use of this variable might be problematic econometrically. Because U is defined as Q/C, entering U as an explanatory variable is nearly the same as entering the dependent variable, $\log Q$, as an explanatory variable.

27. A t-statistic indicates the precision with which the parameter is estimated, with higher t-statistics representing greater precision. As a reference point, a t-statistic exceeding 2.0 indicates that the hypothesis that the parameter is zero can be rejected with 95% confidence.

For plants built in 1960–66, the estimates of β and μ indicate that $MPK/MPF = (0.10/0.97) (F/K) = 0.103(F/K)$. By inserting the levels of F and K for each plant, the ratio of marginal products for each plant is calculated. Comparison with the ratio of input prices determines whether, as suggested by the A-J model, the ratio of input prices exceeds the ratio of marginal products such that the firm is using too much capital relative to fuel for its level of output.

Courville's results are striking. Using capital expressed in real terms (that is, deflated by a price index) and fuel consumption in the first year of each plant's operations, he finds that for *all* 110 plants the ratio of input prices exceeds the ratio of marginal products as the A-J model suggests. Furthermore, this comparison is statistically significant at the 95% confidence level for 105 of the 110 plants.

Courville repeats the tests using different measures of capital and fuel consumption, because the most appropriate measure of these variables is not clear (for example, fuel consumption in the first year of operation versus the year of the plant's greatest output). In each of these sets of tests the A-J effect is confirmed. In the "worse" case (i.e., using the set of measures that least supports the A-J model), he finds the A-J effect to be confirmed with 95% confidence for 71 of the 110 plants. The ratio of input prices exceeds the ratio of marginal products in even more than these 71 plants, though not significantly so.

The same concepts are used to calculate the extra cost that results from overcapitalization. Refer again to figure 1.30. The isocost line through R represents the cost of producing the firm's output with its chosen inputs. The isocost through F represents the cost of producing the same output with the cost-minimizing inputs. The difference between these two costs is the loss due to the inefficiency induced by ROR regulation.

Using the estimated production functions, Courville calculates this loss for each plant. He finds that costs are as much as 40.6% higher than minimum because of the plants' inefficiently high capital/labor ratios. Averaged over all plants, the loss is 11.4%.

Courville's method of testing the A-J model focuses on result 2, which deals with the input mix of the firm. Bailey (1973) suggests another way to test the A-J model, based on the firm's output. Result 3 states that the regulated firm produces a level of output at which marginal revenue is positive. Since marginal revenue being positive implies that the demand elasticity exceeds one (in magnitude), Bailey

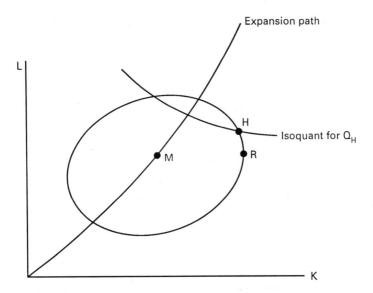

Figure 1.31
Regulated firm under ROR regulation and a maximum price

observes that a test of whether elasticity exceeds one constitutes as test of the A-J model (though not of the A-J *effect*, which is result 2).

The two methods of testing are complementary. Courville's method tests whether the firm uses an inefficient input combination, while Bailey's method tests whether the firm keeps output in the elastic region of demand. It is possible that the regulated firm overcapitalizes in accordance with result 2 but is nevertheless somehow induced by its regulator to increase output into the inelastic portion of demand (where marginal revenue is negative). This inducement might occur, for example, if the regulator applies ROR regulation but also provides oversight on prices. In this situation, the firm is not able to choose its price unilaterally within only the constraint that profits do not exceed the allowed amount. Rather, there is a maximum price the regulator is willing to approve. If demand at this price is so high that marginal revenue is negative, then the firm necessarily produces in the inelastic portion of demand. Yet the firm still uses too much capital relative to labor for its level of output. Figure 1.31 illustrates the situation. Under the type of ROR regulation described by the A-J model, the firm chooses R where the capital/labor ratio is inefficiently high and output is sufficiently low that marginal revenue is positive. Suppose, however, that the regulator also oversees price directly and that the highest price the regulator will approve is P_H. At this price, the quantity demanded is Q_H, which, for illustration, is assumed to be sufficiently large that marginal revenue is negative. The firm is restricted in its choice to any input combination on or above the isoquant for Q_H, because it cannot restrict output below this level by raising price. The firm would choose point H, which contains the most capital, and hence profits, of those points on the constraint curve and above the isoquant. At H, the firm has an inefficiently high capital/labor ratio for its level of output and yet is producing in the inelastic portion of demand.

In this situation, the method used by Courville is expected to detect the presence of overcapitalization, whereas that suggested by Bailey is expected to indicate that output is greater than would occur without direct price control by the regulator. Thus, applying the two tests together assists in identifying the aspects of the A-J model that are applicable in a particular setting.

2

Regulatory Mechanisms to Induce Optimal Outcomes for One-Product Natural Monopolies

2.1 Introduction

The Averch-Johnson model indicates that rate-of-return regulation does not induce a firm to choose the optimal inputs and output. The same method can be used, however, to identify other mechanisms that do induce optimality. In this chapter we examine three types of regulation that are similar to rate-of-return regulation. Each places a limit on the profits the firm is allowed to earn but differs from ROR regulation in the factor on which allowed profits is calculated. Under ROR regulation, allowed profits rise with capital. Under the three mechanisms described in this chapter, allowed profits rise with output, sales (that is, revenue), and costs, respectively. It is shown that, under certain circumstances, these regulatory mechanisms induce the firm to choose a level of output and inputs that is arbitrarily close to the second-best outcome. Bailey's (1973) work in this area is particularly useful in identifying these results.

A mechanism is also introduced that induces the firm to choose the first-best outcome. This mechanism is different in form from ROR regulation in that it does not place a limit on the firm's profit. A regulator might, therefore, consider this form of regulation inappropriate for equity reasons. However, the concepts embodied in this form of regulation—the forces that drive the optimality—are important and serve as the basis for the design of other, more equitable regulatory mechanisms.

To facilitate the discussions of alternative forms of regulation, recall the concepts of first- and second-best outcomes. Total surplus is maximized when price is equal to marginal cost. The first-best outcome consists therefore of using the cost-minimizing input combination to produce the level of output that is demanded when price equals mar-

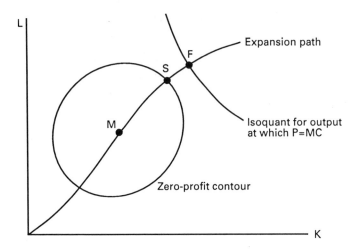

Figure 2.1
First- and second-best outcomes

ginal cost. This outcome is illustrated in figure 2.1 as point F, where the isoquant for the level of output at which price equals marginal cost intersects the expansion path.[1]

This first-best outcome might not be feasible. For many public utilities, fixed costs are so high that average cost exceeds marginal cost at relevant demand levels, such that pricing at marginal cost causes the firm to lose money. If the firm's losses cannot be subsidized, then price must be raised to average cost. The second-best outcome consists therefore of using the least-cost input combination to produce the level of output demanded when price equals average cost. This outcome is point S, where the expansion path intersects the zero-profit contour.

Four types of regulation are described. The findings for each can be summarized as follows:

1. Return-on-output (ROO) regulation. The firm is allowed to earn a certain amount of profit on each unit of output it sells. The firm is free to choose its inputs, output level, and price as long as its profits

---

1. Point F is necessarily further out along the expansion path, representing more output, than the profit-maximizing point M. Profits are maximized when marginal revenues equal marginal cost. Because demand is downward sloping, price exceeds marginal revenue (the firm must lower its price in order to sell more output). Therefore, at the profit-maximizing point; price exceeds marginal cost. For price to equal marginal cost, price must be lowered, thereby increasing output.

do not exceed the allowed amount per unit of output. Under this form of regulation, the firm increases its output beyond the level it would choose if it were not regulated. The firm also chooses an efficient input combination for its level of output and does not waste inputs. If the regulator sets the allowed return on output sufficiently low, the firm can be induced to expand output practically to the second-best level. The second-best outcome cannot be achieved exactly; however, it can be approached arbitrarily closely.

2. Return-on-sales (ROS) regulation. The firm is allowed to earn a certain amount of profit on each dollar of revenue. If marginal revenue is positive up to the second-best output (that is, if the second-best output is in the elastic portion of demand), then the firm under ROS regulation behaves exactly the same as under ROO regulation. This equivalence is due to the fact that when marginal revenue is positive, revenues rise with output such that tying allowed profits to revenues is the same as tying them to output. With positive marginal revenue, the firm can be induced to move arbitrarily closely to the second-best outcome. Unlike ROO regulation, however, the firm under ROS regulation will not expand its output into the inelastic portion of demand where marginal revenue is negative. In this region, an expansion of output decreases revenues and hence allowed profit under ROS regulation. ROO and ROS regulation differ when demand is inelastic because expanding output increases allowed profit under ROO regulation, but decreases it under ROS regulation. If the second-best output is in the inelastic portion of demand, ROS regulation can induce the firm to move only part of the way to second-best, namely, only to the point where marginal revenue starts to be negative.

3. Return-on-cost (ROC) regulation. The firm is allowed a certain amount of profit on each dollar it expends. The firm behaves the same under ROC regulation as under ROS regulation. Specifically, the firm expands output, using least-cost production, but will not enter the inelastic portion of demand. The reasons for this behavior, however, are somewhat different than with ROS regulation. Under ROC regulation, the firm increases its allowed profit by increasing its costs. As long as marginal revenue is positive, the firm benefits from increasing its output along with its costs, because the extra revenues obtained from the extra output help to offset the costs. That is, by expanding outputs, feasible profits rise along with its allowed profit, or at least fall by less than if output were not expanded. However, if marginal

revenue is negative, the firm obtains more revenues by *not* increasing output. Consequently, at the point at which marginal revenue starts to be negative, the firm increases cost (to increase its allowed profit) but does not increase its output (so as to keep its feasible profit as high as possible). In short, the firm starts wasting at this point.

4. Price discrimination. Primary price discrimination occurs when the firm charges a different price to each customer. The firm that is allowed to engage in primary price discrimination will attain the first-best optimum. The reason is simple. The firm charges each customer the maximum the customer is willing to pay for the good, thereby extracting all surplus. Because all surplus accrues to the firm in the form of profit, the firm maximizes its own profit by choosing the surplus-maximizing output, which, by definition, is the first-best. The firm earns large profits; however, in theory, this profit can be taxed and redistributed to consumers in a way that will not affect the firm's behavior.

2.2 Return-on-Output Regulation

Consider a regulatory mechanism that ties the allowed profits of the firm to the firm's output. Under return-on-output (ROO) regulation, the firm is free to choose its input and output levels, but is not allowed to earn (economic) profits in excess of a "fair" return per unit of output. The fair return is set by the regulator and stated in terms of dollars of profit per unit of output. For example, the regulator of an electric utility might state that the firm can earn up to one-tenth of a cent of profit per kilowatt-hour sold.

The profit constraint is expressed as $\pi \le kQ$, where k is the allowed profit per unit of output.[2] At any input combination, the maximum allowed profit is k times the maximum output that can be produced with the inputs. The constraint surface therefore takes the same shape as the production function, rescaled by k. Figure 2.2 depicts this surface. Each isoquant, which represents input combinations whose maximum output is the same, is a contour on the constraint surface,

---

2. The constraint can also be expressed in terms of the firm's price. Because $\pi = PQ - wL - rK$, the profit constraint can be rewritten as $PQ \le kQ + wL + rK$. Dividing through by Q, we have $P \le k + (wL + rK)/Q$, or $P \le k + AC$, where AC is average cost. That is, the firm can mark up price above average cost by at most the amount k—the allowed profit per unit of output.

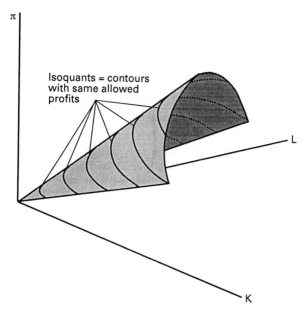

Figure 2.2
Maximum allowed profits under return-on-output regulation

representing the input combinations with the same maximum allowed profits.[3]

The constraint surface slices the profit hill, as depicted in figure 2.3. The firm chooses the highest point on the sliced-off profit hill, which is point E.

The position of point E can be visualized more readily by transposing the information in figure 2.3 onto the two-dimensional graph of input combinations, figure 2.4. The intersection of the constraint surface and the profit hill in figure 2.3 is the constraint curve in figure 2.4. This curve is the set of input combinations at which the maximum profit the firm is able to earn, given technology and demand, is equal to the maximum profit the firm is allowed to earn. At any input combination inside this constraint curve, feasible profit exceeds allowed profit; and vice versa for points outside the constraint curve.

---

3. Note that the constraint surface as defined here gives the maximum allowed profits at each input combination. Allowed profits will be less than this maximum amount if the firm produces less output than is maximally feasible with given inputs, that is, if the firm wastes. Result 3 states that the firm under ROO regulation does not waste, such that the maximum allowed profits can legitimately be considered the constraint surface.

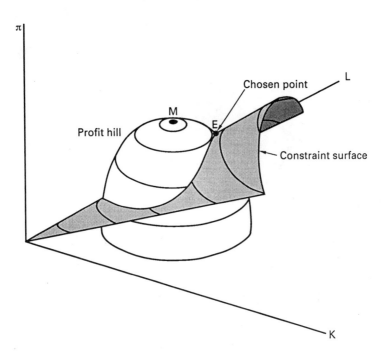

Figure 2.3
Profit hill and constraint for firm under ROO regulation

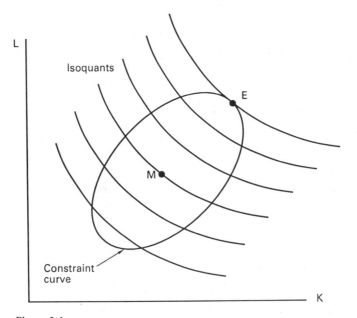

Figure 2.4
Constraint curve and chosen point under ROO regulation

All points on the constraint curve provide the firm with the same profit per unit of output, namely k. Because profit per unit is constant on the constraint curve, absolute profits increase as output increases. The firm therefore chooses the point on the constraint curve with the greatest output, which is E. At this point there is tangency between the constraint curve and an isoquant. If the firm were to increase output beyond this point, going outside the constraint curve, the firm would be allowed to earn more profits but would not be able to.

Several results are now apparent.

Result 1: A firm under ROO regulation produces more output than if unregulated.

For the regulation to be binding, the constraint surface must slice off the top of the profit hill. The point M is therefore inside the constraint curve of figure 2.4. Because the regulated firm chooses the point on the constraint curve with the highest output, it necessarily chooses greater output than is produced at any point within the constraint curve.

Result 2: A firm under ROO regulation uses the efficient input combination for its level of output. That is, the firm produces on the expansion path.

Suppose the contrary, that the chosen point is not on the expansion path. This supposition is depicted in figure 2.5, in which the chosen point E is not on the expansion path. Consider point G, where the isoquant through E intersects the expansion path. Profits at G exceed profits at E because costs are lower at G (by definition of the expansion path) and revenues are the same at both points. However, G is outside the constraint curve, meaning that profits at G are less than k per unit of output. Because output is the same at G and E, and profits per unit of output are k at E and less than k at G, absolute profits at G are less than at E, contradicting the first comparison. Therefore, E cannot be off the expansion path.

Result 3: A firm under ROO regulation does not waste. That is, the firm produces as much output as possible with its inputs.

If the firm starts with no inputs and moves out the expansion path, its feasible profits increase until it reaches the top of the profit hill, after which feasible profits decrease. Figure 2.6 illustrates the relation between feasible profits and output with and without waste. The upper curve gives the profit the firm obtains at each level of output if it uses the cost-minimizing set of inputs. The lower curve gives the profit

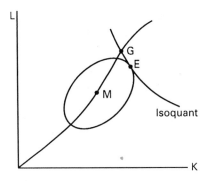

Figure 2.5
Firm under ROO regulation chooses point off expansion path: impossible

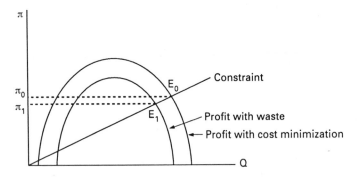

Figure 2.6
Firm under ROO regulation will not waste

the firm obtains if it uses more inputs than necessary to produce the output, that is, if it wastes inputs. Allowed profit, as represented by the constraint plane, increases with output and is the same for each level of output whether or not the firm uses more inputs than necessary to produce the output. Without wasting inputs, the firm chooses point E_0 and earns profit π_0. If the firm wastes, it chooses point E_1 and earns profit π_1. Since $\pi_0 > \pi_1$, the firm chooses not to waste.

Unlike the analogous result for ROR regulation, the fact that a firm under ROO regulation does not engage in pure waste does not depend on marginal revenue being positive. In fact, ROO regulation might induce the firm to increase output sufficiently such that it produces in the inelastic region of demand where marginal revenue is negative. Consider figure 2.7 in which Q_0 denotes the output at which marginal revenue is zero. For all output levels above Q_0, marginal

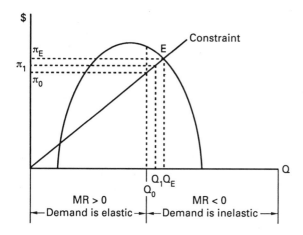

Figure 2.7
Firm under ROO regulation could produce in inelastic portion of demand

revenue is negative. The graph is constructed such that Q_0 is less than the output at which the constraint curve intersects the profit hill. (If Q_0 were beyond E, marginal revenue would be positive throughout the relevant range, such that the issue of negative marginal revenue does not arise.) We can show that the firm increases output beyond Q_0 into the inelastic region of demand. At Q_0, the firm is able to earn more profits than it is allowed to earn. If it remains at Q_0, it must therefore waste an amount of money equal to the difference between its allowed profit and its feasible profit, and ends up earning the allowed profits, π_0. If the firm were to increase its output to Q_1, its feasible profit would decrease because its revenues would decrease (marginal revenue becomes negative) and its costs would increase. However, its allowed profits would increase. The profit that the firm could keep would rise to π_1. The firm would therefore increase output until it reached the point at which its feasible profits equaled its allowed profits. Increasing output beyond this point would increase allowed profits but decrease feasible profits to a point *below* allowed profits, such that the firm would not choose to increase output further.

Another way of stating this argument is perhaps more straightforward. The most profit the firm could make if it stayed within the elastic portion of demand is π_0 in figure 2.7. By expanding output into the inelastic portion of demand, the firm can make greater profits, with a maximum of π_E.

Result 4: If the allowed rate of profit on output is lowered, the output of the regulated firm increases.

As k is lowered, the constraint surface slices off more of the profit hill. The new constraint curve therefore encompasses the original constraint curve, as depicted in figure 2.8. The firm moves out the expansion path to the intersection with the new constraint curve, increasing output and using inputs efficiently.

Result 5: If the allowed rate of profit on output is set at zero, the firm is indifferent among many input and output combinations, including the option of not using any inputs or producing any output.

The result is essentially the same as the analogous statement regarding ROR regulation, namely, that if the firm earns zero profit over a range of output and input levels, and cannot earn more than zero profit, it has no incentive to choose one outcome over another.

Recall that the goal of the regulator is to induce the regulated firm to operate at point S in figure 2.9, where the zero-profit contour intersects the expansion path. Result 4 indicates that the regulator, by lowering k toward zero, can induce the firm to move out the expansion path toward S. Result 5 implies that by lowering k all the way to zero, the regulator will not necessarily induce the firm to take the final step to S; the firm might choose to close down instead. Taken together, the results on ROO regulation indicate that the regulator can induce the firm to move arbitrarily close to the desired price and output level and to use the cost-minimizing input combination. That

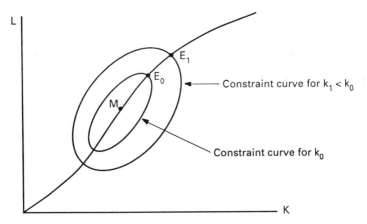

Figure 2.8
Output increases when k is lowered

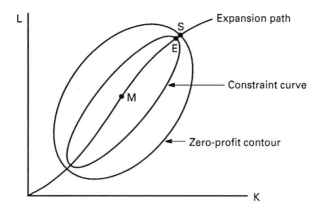

Figure 2.9
Firm's chosen point can be arbitrarily close to second-best

is, the firm can be induced to choose a point very close to S even though S itself cannot necessarily be attained.

This ability of ROO regulation to move the firm arbitrarily close to the desired input and output levels contrasts with the situation under ROR regulation. With ROR regulation, the firm cannot be induced to enter the inelastic portion of demand. Consequently, if point S is in the inelastic portion of demand, ROR regulation is not able to induce the firm to move close to S no matter what rate of return is allowed. Furthermore, ROR regulation does not move the firm along the expansion path, but rather induces the firm to operate with an inefficient input mix.

A difficulty with ROO regulation arises if the firm has the ability to influence its demand curve. If the firm can use advertising or other means to increase its demand, ROO regulation establishes an incentive to engage in these demand-stimulating activities. Conversely, if the firm has the ability to reduce its demand, ROO regulation gives it an incentive not to do so even if demand reductions are desirable from a social perspective. Conservation is an important case in point. Under ROO regulation, the firm would have an incentive not to undertake conservation programs that induce consumers to reduce their consumption even if these programs were cost-effective from a social perspective.[4]

---

4. Cost effective in this context means that total surplus is greater if resources are expended on the programs that reduce demand than on producing the output needed to meet current demand.

2.3 Return-on-Sales Regulation

The revenues generated by a firm are often called its sales, or, more precisely, its dollar volume of sales. If the sales of a firm are easier to measure than its quantity of output, the regulator might want to use sales as the basis for determining allowed profit. Return-on-sales (ROS) regulation allows the firm to choose its outputs and inputs under the constraint that its profits do not exceed a portion of its revenues: $\pi \le kPQ$, where k is the allowed proportion of revenues that can be retained as profit.

If marginal revenue is positive over the relevant output levels, then allowed profit increases with the quantity of output, because revenues increase. Consequently, the analysis of ROS regulation when marginal revenue is positive is essentially the same as that for ROO regulation. The conclusions are the same: if marginal revenue is positive over the relevant output range, ROS regulation induces the firm to increase output, not waste, and to choose the efficient input mix for its level of output. Furthermore, output increases as the allowed proportion of revenues that can be retained in profits decreases, such that the firm can be induced, by lowering the allowed proportion toward (but not to) zero, to produce arbitrarily close to the second-best output level, using cost-minimizing inputs.

If marginal revenue is negative, allowed profit drops when output rises, because revenue decreases. Consequently, ROS regulation differs radically from ROO regulation if the optimal output level is in the inelastic portion of demand. Under ROO regulation, the firm will not expand output into the inelastic region (where marginal revenue is negative) because doing so would decrease its allowed profit.

Figure 2.10 illustrates the situation. The profit hill denotes the maximum profits the firm can attain at each output level given demand and technology. Q_S is the optimal output, where price equals average cost such that profit is zero. Q_0 is the output level at which marginal revenue is zero. Revenues, and hence allowed profit, rise with output up to Q_0 (because marginal revenue is positive in this range) and then decline. Because the firm is allowed to earn more profit at Q_0 than at any other output, it chooses Q_0. Two conclusions are implied. First, the firm produces less than the optimal level of output:[5] Q_0 is less

5. The allowed proportion k determines the height of the allowed profit surface at each output level, but does not affect the location of the top of this surface: revenues and

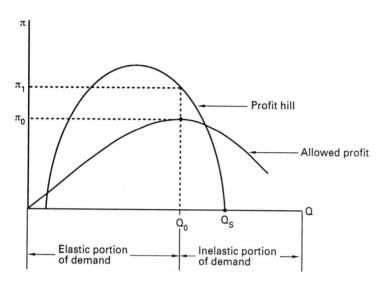

Figure 2.10
ROS regulation when marginal revenue becomes negative

than Q_S. Second, the firm does not cost-minimize in its use of inputs. At Q_0 the firm is able to attain profit of π_1 if it uses inputs efficiently; however, it is only allowed to earn π_0. To ensure that its profit does not exceed the allowed amount, the firm must use inputs inefficiently, through pure waste (that is, by producing less than is possible with the inputs) and/or by choosing an inefficient input mix. Costs exceed their minimizing level by the difference between π_0 and π_1. Furthermore, because k affects the level of allowed profits but not the firm's choice of output, lowering k simply increases the inefficiency costs.

The general conclusion is that ROS regulation induces desirable behavior on the part of the firm if marginal revenue is positive throughout the relevant range of output, but not if the optimal output is in the inelastic portion of demand.

2.4 Return-on-Cost Regulation

Allowed profit can also be based on the costs of the firm. Return-on-cost (ROC) regulation imposes a constraint on the firm of the form

---

thus allowed profit are highest where marginal revenue is zero for any value of k (insofar that k is sufficiently low such that allowed profits has a maximum within the profit hill).

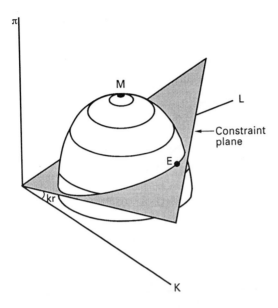

Figure 2.11
Firm under ROC regulation

$\pi \leq k(wL + rK)$, where k is the proportion of costs the firm is allowed to retain as profit.[6] As with ROS regulation, the implications of this form of regulation are very different if marginal revenue is consistently positive than if the optimal output falls in the inelastic portion of demand. Consider first the situation of positive marginal revenue throughout the relevant range.

The constraint surface is a plane with a slope kr in the capital direction and slope kw in the labor direction. The contours of this surface are the isocost lines, with "higher" isocost lines corresponding to greater costs and hence greater allowed profits. As shown in figure

---

6. This form of regulation is equivalent to allowing the firm to mark up price over average costs by the proportion k:

$$\pi \leq k(wL + rK)$$
$$PQ - (wL + rK) \leq k(wL + rK)$$
$$PQ \leq (1 + k)(wL + rK)$$
$$P \leq (1 + k)AC,$$

where AC is average cost. Note that this markup is different from that discussed in section 2.2 regarding ROO regulation. Under ROO regulation, the firm is allowed to mark up its price by a certain dollar amount over average cost. Under ROC regulation, the firm can mark up by a given proportion of average costs, such that the dollar amount of markup varies.

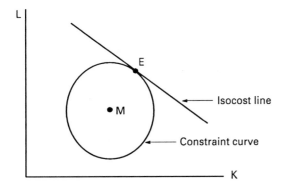

Figure 2.12
Choice of firm under ROC regulation: tangency of constraint curve with an isocost line

2.11, the constraint surface slices the profit hill. The firm chooses point E, the highest point on the sliced-off profit hill.

Figure 2.12 depicts the chosen point with the π dimension suppressed. Profits as a proportion of costs are the same for all points on the constraint curve, such that absolute profits are higher for those points with higher costs. The firm therefore chooses the point on the constraint curve that touches the highest isocost line, at which there is tangency between the isocost line and the constraint curve.

Knowing that the firm chooses this point of tangency allows us to readily demonstrate several results.

Result 1: A firm under ROC regulation and facing positive marginal revenue produces on the expansion path, using the efficient input mix for its level of output.

Suppose the contrary, as illustrated in figure 2.13. The firm chooses point E, which is not on the expansion path. Point H is the intersection of the expansion path with the constraint curve. Point G is the intersection of the constraint curve with the isoquant that goes through H. (Because the isocost at H cuts the constraint curve instead of being tangent, the isoquant also cuts the constraint curve. This isoquant therefore intersects the constraint curve at a second point, G.) Because G and H are on the same isoquant but H is on the expansion path, $\pi_H > \pi_G$. We can also show, however, that $\pi_G > \pi_H$. Because H is on the expansion path, which represents cost minimization, costs are lower at H than G. Both G and H are on the constraint curve, such that profit at each point is the same proportion of costs at each point.

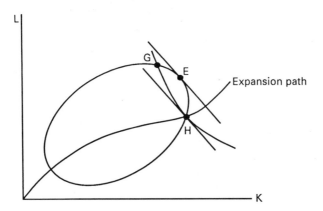

Figure 2.13
Firm chooses a point off the expansion path: impossible

Therefore, absolute profit is lower at H than G. This contradiction implies that the firm's chosen point must be on the expansion path.

Result 2: The firm under ROC regulation and facing positive marginal revenue produces more output than the unregulated firm.

Result 3: The firm under ROC regulation and facing positive marginal revenue does not waste inputs.

Result 4: If the allowed proportion k of costs to be retained as profit is lowered toward (but not to) zero, then the firm under ROC regulation and facing positive marginal revenue increases output, using inputs efficiently.

These results are straightforward applications of previous concepts. They are illustrated in figures 2.14, 2.15, and 2.16, respectively. It is interesting that the firm does not increase its costs through wasting inputs even when it is allowed to earn more profits by doing so. This result is critically dependent on marginal revenue being positive. If the firm purchases nonproductive inputs (that is, if it wastes), then its allowed profit increases but its feasible profit decreases (because costs increase without an increase in revenues). If instead the firm uses the same amount of money to purchase inputs but uses them productively, allowed profit rises by the same amount and yet feasible profit either rises or drops by less (because revenues increase, at least partially offsetting the cost of the extra inputs). ROC regulation gives the firm an incentive to increase costs, but as long as marginal revenue is positive, the firm earns greater profit by increasing output as much as possible along with costs.

If marginal revenue becomes negative within the relevant range of output, then the cost-based incentive does not translate into a quantity-based incentive. If marginal revenue is negative, the firm loses revenue by selling extra output and gains revenue by selling less output. As a result, the firm is able to earn greater profits by selling less even without reducing inputs: its allowed profit does not change and its feasible profit increases. Conversely, the firm can increase its allowed profit by purchasing inputs (whether productive or not), and yet its feasible profit decreases less when inputs are purchased without increasing output than when using the inputs to produce more.

The firm will increase output beyond its unregulated level only to the point that marginal revenue is zero. If allowed profit exceeds feasible profit at this point, the firm purchases nonproductive inputs, increasing allowed profit while decreasing feasible profit as little as possible. (If the firm used these extra inputs to produce extra output, its feasible profit would decline even more.) Figure 2.17 illustrates the situation. In this graph, the level of labor is assumed constant. As capital is increased, output and revenue increase until marginal revenue is zero. This point is labeled K_0. If capital is increased beyond this point and the capital is used to produce and sell extra output, the firm's feasible profits decrease along the downside of the profit hill. However, if the firm purchases extra capital but does not produce more output, its feasible profits decrease by less. (By not selling extra output, the firm's revenues do not decrease.) The profit that the firm can obtain by using extra capital but not selling extra output is given by the downward sloping line that starts at capital level K_0. The slope of this line is the cost of capital r: for each extra unit of capital purchased, profits decrease by exactly r. If extra output were produced with the extra capital and sold, then profit would decrease by r plus the decrease in revenues that results from selling the extra output.

The firm in this situation chooses to produce the output at which marginal revenue is zero and yet purchase K_E capital. Because only K_0 capital is needed to produce the level of output, the firm wastes the difference between K_E and K_0. The same type of waste also occurs with labor.

In summary, if the optimal output is in the inelastic portion of demand, then the ROC regulation can be used to induce the firm to increase output and use cost-minimizing inputs only to the point at which marginal revenue is zero. Any attempt to induce the firm to

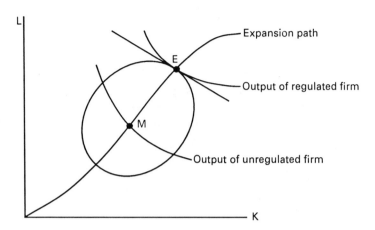

Figure 2.14
Firm under ROC regulation will produce more output than if unregulated

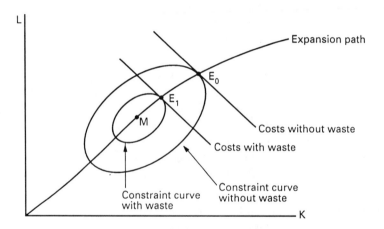

Figure 2.15
Firm under ROC regulation will not waste inputs

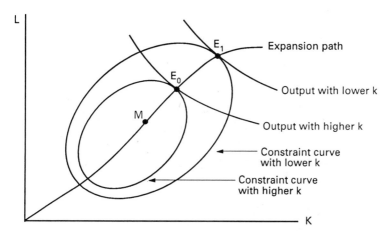

Figure 2.16
Firm under ROC regulation will increase output when allowed profit is lowered

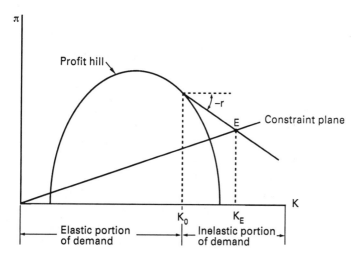

Figure 2.17
ROC regulation

increase output further, by lowering the allowed profits, simply induces the firm to waste.

2.5   Price Discrimination

Price discrimination exists when a firm charges different prices to different customers and/or for different units of output (e.g., one price for consumption up to a certain quantity and then another price for additional units). Primary price discrimination (also called perfect price discrimination) is defined as a situation in which the firm charges each unit of output at exactly the amount that a consumer is willing to pay for that unit.

Under the regulatory mechanisms described so far, the regulated firm is assumed to charge one price to all of its customers and for all units of output. It has long been recognized (for example, Robinson 1933)[7] that price discrimination by a monopolist results in greater total surplus than if the firm charges only one price. In fact, as shown below, a firm that is able to engage in primary price discrimination chooses the first-best output level and uses cost-minimizing inputs. This fact suggests that a potentially effective form of regulation is for the regulator to allow and assist the firm in price discrimination.

Price discrimination is not always possible, and even if possible, it might violate goals that the regulator holds in addition to the objective of inducing optimal input and output levels. For example, primary price discrimination results in all surplus accruing to the firm and none to consumers, which might not be considered equitable. Furthermore, different customers are required to pay different prices for the same good or service, which can also be considered inequitable. However, before addressing these limitations, let us demonstrate the fact that primary price discrimination leads to the first-best outcome in an efficiency sense.

Consider first the decision process of a non-price-discriminating monopolist, as depicted in figure 2.18. At any level of output, the firm must lower its price in order to sell additional units of output, because market demand is downward sloping. Consequently, marginal revenue is below price at each level of output. The firm maximizes profit by expanding output whenever marginal revenue exceeds marginal cost, eventually choosing the output at which marginal revenue equals

---

7. More recent treatments are provided by Schmalensee (1981) and Varian (1985).

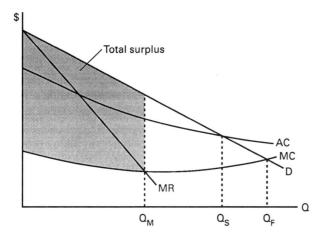

Figure 2.18
Non-price-discriminating monopolist

marginal cost. This output is labeled Q_M, and at this output total surplus (excluding fixed costs) is the shaded area.

The monopolists' output is below the socially optimal level and total surplus is less than maximal. The first-best output is Q_F, at which price equals marginal cost. At this output, the total surplus is the area below the demand curve and above the marginal cost curve up to Q_F. If the firm is a natural monopoly, marginal cost is below average cost, and the firm would lose money at the first-best output. The second-best output is Q_S, which is the largest output consistent with non-negative profits.

Suppose that the firm is able to engage in primary price discrimination, pricing each unit separately. For each unit of output, the firm charges the maximum that any customer is willing to pay for the unit. The firm sells its first unit of output to the customer most willing to pay for that unit. In figure 2.19, this price is P_1, because at a price of P_1 one unit of output is demanded. Then the firm sells its second unit to the customer who is second-most willing to pay; the price for this unit is P_2. Note that the firm still charges P_1 for the first unit: it does not have to lower its price for previous units in order to sell more units. The firm sells extra units whenever the price it can receive from an extra unit, as indicated by the demand curve, exceeds the extra cost incurred in producing the extra unit; that is, whenever demand exceeds marginal cost. The firm chooses the output at which demand equals marginal cost, which is the first-best output Q_F.

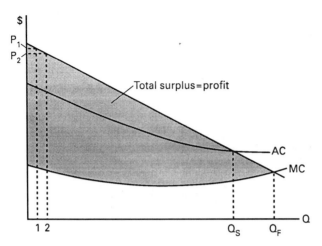

Figure 2.19
Monopolist with primary price discrimination

The firm in both situations sells extra output whenever the extra revenue it obtains exceeds the marginal cost of producing the extra unit. When only one price is charged for all units, the extra revenue from an extra unit is less than the price the firm can obtain for that one unit, because price must be lowered on all units of output, not just the marginal unit. However, when each unit can be priced separately, the extra revenue from selling extra output is exactly the price the firm receives for the one extra unit, since the prices for other units do not change. Essentially, the demand curve is the marginal revenue curve under primary price discrimination. The firm maximizes profits by choosing output at which marginal revenue equals marginal cost, which in the case of price discrimination is where demand equals marginal cost.

The basic task of regulatory economics is to ensure consistency between the firm's goal of maximizing profit and the regulator's goal of maximizing surplus. The manner by which primary price discrimination attains this consistency constitutes a fundamental solution to the problem. Under primary price discrimination, the firm extracts all surplus: it charges each customer exactly the customer's willingness to pay. Because the firm obtains all surplus as profit, profit maximization and surplus maximization are identical: the firm naturally chooses the optimal outcome. This transfer of all surplus to the firm is clearly the most straightforward way (at least theoretically) to provide consistency between the regulator's goal and the firm's profit motive.

Note that primary price discrimination, unlike the other regulatory mechanisms discussed in this chapter, brings the firm to the first-best, not second-best, output. The possibility of attaining first-best is an interesting consequence of price discrimination. Without price discrimination, the largest output the firm can produce and not lose money is the second-best level, at which price equals average cost and profits are zero. However, with a different price for each unit, the firm is able to earn larger profits at any level of output sold. Consequently, the firm earns positive profits at this second-best output. (Its profits are the area below demand and above marginal cost up to this output level.) Because profits are positive at this output, the firm can expand output without its profits becoming negative. In fact the firm makes *more* profit by expanding output beyond the second-best level. At Q_S, the price the firm can charge for an extra unit (as given by the demand curve) exceeds the cost of producing the extra unit (as given by the marginal cost curve). As a result, primary price discrimination allows, and induces, the firm to produce more output than would be possible (given that the firm cannot lose money) under regulatory mechanisms that require one price for all units of output.

The potential advantages of price discrimination are obvious. There are, however, some limitations, both practical and ethical.

1. The existence of price discrimination provides an incentive to customers to establish resale markets, which undermine the monopolist's attempt to price discriminate. A customer that is charged a low price by the monopolist would, if possible, sell the units to a customer who is being charged a higher price by the monopolist. The monopolist would find itself selling only to the low-priced customer, because the customer that is charged the higher price would buy at resale from the low-priced customer. The attempt to charge different prices would therefore result in sales at only one price, namely the lowest price offered to any customer.

The monopolist might be able to prevent resale. For example, a monopolist in trash collection can reduce the potential for resale by placing a limit on the number of barrels of trash that will be collected from each customer.[8] However, in many situations, resale cannot be readily prevented by the monopolist.

---

8. Without this limit, any customer that is charged a lower per-barrel fee than his neighbors has an incentive to charge his neighbors to put their barrels in his collection area, with the charge being below the per-barrel charge of his neighbors but above his own per-barrel charge. With the limit on number of barrels, this resale of service would be restricted.

The prevention of resale is generally more feasible for regulated than unregulated firms. In a regulated setting, the regulator—usually an arm of the government—can establish and, more important, enforce rules against resale to an extent not possible by the firm itself. Consequently, a regulator that wishes to use price discrimination as a way to induce first-best output and input levels might find it possible to enforce the discrimination even if the firm itself could not.

2. To extract the entire surplus, the firm must know the willingness to pay of each customer for each unit of output. This amount of information is usually beyond the scope of most firms. However, the firm need not actually extract all surplus in order to produce the first-best output. Suppose the firm knows whether or not it can sell an extra unit of output for more than its marginal cost, though it does not necessarily know the maximum that it can obtain for the unit. In this case, the firm sells extra output whenever a customer is willing to pay more than the marginal cost. The firm therefore produces the first-best output level even though it attains less than the full surplus.

3. Assuming the firm has full information, primary price discrimination results in the firm making large profits, consisting of the entire surplus. Thus, even though the optimal output is attained, the benefits of attaining this output all accrue to the monopolist. The regulator might consider this distribution of benefits to be inequitable.

In theory, it is possible to tax the monopolist at a rate that is a fixed proportion of its profits, and then refund the tax revenues to the firm's customers. In this way, the surplus is shared between the firm and its customers. The firm's actions would be the same with or without the tax since the output and input levels that maximize its profits also maximize, say, 50% of its profits. Of course, the issue then arises of whether the regulator has the authority to tax the firm and how the tax funds can be distributed to consumers without the distribution essentially changing the price consumers pay for the firm's output.[9]

4. It might be considered inequitable for different customers to pay different prices for the same goods or services. That is, the basic premise of price discrimination might conflict with the regulator's goals re-

9. If the size of the refund to each customer is based on the number of units purchased or the total amount paid by the customer, then the refund constitutes a change in price. If, however, an equal refund is made to all of the firm's customers independent of consumption level or payments, then people who would not buy the firm's output without the refund would choose to buy a small quantity in order to obtain the refund.

garding equity, even though the regulator's goals regarding input and output are met.

Regulators usually allow different prices to be charged for different groups of customers. For example, electricity is priced differently for residential customers than for commercial and industrial customers; and among residential customers, different prices are often charged for electrically heated households than for those with gas or other heat. This implies that regulators often consider it equitable to price discriminate on the basis of some factors. The question is therefore not whether price discrimination is equitable per se, but rather the extent to which the regulator can equitably distinguish customers for the purpose of price discrimination.

The practical and ethical difficulties of primary price discrimination are formidable. Our purpose in describing price discrimination is not necessarily to recommend it as a form of regulation. The point is rather to illustrate the concept that consistency between social goals and the firm's profit drive can most simply be attained by enabling the firm to secure as profit *all* social benefits (and then, perhaps, taxing and redistributing these benefits). In chapter 6, regulatory mechanisms are introduced that utilize this concept in a fashion that can be more equitable and yet just as effective from an efficiency perspective.

3   The A-J Model under Uncertainty

3.1 Motivation

So far we have assumed that the firm knows exactly the profit it is able to earn with each combination of inputs. In actuality, a firm's profits are affected by many factors that are beyond its control and cannot be predicted perfectly. Several examples suggest the prevalence of this uncertainty. (1) Weather greatly affects the sales of energy utilities. When summers are mild, electric customers do not use their air conditioners as much as in hot summers, and as a result, the utility earns less profit. Similarly, mild winters reduce demand for gas and electricity for heating compared to more severe winters. Weather varies from year to year in unpredictable ways, such that the utility cannot fully know beforehand the profits that will result from its actions. Even over a period of years, cumulative profits may be higher or lower than expected due to long-term differences in actual weather from that predicted. (2) Firms must plan new capital facilities (e.g., power plants for energy utilities or fixed guideways for transit) years before the facilities will be operational. At the time the decision is made to construct new facilities, predictions are made concerning the building costs and the level of demand that will prevail when the facility is completed. Inevitably, actual costs and demand will differ from those predicted, and profits will not be as expected. (3) Operational costs for a firm vary from day to day due to such mundane factors as the number of employees unable to work on a particular day due to illness. When averaged over a period of time, costs might tend to stabilize. However, costs never become perfectly stable, and, more important, there may be no stabilizing tendency at all if shocks (such as strikes, unexpected inflation, and so on) occur more rapidly than the averaging over time can accommodate. Inevitably, the firm does not know, at the time of making decisions, exactly what its profits will be as a result of the actions it decides to take.

This uncertainty has important implications for the behavior of the firm and consequently for the design of appropriate regulation. The issue has been examined fairly extensively in relation to the Averch-Johnson model. Theorists have generalized the A-J model to incorporate the fact that the regulated firm is uncertain about the profits that result from its input choice. Peles and Stein (1976) show that some of the seemingly implausible implications of the standard A-J model (such as that the regulated firm increases its use of capital when the fair rate of return is lowered) do not occur when uncertainty is introduced. Das (1980) demonstrates, however, that the basic A-J result (namely, that the regulated firm uses an inefficiently high capital/labor ratio for its level of output) still holds when uncertainty is introduced. As such, these analyses strengthen the plausibility of the A-J model by removing problematical aspects while retaining its central message.

These investigations are also important, and perhaps more important, for their general implications beyond the confines of the A-J model. In particular, these analyses elucidate a fundamental concept regarding appropriate regulation in the face of uncertainty. They provide a case study of the fact that an asymmetric treatment of uncertainty—by which losses by the firm are treated differently by the regulator than extraordinary profits—leads to distortions in the firm's actions that operate against optimality.

This lesson has broad implications. There is often a tendency for regulators, in an attempt to protect the public, to treat extraordinary losses and gains differently. For example, if a firm makes a decision that later proves to have been wrong (e.g., to build a power plant that ends up being unneeded, or ends up costing much more than expected), there is a tendency to force the firm (namely, the shareholders) to bear part of the cost of the "mistake" rather than pass on the entire cost to the firm's customers. On the other hand, if the utility makes a decision that results in much greater profits than expected (e.g., negotiates long-term contracts for the supply of inputs just before the spot price of these inputs unexpectedly skyrockets), then there is a tendency for the gains to be passed on to customers, because allowing the firm to retain the extra profits would result in the firm earning more than a "fair" return. As the analysis in this chapter indicates, this asymmetry can actually induce the firm to make decisions in a way that ultimately works against the goals of the regulator and the welfare of customers.[1]

As a basis for comparison, section 3.2 describes the behavior of an *unregulated* firm facing uncertainty. Section 3.3 identifies the effect of rate-of-return regulation on the way uncertainty is perceived by the firm and the behavior of the regulated firm given this uncertainty. Several results are then demonstrated in section 3.4. The discussion throughout the chapter is motivated by the concepts of Peles/Stein and Das. However, our methods are different and less general, designed to allow the concepts to be visualized and to focus on the essential meanings that drive the analysis. In addition, we include some interesting results not discussed by these authors but implied by their work.

The findings can be summarized as follows for a firm in an uncertain world that is subjected to ROR regulation.

• Except in rare cases, the firm earns on average *less* than the allowed rate of return.

• Except in rare cases, the firm engages in pure waste.

• Contrary to the standard A-J result without uncertainty, the firm might utilize *less* capital than if it were not regulated. The reason is straightforward. If the risk the firm faces increases with the amount of capital that it employs, then ROR regulation provides the firm with two countervailing incentives. First, the firm has an incentive to *increase* capital so as to increase its allowed profit. Second, the firm has an incentive to *decrease* capital in order to reduce the asymmetrical risk it faces under ROR regulation. Either of these incentives could dominate, resulting in either an increase or decrease in capital.

• Contrary to the standard A-J result, lowering the fair rate of return can induce the firm to *reduce* its capital.

• The firm nevertheless chooses an inefficiently high capital/labor ratio for its level of output.

If the firm utilizes less capital than when unregulated, this last result implies that the firm also reduces its labor and output. The overall

---

1. If the "mistakes" of the firm are actually due to unreasonable behavior, requiring the firm to incur the subsequent loss is perhaps appropriate as a deterrent against such behavior. The point is simply that there is a tendency to apply a stronger standard of scrutiny to losses than to gains, forgetting that in an uncertain world both unexpected losses and unexpected gains are inevitable.

picture of ROR regulation under uncertainty is even more distressing than without uncertainty: in addition to utilizing an inefficient input mix, the firm probably wastes inputs and could easily produce less output than if it were not regulated.

3.2 Behavior of the Unregulated Firm under Uncertainty

Suppose that some intervening factor affects the profits that the firm is able to obtain at any input combination. For simplicity, let us suppose that the firm faces two possible events, called good luck and bad luck, where good luck means that the firm is able to earn greater profits at each input combination than under bad luck. For example, good luck might consist of prices for inputs dropping such that the cost of building a power plant is lower than expected, whereas bad luck is the opposite. Or, good luck might be an unexpected increase in demand such that the firm is able to earn greater profits at each input level, while bad luck is a drop in demand.[2]

With the exception of the last result of this chapter, the essential concepts concerning uncertainty can be described, and easily visualized, if we assume that there is only one input, which we call capital. At the time of choosing a level of capital (e.g., when deciding whether to build a new plant), the firm does not know whether good luck or bad luck will occur. Furthermore, the firm knows that it will not be able to adjust its capital after it has observed which type of luck has occurred. For example, after a new plant has been built, the sunk costs cannot be recovered if demand ends up being unexpectedly low such that the plant is not needed.

Because the firm does not know its exact profits at each level of capital, it calculates *expected* profits at each level of capital and chooses the level that provides the greatest expected profits.[3] For simplicity,

---

2. Note that good/bad luck simply refers to the effect of the event on the firm's profits. An event that constitutes bad luck for the firm might actually be socially beneficial. For example, mild weather reduces an energy utility's revenues and yet is beneficial for customers if the utility's rates are not raised to recoup its lost revenues.
3. We assume that the firm maximizes expected profits, though this need not be the case for all firms. A firm might maximize some other function of good- and bad-luck profits. For example, the firm might be more concerned about losing money than gaining, in which case it might maximize the weighted sum of expected profits and some factor that reflects the risk and harm of losing money. The tools used in this chapter can be generalized to allow for these other possibilities. However, the basic concepts regarding uncertainty are most apparent under expected profit maximization.

suppose that there is an equal probability that good luck and bad luck will prevail, such that expected profits are the average of the profits that would occur under good luck and those that would occur under bad luck.

Figure 3.1 illustrates the situation. There are two profit hills, one showing the profits the firm would earn at each level of capital if good luck occurred and another, lower one showing profits if bad luck occurred.[4] The average of these two profit hills is expected profits, denoted by a dotted line. The firm chooses the level of capital that gives it the highest expected profits, which is K_M.

The shape of the good- and bad-luck hills reflects the nature, or

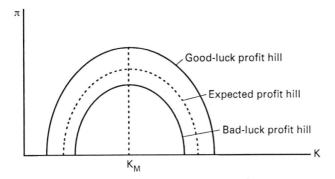

Figure 3.1
Unregulated firm facing independent risk

---

4. These profit hills, and the ensuing discussion, also have meaning in a two-input situation under a particular assumption about how each input is chosen. Suppose the inputs are capital and labor, and that capital is chosen before luck is revealed but that labor can be adjusted appropriately for the type of luck that occurs. This assumption is consistent with the idea that, for example, the sunk costs of a new plant cannot be recovered if demand ends up being insufficient to warrant the plant, but that the firm's labor force can be reduced or expanded in response to unanticipated events. Under this assumption, the good-luck profit hill gives the maximum profits that the firm can attain at each level of capital if good luck prevails and the firm adjusts its labor to be optimal given this good luck; and similarly for the bad-luck hill. All of the results in this chapter, with the important exception of the last one, are equivalently derived under this alternative interpretation of the profit hill.

All of the results, including the last one, can also be derived under the assumption that both labor and capital are chosen in advance and cannot be adjusted after the good or bad luck has occurred. However, the graphical methods in this chapter, while still suggestive, are not exactly accurate for the necessary demonstrations. The reason for this is that the firm would not necessarily choose beforehand the amount of labor that is optimal for the level of capital after the type of luck has been revealed. Consequently, the expected profit hill is not necessarily the average of the good- and bad-luck hills when expressed in the capital dimension only.

type, of uncertainty the firm faces. Two types of risk can be distin-
guished. (1) Independent risk refers to a situation in which the difference between good- and bad-luck profits is the same at all levels of
capital. That is, the degree of risk is independent of the amount of
capital employed. (2) Dependent risk occurs when the difference between good- and bad-luck profits varies with the amount of capital
employed. That is, the degree of risk the firm faces depends on, and
can be affected by, the firm's choice of capital.

In figure 3.1, risk is assumed to be independent: the good- and bad-
luck profit hills are the same distance apart at each level of capital. As
a result, the two hills reach their maxima at the same level of capital.
The expected profit hill therefore reaches its maximum at the same
level of capital as the good- and bad-luck hills. The firm chooses under uncertainty the same level of capital as it would if it knew with
certainty which type of luck would occur.

Figure 3.2 illustrates a situation with dependent risk. As is usual
with dependent risk, the difference between good- and bad-luck profits increases with capital. (As the firm uses more capital, it is usually
more vulnerable to unexpected changes in input prices and demand
because it has invested a larger amount of money in capital that cannot be altered after these unexpected changes have occurred.) The
top of the expected profit hill occurs where the slope of this hill is
zero. This point can be identified exactly by comparing the slopes of
the good- and bad-luck hills. In particular, because expected profits
is the average of good-luck and bad-luck profits, the slope of the
expected profit hill is the average of the slopes of the good- and

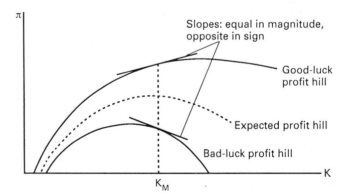

Figure 3.2
Unregulated firm facing dependent risk

bad-luck profit hills. The maximum of the expected profit hill occurs therefore at the level of capital at which the slope of the good-luck hill is equal in magnitude and opposite in sign to the slope of the bad-luck hill, such that the average of these two slopes is zero. This point is labeled K_M.[5] The firm in this case chooses more capital than it would if it knew with certainty that bad luck would prevail and less than if it knew good luck would occur.

3.3   Behavior of the Firm Facing Uncertainty under Rate-of-Return Regulation

Under ROR regulation, the firm is not allowed to earn more than a fair return on capital. This constraint interacts with the firm's good- and bad-luck profit hills, slicing off any parts that exceed the allowed amount. The firm's expected profits is the average of its sliced-off good-luck and bad-luck hills.

As figure 3.3 illustrates, under good luck, the firm would earn excessive profit over a range of capital levels; this part of the good-luck hill is sliced off by the constraint plane. Under bad luck, the firm, in this example, earns less than the allowed profit at all capital levels. The expected profit hill of the firm is the average of the bad-luck hill and the sliced-off good-luck hill; this average is denoted by the dotted line.[6] The maximum expected profits in this example occurs at capital K_R, at which the bad-luck hill slopes downward just as steeply (no more or less) as the constraint plane slopes upward, such that the average of their slopes is zero.

It is useful to identify the choice that the firm would make if it somehow knew the type of luck that would prevail. If the firm knew for sure that good luck would prevail, it would choose capital K_G, which provides the greatest profit under the sliced-off good-luck hill. If the firm knew for sure that bad luck would prevail, it would choose capital K_B, which is the top of the bad-luck hill. Because the firm does

---

5. The same relation holds with independent risk, though trivially. At the level of capital that maximizes expected profits, the slopes of the good-luck and bad-luck hills are each zero, such that their magnitudes are equal and their signs are irrelevant.
6. Note that this dotted line has a kink at the level of capital at which the constraint plane intersects the good-luck hill. For levels of capital immediately below this amount, expected profits is the average of allowed profits, which is the upward-sloping constraint plane, and bad-luck profits, which are downward sloping. For greater amounts of capital, expected profits is the average of the good-luck and bad-luck hills, both of which are downward sloping in this range.

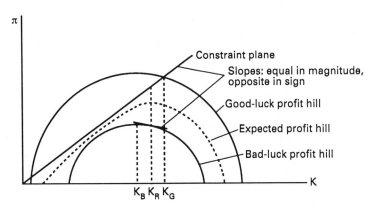

Figure 3.3
Example of regulated firm under uncertainty

not know the type of luck that will occur, it chooses K_R, which is between K_B and K_G.

In figure 3.3, the constraint plane slices the good-luck hill but not the bad-luck hill, and the chosen level of capital is strictly between K_B and K_G. Depending on the shapes of the good- and bad-luck hills and the allowed rate of return, the constraint plane may slice *both* the good- and bad-luck hills[7] and the chosen level of capital might equal K_B or K_G. Figure 3.4 illustrates these possibilities. In panel (a) the constraint plane slices both the good- and bad-luck hills. The chosen level of capital is identified the same as in figure 3.3, namely, where the negative slope of the bad-luck hill is the same in magnitude as the positive slope of the constraint plane. At this point, K_R is strictly between K_B and K_G. In panel (b) the constraint plane also intersects both hills. However, in this case, the bad-luck hill is steeper on the downward-sloping side than in panel (a). For all levels of capital beyond K_B, the bad-luck hill slopes down more steeply than the constraint plane slopes up. Expected profits therefore decrease beyond K_B. The firm chooses $K_R = K_B$, where expected profit is highest. In this situation, the regulated firm facing uncertainty chooses the same amount of capital as it would if it knew for sure that bad luck would prevail. Panel (c) depicts the opposite situation. Beyond K_B, the bad-luck hill slopes down *less* steeply than the constraint plane slopes up. Expected profit is highest at the level of capital at which the constraint plane inter-

---

7. For the regulation to be effective, the constraint plane must slice off part of the good-luck hill. As in chapter 1, the possibility that regulation has no effect is ignored.

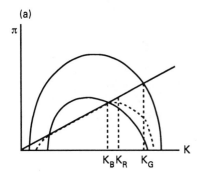

(a)

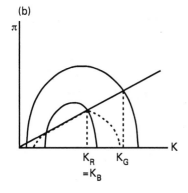

(b)

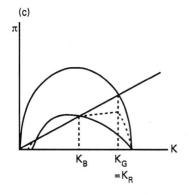

(c)

Figure 3.4
Other examples of regulated firm under uncertainty

sects the good-luck hill. This is the amount of capital the firm would choose if it knew with certainty that good luck would prevail.

Figures 3.3 and 3.4 indicate that the regulated firm under uncertainty chooses a level of capital at or between, but not beyond, the levels it would choose if it knew for sure which type of luck would prevail: $K_B \leq K_R \leq K_G$. The exact level of K_R within this range depends on the shapes of the good- and bad-luck hills and the slope of the constraint plane.

3.4 Results

Some results can now be demonstrated regarding the behavior of the regulated firm under uncertainty.

Result 1: If K_R is strictly greater than K_B (that is, except in cases like panel (b) of figure 3.4), then the expected rate of return for the regulated firm is lower than the allowed rate of return. The regulated firm earns less profit on average than it is allowed to earn.

In figure 3.5, the firm chooses K_R. If good luck prevails, the firm is capable of attaining profit π_G. However, because this profit exceeds the allowed amount, the firm is allowed to retain only π_A, the allowed profit. If bad luck prevails, the firm earns π_B. Expected profit, π_E, is the average of π_A and π_B, which is less than allowed profit π_A.

This phenomenon occurs whenever it is possible for the firm to earn *less* than the allowed rate of return but the regulator prevents

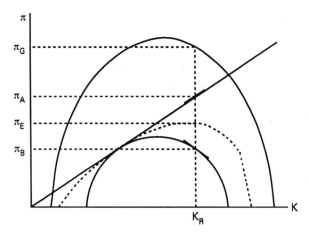

Figure 3.5
Regulated firm's expected profits are less than allowed profits

the firm from earning *more* than the allowed rate. The one case in which the firm's expected profits equal the allowed profits is when, as in panel (b) of figure 3.4, the firm earns exactly the allowed profit rate under both good and bad luck. Except in this rare situation, the firm on average earns less than the fair return.

There is a simple but often overlooked message in this result. If the regulator considers f to be the fair rate of return, the allowed rate should be set above f for the firm to have an expected profit of f. This concept is particularly meaningful in the context of demand fluctuations (due, for example, to weather). If the firm makes less than the allowed rate of return in "bad" years and yet is not allowed to make more than the fair return in "good" years, the firm's average return over time is less than the allowed return. If the regulator truly considers a certain rate of return to be fair, the allowed rate in each year must be set above this fair rate in order for the average rate that the firm earns over several years to end up being fair.

One way in which regulators have addressed this issue is to allow losses from one year (or, more precisely, the amount by which profits fall short of the allowed level in one year) to be made up in future years. That is, allowed profits in future years are raised until the losses are recouped. An accounting procedure is used to keep track of the cumulative sum of excess and deficient profits over time. When the sum is zero, the firm has earned the fair return over the period of time. This practice, and variants of it, are employed extensively, especially in relation to weather-related fluctuations in demand.

Result 2: If K_R is strictly less than K_G (that is, except in cases like panel (c) of figure 3.4), then the regulated firm wastes if good luck prevails. On average, inputs are wasted.

Figure 3.5 illustrates the situation. If good luck occurs, the firm can earn π_G if it operates efficiently. However, because it is only able to earn π_A, the firm must engage in some form of waste to reduce its profits by the amount $\pi_G - \pi_A$. This waste can take the form of producing less output than is maximally possible with the available capital.[8] This phenomenon of expected waste occurs whenever the firm, at its chosen capital level, is able to earn more than the allowed rate when luck is good. The one situation in which waste does not occur

---

8. If the firm uses labor along with capital and chooses its labor after knowing that good luck occurred, waste can be in the form of utilizing too much or too little labor relative to the cost-minimizing quantity.

is when, as in panel (c) of figure 3.4, the firm is able, if fully efficient, to earn only as much as the allowed rate when good luck occurs.

The relation of result 2 to the analogous result in chapter 1 provides insight into the source of waste in regulated firms. Recall that the standard A-J model implies that a regulated firm facing a fair rate of return that exceeds the cost of capital does not waste in the sense of producing less than is maximally possible with its inputs. The A-J model has often been criticized for this implication because it seems to contradict causal empiricism regarding the operations of regulated firms. The introduction of uncertainty into the A-J model provides information on a possible source of observed waste. In particular, waste can result from an asymmetric treatment of uncertainty. Waste occurs whenever the firm's allowed profit at its chosen capital level is less than the profit it is maximally able to earn with that capital. Thus waste can occur even if the firm is under some form of regulation other than ROR regulation, as long as the regulatory mechanism treats excess and deficient profits differently and the firm is maximally able to earn more than the allowed profit if good luck prevails.

If bad luck prevails, the firm does not waste. However, this fact has less importance than it might seem to. The explanations and graphs in this chapter are expressed in terms of two possibilities, good and bad luck. However, in the real world the possibilities are infinite. There is a continuum of profit hills, ranging from the very worst possible luck to the very best luck possible. For many of these (and perhaps all except the very worst luck) the firm wastes to some degree after its luck has been revealed.

Result 3: Under independent risk, the regulated firm utilizes more capital than the unregulated firm. However, under dependent risk, the comparison can go either way; in particular, the regulated firm might utilize less *capital than the unregulated firm.*

If risk is independent of the firm's choice of capital, the unregulated firm faces good- and bad-luck hills that reach their maxima at the same level of capital. The unregulated firm chooses this level of capital. At this level of capital, denoted as K_M in figure 3.6, the good- and bad-luck hills each has a slope of zero (such that the slope of the unregulated firm's expected profit hill is also zero).

When regulation is imposed, the top of the good-luck hill is sliced off; however, suppose for now that, as in figure 3.6, the top of the bad-luck hill is not sliced off. At the level of capital that the unregulated firm chooses, K_M, the slope of the regulated firm's expected profit

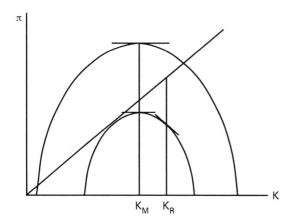

Figure 3.6
Regulated firm uses more capital than unregulated firm when risk is independent

hill is the average of the constraint's slope (which is positive) and the slope of the bad-luck hill (which is zero at K_M). Because the average of a positive number and zero is positive, the expected profit hill for the regulated firm is necessarily upward sloping at K_M, meaning that the regulated firm obtains greater expected profit at a higher level of capital. The firm therefore chooses greater capital, namely, K_R in the graph.

If the constraint plane slices off the top of the bad-luck hill as well as the good-luck hill, the same conclusion obtains. In this case, the regulated firm's expected profit hill near K_M is the constraint plane (see figure 3.4), which has a positive slope.

Consider now the possibility of dependent risk. In this case the regulated firm might actually choose *less* capital than if unregulated. Figure 3.7 illustrates such a situation. The unregulated firm chooses K_M, at which the slope of the good-luck hill is equal in magnitude and opposite in sign from that of the bad-luck hill (such that the slope of its expected profit hill is zero.) When the constraint is imposed, the slope of the regulated firm's expected profit hill at K_M becomes the average of the slopes of the constraint and the bad-luck hill. If, as in the figure, the bad-luck hill at K_M slopes down more steeply than the constraint plane slopes up, then the regulated firm's expected profit hill has a negative slope at K_M.[9] Because expected profits for the reg-

---

9. Another way to describe the situation is that the constraint plane slopes up less steeply than the good-luck hill at K_M. (Both slope upward, but the good-luck hill does

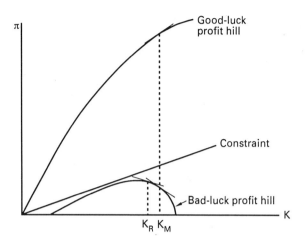

Figure 3.7
Regulated firm might use less capital than unregulated firm when risk is dependent

ulated firm are downward sloping at K_M, the firm obtains greater expected profits by utilizing less capital.

There is a clear reason for the firm facing dependent risk to reduce its capital when regulation is imposed. Without regulation, the firm might incur losses for reasons beyond its control, but it might also happen to obtain extraordinary profit. When regulation is imposed, the firm is still at risk of incurring the losses, but it is prevented from retaining any extraordinary profit that might occur, insofar as these exceed allowed profit. The larger the degree of uncertainty, the more the regulated firm is at risk of loss without a compensating chance of gain. As a result, the firm has an incentive to reduce its risk; and if risk is related to its use of capital, the firm has an incentive to reduce its capital. ROR regulation with dependent risk therefore provides the firm with two opposing incentives: to increase capital so as to increase allowed profits, and to decrease capital so as to decrease risk. Which of these two incentives dominates, and therefore whether the firm increases or decreases its capital when regulation is imposed, depends on the allowed rate of return and the relation of risk to capital.

Result 4: If K_R is strictly between K_B and K_G, then lowering the allowed rate of return reduces the regulated firm's use of capital, under either independent or dependent risk.

---

so more steeply than the constraint plane.) The good-luck and bad-luck slopes average to zero at K_M. Because the constraint has a smaller slope than the good-luck hill, the average of the constraint's slope with the bad-luck slope is necessarily negative.

The interesting aspect of this result is that it holds for independent risk, even though by result 3 the firm increases its use of capital when regulation is imposed. We therefore demonstrate the result with independent risk; the case of dependent risk is analogous.

In figure 3.8 the firm chooses capital K_0 under the original allowed rate of return. At this level of capital, the slope of the bad-luck hill is equal in magnitude and opposite in sign to the slope of the original constraint. When the allowed rate of return is reduced, the constraint plane rotates downward, becoming less steep. Because the slope of the bad luck hill at K_0 is equal in magnitude to the slope of the original constraint, it is greater in magnitude than the slope of the new constraint. Therefore, the average of the slopes of the bad-luck hill at K_0 and the new constraint is necessarily negative. Because the firm's expected profit hill with the new constraint is downward sloping at K_0, the firm obtains greater expected profits with a lower level of capital.

The result is essentially due to the fact that the expected profit hill is the average of the constraint and the bad-luck hill, such that reducing the slope of the constraint reduces the slope of the expected profit hill. At the point of zero slope originally, the slope becomes negative under a lower allowed rate.

If K_R is originally equal to either K_B or K_G (that is, the level of capital that the firm would choose if it knew for certain that bad luck or good luck, respectively, would occur), then lowering the allowed rate of

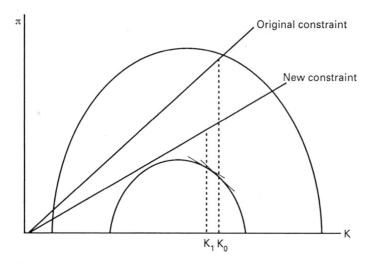

Figure 3.8
Regulated firm uses less capital when fair rate is reduced

return does not decrease the use of capital. In panels (b) and (c) of figure 3.4, lowering the constraint induces the firm to use more capital.

Result 4 is important because, like result 2, it reverses a widely criticized implication of the standard A-J model. Without uncertainty, the A-J model suggests that lowering the allowed rate of return necessarily increases the firm's use of capital, which is contrary to the concept that capital leaves industries whose profit rates fall.[10]

Results 2 and 3 are descriptive rather than normative, in that they describe how the regulated firm behaves in its choice of capital but do not indicate, directly at least, whether the level of capital is efficient. The following result suggests that the basic A-J effect, namely, that the firm uses an inefficient input mix, holds when uncertainty is introduced even though, as we have seen, other implications of the standard A-J model do not.

Result 5: The regulated firm's capital/labor ratio is inefficiently high.

For this result, it is necessary to include labor in the analysis of the firm's behavior. Assume that the firm chooses labor at the same time as capital; that is, assume that the firm chooses the levels of capital and labor without knowing whether good or bad luck will occur and cannot adjust these levels after its luck has been revealed.

I have not been able to devise a graphical method for demonstrating this result. However, in our situation involving only good or bad luck, a mathematical demonstration turns out to be simple and informative.

Assume that the constraint plane slices off all relevant portions of the good-luck profit hill but does not intersect the bad-luck hill, such that expected profit is the average of the constraint and the bad-luck hill. This is the two-input analog of figure 3.3; other situations can be examined analogously. Let $RB(K,L)$ be the largest revenues that the firm is able to attain under bad luck with inputs K and L. Given wage rate w, interest rate r, and allowed rate of return f, the firm's expected profit is

---

10. This criticism of the A-J model is based on an idea that in reality the supply of capital available to the firm depends on the firm's allowed rate of return, while in the A-J model the firm is assumed to be able to obtain as much capital as it wants at a given interest rate r. The direct way to approach this criticism is to generalize the A-J model to allow for a variable price of capital, with r being a function of the allowed rate of return and perhaps the amount of capital purchased by the firm. The analysis of uncertainty, however, indicates that the expected direction of effect can be obtained even without the generalization to variable r.

$$EP = (1/2)[(RB(K,L) - wL - rK)] + (1/2)[(f-r)K].$$

The first term in brackets is the profit the firm obtains under bad luck. Because we assume that the firm under bad luck cannot feasibly earn as much profit as it is allowed, the profit the firm attains is simply the maximum revenues minus the cost of the inputs. The second term in brackets is the profit under good luck. Because feasible profit is assumed to exceed allowed profit under good luck, the firm keeps only the allowed profit $(f - r)K$. Expected profit is the average of profits under good and bad luck, with a probability of 1/2 for each.

The firm chooses the K and L that maximize expected profit. Taking the partial derivative of EP with respect to capital:

$$\delta EP/\delta K = (1/2)[(RB_K - r) + (f-r)] = 0,$$

or,

$$RB_K = r - (f-r).$$

where RB_K is the marginal revenue product of capital. This marginal revenue product is the extra revenue the firm obtains when it utilizes an extra unit of capital and sells the extra output that it is able to produce with this extra capital. As such it can be expressed as the marginal product of capital times the marginal revenue of the firm's output: $RB_K = MP_K \cdot MR$. Substituting into the above equation:

$$MP_K \cdot MR = r - (f-r). \tag{3.1}$$

Taking the partial derivative of EP with respect to labor:

$$\delta EP/\delta L = (1/2)(RB_L - w) = 0,$$

or, because $RB_L = MP_L \cdot MR$,

$$MP_L \cdot MR = w. \tag{3.2}$$

The ratio of equation (3.1) to (3.2) is:

$$\frac{MP_K \cdot MR}{MP_L \cdot MR} = \frac{r - (f-r)}{w}$$

or

$$MP_K/MP_L = (r/w) - (f-r)/w.$$

If $f > r$, the term being subtracted is positive, such that the ratio of marginal products is *less* than the ratio of input prices. At the cost-minimizing input mix, the ratio of marginal products (the slope of the isoquant) is *equal* to the ratio of input prices (the slope of the isocost). The firm is therefore using an inefficient input mix. Furthermore, because the ratio of marginal products is *less* than the ratio of prices, costs would be lower with less capital and more labor.[11] That is, the firm chooses an inefficiently high capital/labor ratio.[12]

Results 2, 3, and 5 combine to paint an even more distressing picture of ROR regulation than obtains when uncertainty is not considered. When risk is dependent on the level of the firm's operation (as it usually is), then regulating the firm can induce it to reduce its level of capital. At this lower level of capital, the firm uses an inefficiently high capital/labor ratio, which implies that its labor and output are also reduced. Except under rare conditions, the firm also wastes on average. Stated succinctly, ROR regulation in an uncertain world can induce the firm to reduce its output, engage in pure waste, and purchase an inefficient input mix.

The forces driving these results are important to distinguish. By

---

11. This fact is elaborated in section 1.5. Assuming diminishing marginal products, the use of less capital increases the marginal product of capital, and the use of more labor decreases its marginal product. The ratio of marginal products therefore increases, rising toward the ratio of input prices as required for cost minimization.

12. The question naturally arises with regard to result 5: For what level of output is the input mix inefficient? For the analysis of result 5 to be fully consistent and meaningful, we can assume that the output of the firm is the same under both good and bad luck. Luck simply determines the *price* at which the firm can sell this output. (Under good luck, the firm can charge a higher price than under bad luck.) The difference between the good-luck and bad-luck profit hills is therefore attributable to this price difference. In this context, result 5 says that the firm chooses an inefficiently high capital/labor ratio for its level of output, which is the same under both good and bad luck.

Under this interpretation of the good- and bad-luck hills, the constraint on profits prevents the firm from raising price as high as it would otherwise be able to under good luck. Because the regulated price is below the highest price at which the firm could sell its output, demand for the firm's output exceeds the quantity produced when good luck occurs (assuming, as usual, downward-sloping demand). This is perhaps somewhat consistent with reality, in which, for example, an electric utility is not able to meet demand during extremely hot days when most air conditioners are on and running continuously. However, the concept that output is constant is contrary to some of the interpretations provided for other results, particularly result 2 regarding waste. If output is constant and only price differences determine the difference between the good- and bad-luck hills, the firm does not waste in the sense of producing less output than possible. Rather the inefficiency takes the form of excess demand. When price is not used to allocate available supply and excess demand arises as a consequence, customers who are most willing to pay for the output are not necessarily the customers who receive the output. This misallocation incurs a cost on society, which can be considered a form of waste. Consequently, result 2 can be considered to hold under the assumptions for result 5, but with the waste taking a different form.

tying allowed profits to the firm's use of capital, ROR regulation provides the firm with an incentive to substitute capital for labor. By treating the consequences of uncertain events asymmetrically, the firm is induced to reduce its risk, even if doing so means reducing output (by purchasing fewer inputs and/or wasting the inputs that it purchases). This reaction to uncertainty, though examined in the context of ROR regulation, can be expected to occur, in some form, under any regulatory mechanisms that let the firm incur losses (or less than allowed profits) due to chance events but do not allow the firm to retain excess profits when these are also due to chance events. By applying a stricter standard of review to windfall profits than to unexpected losses, the regulator, while trying to serve the interests of the public, actually induces behavior that is contrary to its own goals.

4   Ramsey Prices

4.1 Motivation

Most public utilities produce more than one good or service, or sell their output in more than one market with a different price in each market. For example, power utilities often sell both gas and electricity. Those that sell only electricity nevertheless sell this good in several time periods (such as peak and off-peak periods) and to several types of customers (such as residential, commercial, industrial, and agricultural customers). Local telephone companies sell point-to-point service, often pricing on the basis of the distance of the call. Transit agencies might provide both bus and rail service. And so on. In fact, it is hard to find a public utility that actually provides only one service at one uniform price to all customer groups.

When more than one good is sold, or a good is sold in more than one market, the second-best outcome is not immediately obvious. First-best pricing, as always, is to set all prices equal to marginal cost. However, for a natural monopoly, marginal-cost pricing can result in the firm's losing money. If the firm cannot be subsidized, price must be raised above marginal costs until profit rises to zero. In a one-good situation, the requirement of zero profit is sufficient to determine the second-best price: price is necessarily equal to average cost when profits are zero. Consequently, the second-best price for one good is average cost. However, with more than one good, many different price combinations result in zero profit. For example, for a utility selling gas and electricity, the price of gas can be raised sufficiently for the firm to break even overall while still holding the price of electricity at its marginal cost; or, the price of electricity can be raised, holding gas price at its marginal cost; or, the prices of both can be raised somewhat above their marginal costs. There are an infinite number of possibilities. Of the various price combinations that provide zero profit, which is best from a social welfare perspective?

This question was first addressed by Ramsey (1927) in the context of optimal taxation. He developed a method for determining the tax rates for various goods that would provide the government with sufficient revenue while reducing consumer surplus as little as possible. As Baumol and Bradford (1970) have pointed out, optimal taxation rules are directly applicable for determining second-best prices for multiproduct natural monopolies. It is traditional, therefore, to refer to these second-best prices as Ramsey prices.

The following sections describe the goal that is implicit in Ramsey pricing, state the rule (or formula) that is used to calculate these prices, and demonstrate that the prices obtained by applying this rule attain the desired goal. The final section illustrates these concepts with an empirical example of pricing for urban transit.

The findings of the chapter can be summarized as follows. Of all possible price combinations for a multiproduct firm, Ramsey prices provide the greatest total surplus while allowing the firm to break even. At the Ramsey price, profits are zero, and

1. the output of each good is reduced by the same proportion relative to the outputs that would be produced when prices are at marginal cost; and

2. the amount by which price exceeds marginal cost, expressed as a percentage of price, is greater for goods with less elastic demand.

The first of these statements applies exactly only when demand is linear; otherwise, output is reduced *approximately* the same for each good. The second statement, called the "inverse elasticity rule," applies with both linear and nonlinear demand. The two statements are equivalent, but are simply described in different terms. That is, if prices are raised inversely to elasticity, outputs will be reduced by the same proportion for all goods, and vice versa.

It is important to note that Ramsey prices might not be considered equitable in certain situations. Inelastic demand can reflect a lack of options by consumers (e.g., demand for medical care, demand for bus service by low-income households without cars). Yet, under Ramsey concepts, prices for goods and services that consumers have no option but to buy would be raised *more* than prices for less essential goods. The regulator must address these equity issues in deciding whether to implement (or, more precisely, induce the firm to implement) Ramsey prices.

4.2 Description of the Ramsey Rule

If a multiproduct firm is a natural monopoly, then pricing each good at its marginal cost can result in the firm losing money. Suppose that the firm cannot be subsidized and consequently cannot continue to operate with negative profit in the long run. To remain solvent, the firm must set prices sufficiently above marginal cost to break even, that is, earn zero profit. However, there are many price combinations for the goods that will result in zero profit. The question is: Which of these price combinations is best from a social surplus perspective?

Let us first define the term "best." Because prices are raised above marginal cost, there is necessarily some loss of surplus associated with the higher prices. The amount by which total surplus decreases depends on the exact prices charged. Each price combination that provides zero profits (and hence is feasible for the firm to charge) results in a different amount of surplus loss. The "best" price combination is the one that results in the smallest loss in surplus.

Total surplus consists of consumer surplus plus firm profits (that is, producer's surplus). Because all price combinations that result in zero profit provide the same producer's surplus, the price combination that reduces total surplus the least also reduces consumer surplus the least. Therefore, the "best" price combination can also be considered to be that which results in the smallest loss of consumer surplus relative to marginal-cost pricing.

Ramsey, and others, have derived formulae for calculating the prices that result in the smallest surplus loss when prices must be raised above marginal cost in order for the firm to remain solvent. We present below a numerical example that illustrates the meaning of these formulae and indicates why they necessarily result in the prices that minimize the loss in surplus. In the following section, a more rigorous demonstration of the formulae is provided.

Consider a firm producing two goods, or selling one good in each of two markets. Generalization to cases with more than two goods is straightforward. Suppose that demand in the two markets is $P_1 = 50 - .0075Q_1$ and $P_2 = 40 - .004Q_2$, respectively. The firm incurs setup costs of $19,800 and marginal costs of $20 for each unit

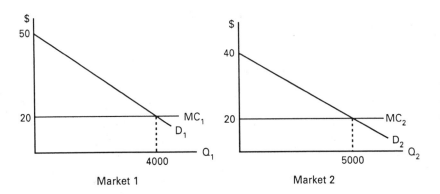

Figure 4.1
Demand and costs in numerical example

of either good produced. Its cost function is therefore $TC = 19,800 + 20Q_1 + 20Q_2$. The relevant curves are graphed in figure 4.1.

If the firm priced at marginal cost, it would sell 4,000 units in market one and 5,000 in market two. Its revenues would cover its variable costs, but not its fixed costs. It would therefore incur a loss of $19,800 when pricing at marginal cost. To stay in business, the firm must raise its price for one or both of the goods.

Several options are available. The firm could keep the price in market one at marginal cost and raise price sufficiently in market two to break even. With $P_2 = 25.44$, revenues in market two exceed the variable costs of production for that market by $19,800, which are its fixed costs of production. Therefore, with $P_1 = 20.00$ (that is, marginal cost) and $P_2 = 25.44$, the firm would break even.[1] Alternatively, the firm could keep P_2 at marginal cost and raise price sufficiently in market two to break even. With $P_1 = 26.25$ and $P_2 = 20.00$, the firm earns zero profit. Or, the firm could raise each price above marginal cost. If P_1 is raised $1 above marginal cost, to 21.00, then the firm would break even with P_2 raised to 23.98. With P_1 raised to 22.00, a price of 22.88 in market two is sufficient to break even. And so on. An infinite number of price combinations will result in zero profits for the firm. Some of these (for $1 increments in P_1) are listed in table 4.1.

---

1. At $P_2 = 25.44$, demand in market two is 3,640. Revenue in market two is $P_2 \cdot Q_2 = 92,600$ (rounded). Revenue in market one is $P_1 \cdot Q_1 = (20)(4,000) = 80,000$. Total cost is $19,800 + (20)(4,000) + (20)(3,640) = 172,600$. Profit is therefore $92,600 + 80,000 - 172,600 = 0$.

Table 4.1
Price combinations that result in zero profit

P_1	P_2	Demand in market 1 Q_1	Demand in market 2 Q_2	Revenue in market 1 P_1Q_1	Revenue in market 2 P_2Q_2	Total cost $19800 + 20Q_1 + 20Q_2$	Profit	Consumer surplus in market 1	Consumer surplus in market 2	Total consumer surplus
20.00	25.44	4,000	3,640	80,000	92,600	172,600	0	60,000	26,499	86,499
21.00	23.98	3,867	4,005	81,200	96,040	177,240	0	56,067	32,080	88,147
22.00	22.88	3,733	4,280	82,130	97,930	180,060	0	52,267	36,637	88,904
23.00	22.00	3,600	4,500	82,800	99,000	181,800	0	48,600	40,500	89,100
24.00	21.27	3,467	4,683	83,200	99,600	182,800	0	45,067	43,852	88,919
26.25	20.00	3,167	5,000	83,140	100,000	183,140	0	37,605	50,000	87,605

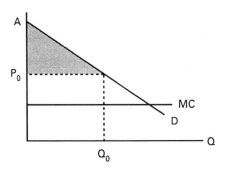

Figure 4.2
Consumer surplus

Each of these price combinations is equally acceptable to the firm. However, consumers are better off at some of these price combinations than at others. To determine which price combination is best for consumers, we calculate the consumers' surplus at each price combination.

Recall that consumer surplus in a market is the area under the demand curve and above price, the shaded area in figure 4.2. For linear demand, this area can be calculated fairly easily. It is the area of a triangle whose width is the quantity sold (Q_0) and whose height is the difference between the price and the y-intercept of the demand curve ($A - P_0$). Because the area of a triangle is one-half the width times the height, consumer surplus in this figure is $(1/2)Q_0(A - P_0)$.

Applying these ideas to the two markets in our example, we find that consumer surplus is \$86,499 when $P_1 = 20.00$ and $P_2 = 25.44$,[2] which is one of the price combinations that result in zero profit. Consumer surplus for each other price combination that provides zero profit is given in the last column of table 4.1.

Consumer surplus is greatest at $P_1 = 23$ and $P_2 = 22$. These are therefore the second-best prices: of those price combinations that provide the firm with zero profit, this price combination provides consumers with the greatest surplus.[3]

---

2. In market one, consumer surplus is $(1/2)(4,000)(50 - 20) = 60,000$. In market two, $(1/2)(3,640)(40 - 25.44) = 26,499$. Surplus in both markets is therefore $60,000 + 26,499 = 86,499$.

3. Total surplus is the sum of consumers' surplus and producers' surplus (that is, profit). Because profit is the same (zero) for all these price combinations, the price combination that provides the greatest consumer surplus also provides the greatest total surplus.

Two characteristics of these prices warrant notice; both are aspects of the Ramsey rule for second-best pricing.

1. *Output is reduced by the same proportion in each market relative to marginal-cost pricing.*

If prices are at marginal cost in both markets ($P_1 = P_2 = 20$), output in market one is 4,000, and in market two, 5,000. At the second-best prices, output is 10% lower in each market. (In market one, output decreases by 10% from 4,000 to 3,600; and in market two, output decreases from 5,000 to 4,500, for a 10% drop.) This occurrence is not a coincidence. When demand curves are linear, second-best prices always result in output being reduced by the same proportion in all markets, relative to output levels that result when prices equal marginal costs.

There is an intuitive reason for this occurrence. Marginal-cost pricing results in the first-best output level for each good. For a natural monopoly to break even, prices must be raised, meaning that output must decrease below its optimal level. If output decreases by *the same proportion* for all goods, then *relative* output levels remain at their first-best levels, even though absolute outputs change. For example, in our numerical example, first-best output is 4,000 in market one and 5,000 in market two, such that the first-best ratio of outputs is 4/5. When output is reduced by 10% in each market, the ratio of outputs remains at its optimal level of 4/5 (now 3,600/4,500). The second-best prices are those that retain the first-best ratio of outputs, even though, by necessity, the absolute output levels are not first-best.

This concept can be expressed algebraically. Let Q_1 and Q_2 be the output in markets one and two, respectively, under second-best prices. Let ΔQ_1 and ΔQ_2 be the changes in output from marginal-cost pricing to second-best pricing. (That is, ΔQ_1 is output in market one when prices are second-best minus the output that would occur under marginal cost prices; and similarly for ΔQ_2. In our example, $Q_1 = 3,600$, $Q_2 = 4,500$, $\Delta Q_1 = 400$, and $\Delta Q_2 = 500$.) At the second-best prices with linear demand, the following relation necessarily holds:

$$\Delta Q_1/Q_1 = \Delta Q_2/Q_2. \qquad (4.1)$$

That is, the percentage change in output from its marginal-cost level is the same in both markets.

This relation gives us another way of thinking of the second-best prices. If a firm is charging marginal-cost prices and losing money, prices can be raised and output reduced in a number of ways to allow the firm to break even. For example, price can be raised considerably in one market and not much in another, or vice versa. Of all the possible ways of raising prices to allow the firm to break even, the price changes that keep the ratio of outputs unchanged (that is, keeps this ratio at its first-best level) are the changes that result in the least loss to consumers and hence are second best.

This fact provides a mechanism for calculating second-best prices. Start at marginal-cost prices and determine the ratio of outputs at these prices. Raise prices a little in each market in such a way that this output ratio is unchanged, that is, that output in each market is reduced by the same proportion. With these slightly higher prices, the firm will have somewhat smaller losses. Raise prices again, still keeping the output ratio constant, and the firm will incur even smaller losses. Continue raising prices in this way until the firm breaks even: these are the second-best prices.

2. *Price is raised more in the market with less elastic demand.*

Recall that the elasticity of demand is a measure of price responsiveness in a market and is defined as the percent change in output that results from a percent change in price. The elasticity is calculated as $\epsilon = (\Delta Q/Q)/(\Delta P/P)$, or, rearranging, $\epsilon = (\Delta Q/\Delta P)(P/Q) = (1/m)(P/Q)$, where m is the slope of the demand curve (with the demand curve giving price as a function of quantity, as in our example).

At the second-best prices in our numerical example, the elasticity of demand in market one is $-.85$ (calculated as $(1/-.0075)(23/3,600)$), and the elasticity of demand in market two is -1.2 (calculated as $(1/-.004)(22/4,500)$). Comparing the second-best price in each market with the elasticity in the market, we find that price is *higher* in the market with *lower* elasticity: the price in market one is higher than in market two (23 compared to 22) and the elasticity of demand is lower ($-.85$ compared to -1.2, where "lower" means smaller in magnitude, representing less price response).

This occurrence is not a coincidence. Second-best pricing always results in raising price farther above marginal cost in the market with a lower elasticity of demand. This characteristic of second-best prices is often called the inverse elasticity rule: prices are raised in inverse relation to the elasticity of demand in each market (raising prices more in markets with lower elasticity and less in markets with higher elasticity).

This result has intuitive meaning. Raising prices has two effects. First, it transfers money from consumers to the producer, because consumers have to pay more for the goods they purchase. Second, it reduces the quantity of goods sold, because consumers generally demand fewer of the good when its price is higher. The degree to which each of these two effects occurs depends on the elasticity of demand. If, as in panel (a) of figure 4.3, demand is highly inelastic (that is, consumers are not very responsive to price), then raising price from P_0 to P_1 transfers a considerable amount of money to the firm (its profits increase by the shaded area) and reduces the quantity sold by very little. However, when demand is more elastic (that is, consumers are more price responsive), as in panel (b), the same price increase results in a smaller transfer of money from consumers to the firm and a larger reduction in output. If the firm is losing money, a certain amount of money must be transferred to the firm for it to break even. More funds can be obtained with less disruption in consumer's consumption patterns (that is, less reduction in output) by raising price in the market with inelastic demand than in the market with elastic demand. This fact is essentially what the inverse elasticity rule is stating: raise price more in the market with a lower elasticity of demand.

The precise statement of this characteristic of second-best prices is somewhat more complex than the inverse elasticity rule might suggest. In our example, marginal cost is constant and the same for both markets. An accurate statement of the rule allows for differences in marginal cost. We give this statement below for situations in which demand in each market is independent of the price charged in the other market; that is, no cross-elasticities of demand. In a later section, we generalize to situations with cross-elasticities.

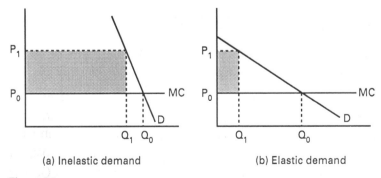

(a) Inelastic demand   (b) Elastic demand

Figure 4.3
Price increase in markets with different demand elasticities

The general rule, when there are no cross-elasticities, is that, at the second-best prices

$$((P_1 - MC_1)/P_1) \cdot \epsilon_1 = ((P_2 - MC_2)/P_2) \cdot \epsilon_2, \qquad (4.2)$$

where ϵ is the elasticity of demand. The term $P_1 - MC_1$ is the amount by which price in market one exceeds marginal cost for that good. Dividing this by P_1 gives the amount by which price exceeds marginal cost expressed as a proportion of price. The equation states that, at second-best prices, if the percentage by which price exceeds marginal cost in each market is multiplied by the elasticity of demand in that market, the resulting product is the same for all markets.

This equation holds in our numerical example. In market one, elasticity is $-.85$, price is 23, and marginal cost 20. Price exceeds marginal cost by 3, which is 13% (2/23) of the price. The product of the elasticity and the percent increase of price over marginal cost is $-.11$ ($= -.85 \cdot .13$). In market two, elasticity is -1.2, price is 22, and marginal cost is 20. Price exceeds marginal cost by 9% of price, which, when multiplied by elasticity, is $-.11$. In both markets, the elasticity of demand multiplied by the proportion by which price exceeds marginal cost is the same, as stated in the above equation.

Equation (4.2) is the algebraic expression of the inverse elasticity rule. For this equation to hold, price must be raised farther above marginal cost in markets with lower elasticities of demand. That is, if ϵ is smaller in one market than another, the term $(P - MC)/P$ must be higher in that first market so that the product $(P - MC)/P \cdot \epsilon$ can be the same in both markets. Thus the equation requires higher prices in markets with lower elasticities.

It is important to note that equations (4.1) and (4.2) are not two separate rules. Rather, they are two different ways of stating the same rule. Equation (4.1) states that second-best prices are attained by reducing output in each market by the same proportion. Equation (4.2) states that second-best prices are attained by increasing price in the market with the lower elasticity. However, equation (4.1) implies equation (4.2) and vice versa: if outputs are reduced by the same proportion in all markets, price necessarily rises more in markets with lower elasticity. Consider figure 4.4. First-best output is Q_F in each market, which is obtained when prices are set to marginal costs. If output is reduced by the same proportion in each market to Q_S, the price in the first market rises to P_1 and that in the second market to P_2. That is, a given proportion reduction in output in both markets

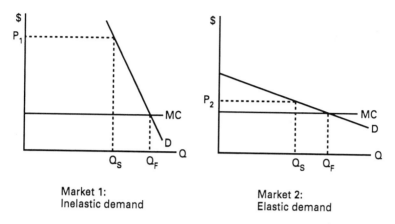

Market 1:
Inelastic demand

Market 2:
Elastic demand

Figure 4.4
Ramsey prices

results in a higher price in market one than in market two. This is reasonable. Because there is less response to price in market one than market two, a larger price increase is needed in market one to induce a given percent reduction in quantity demanded. This illustration implies that, generally, for the output ratio to remain unchanged, price must be raised more in the market with lower elasticity.

Because the two equations are alternative ways of saying the same thing, each equation alone is, or both collectively are, called the Ramsey rule for second-best pricing. Either can be used to calculate second-best prices. That is, prices can be raised above marginal cost in such a way that output ratios remain constant, with the prices raised in this manner until the firm breaks even. Or, price in each market can be raised by an amount that is inversely related to the elasticity of demand in that market until the firm breaks even. Either method will result in the same prices.

4.3 A More Rigorous Derivation of the Ramsey Rule

In the previous section, a numerical example was used to motivate and illustrate the Ramsey rule. We asserted, without proof, that the results obtained in the numerical example occur in all such situations. We now present a more rigorous demonstration of the Ramsey rule. This demonstration is intended to be pedagogic, in that the emphasis is on understanding the meaning of the Ramsey rule and why it is generally true. The analysis avoids the use of calculus so that (1) readers who are not comfortable with calculus can obtain a clear understanding of the result, and (2) readers who know calculus will have the opportunity to think about the meaning behind the equations, which is often obscured in purely mathematical proofs. A formal analysis is provided by Baumol and Bradford (1970).

Suppose the following:

1. A firm produces two goods, labeled x and y.

2. Pricing the two goods at their marginal cost results in the firm losing money.

3. It is not possible for the firm to operate while losing money. That is, the firm cannot be subsidized.

4. Demand for the two goods is independent, in that the price of one good does not affect the demand for the other good. That is, cross-price elasticities are zero.

5. Demand for each good is linear.

The first assumption allows us to show results on two-dimensional graphs; generalization to three or more goods is straightforward. The second assumption is consistent with the firm being a natural monopoly. The third assumption reflects the way natural monopolies are generally regulated in the United States. It can be relaxed to allow the firm to lose up to a certain amount of money (the amount of its subsidy); the Ramsey rule is still applicable as long as the firm would lose more than the subsidy amount if it priced at marginal cost. The fourth and fifth assumptions are for convenience of exposition only. With these two assumptions, the Ramsey rule takes a form that is particularly intuitive. In a later section we discuss how allowing for nonlinear demand and cross-elasticities generalizes the form of the Ramsey rule.

We state the Ramsey rule first and then derive it.

Ramsey rule: Given a situation described by assumptions (1)–(5), the prices that provide the greatest surplus while also allowing the firm to break even are those at which profits are zero and

$$\frac{\Delta Q_1}{Q_1} = \frac{\Delta Q_2}{Q_2}, \tag{4.1}$$

or, alternatively,

$$\frac{(P_1 - MC_1)}{P_1}\epsilon_1 = \frac{(P_2 - MC_2)}{P_2}\epsilon_2, \tag{4.2}$$

where ϵ is the price elasticity of demand and ΔQ is the change in output from its level when prices are at marginal cost.

We first introduce two graphical devices: the zero-profit contour for the firm and isobenefit contours for consumers. Then, by combining these two concepts, we determine the prices and outputs at which consumers obtain the greatest surplus while the firm breaks even.

Consider first the firm. The profit the firm earns is completely determined once the firm sets its prices for the two goods. Given the price of each good, the demand curve for each good determines the quantity sold. Given the quantity sold, the technology and input prices the firm faces (as embodied in the firm's cost curves) determine the minimum cost of producing the goods. The profit of the firm is simply its revenues (the product of its price and output levels) minus its costs.

The relation between profit and prices has the form of a hill, as shown in figure 4.5. When prices are very low, the firm loses money, because its prices are not high enough to cover its costs. As prices are raised, the firm's profit increases (losses decrease) and the firm starts to earn positive profit. Profit continues to increase as prices are raised. Eventually, however, prices are raised so much that demand for the goods is choked off and profit starts to drop. That is, beyond a certain point, increasing prices decreases demand sufficiently that the profit of the firm declines. Eventually, at high enough prices, profit again becomes negative.

The relevant information can be depicted in two dimensions. To

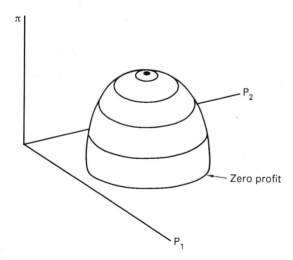

Figure 4.5
Relation of profit to prices

remain solvent, the firm must earn at least zero profit. The base of the profit hill in figure 4.5 (or, more precisely, the points at which the profit hill is cut by the $P_1 - P_2$ plane) is the set of price combinations that result in the firm earning exactly zero profits. These price combinations are depicted in two dimensions by suppressing the profit dimension, as in figure 4.6. The "zero-profit contour" in this latter figure is the set of prices that result in zero profit. Note that any price combination that is inside this zero-profit contour results in strictly positive profit, and any price combination that is outside results in negative profit. To remain solvent, the firm must charge prices that are either inside or on the zero-profit contour.

Figure 4.6 illustrates the issue that Ramsey prices address. If prices were set to marginal cost, the firm would be at point F (first-best prices), which is outside the zero-profit contour. To remain solvent, the firm must increase one or both of the prices so as to move to the zero-profit contour. The question is: Of all the price combinations that the firm could move to on the zero-profit contour, which one is best for consumers?

We now introduce a graphical method for representing consumers' surplus. At any set of prices, consumers obtain some amount of surplus. This surplus increases when the price of either good decreases; that is, consumers benefit from reduced prices. Conversely, surplus decreases as the price of either good increases. The relation between consumer surplus and prices can be represented, as in figure 4.7, as a surface that is highest when prices are zero and drops when prices rise.

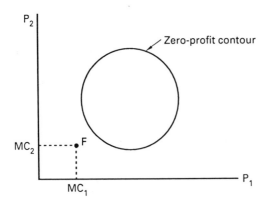

Figure 4.6
Zero-profit contour

The information in figure 4.7 can be represented in two dimensions by making a contour map of the surface (i.e., a topological map). Figure 4.8 is a contour map of the three-dimensional surface in figure 4.7. Each contour in figure 4.8 is the set of prices that result in a particular level of surplus for consumers. For example, all price combinations on the contour labeled b_1 result in $\$b_1$ of surplus for consumers. Each of these contours is called an "isobenefit contour" because it represents a set of price combinations that provide the same ("iso") level of benefits to consumers.[4]

Consumer surplus is greater on isobenefit contours that are closer to the origin (closer to zero prices.) In the figure, this means that consumer surplus level b_3 is greater that b_2, which in turn is greater than b_1. Consumers are therefore made as well off as possible by moving as far inward on the isobenefit mapping as possible.

The goal of Ramsey pricing is to make consumers as well off as possible while allowing the firm to break even. To determine which prices accomplish this goal, the isobenefit mapping for consumers is superimposed with the zero-profit contour for the firm, as in figure 4.9. The Ramsey prices are found by examining all of the price combinations on or inside the zero-profit contour (because these are the prices that allow the firm to remain solvent) and determining which of these touches the lowest isobenefit contour (because the lowest, or most inward, contour represents the highest consumer surplus). This price combination is labeled S (second-best). In particular, the Ramsey prices in this situation are P_1^S and P_2^S.

Note that at the Ramsey price combination S, the isobenefit contour is tangent to the zero-profit contour.[5] The isobenefit and zero-profit contours being tangent at S means that they have the same slope at

---

4. The isobenefit contours are downward sloping. This feature reflects the fact that, if one price is raised, the other price must be lowered for consumer surplus to remain unchanged. (Consumers are hurt by an increase in one price; to keep consumers' welfare unchanged—no better or worse—consumers must be helped a commensurate amount by lowering the other price.) Also, the isobenefit contours bow inward, becoming less steeply sloped as P_1 is raised and P_2 is lowered. This feature reflects the expectation that changing a price has less impact on consumer surplus when that price is relatively high (and hence consumption of the good is low) than when price is lower.
5. Stated alternatively: if the isobenefit contour and zero-profit contour are *not* tangent at a particular price combination, that price combination cannot be Ramsey. Consider point G. At this point, consumer surplus can be increased without hurting the firm by moving along the zero-profit contour to lower isobenefit contours (that is, toward S). Because consumer surplus can be higher than at G with the firm still breaking even, G cannot be the Ramsey price.

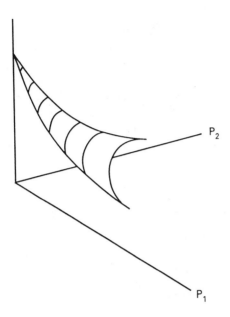

Figure 4.7
Relation of consumer surplus to prices

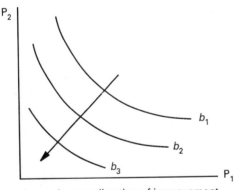

Arrow denotes direction of improvement

Figure 4.8
Isobenefit contours

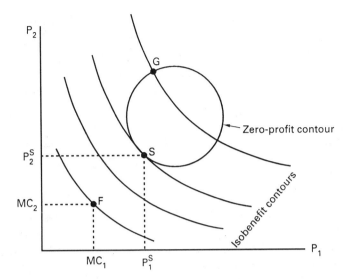

Figure 4.9
Ramsey prices

that point. The Ramsey rule (that is, equations 4.1 and 4.2) is derived from this fact.

Three steps are required to demonstrate the Ramsey rule. First, we derive a formula for the slope of the isobenefit contour. Second, we derive a formula for the slope of the zero-profit contour. Third, we set these two formulas equal to each other (because the slopes of these two contours are equal at the Ramsey prices). This equation, when rearranged, takes the form of equation (4.1) or (4.2), that is, becomes the Ramsey rule. The three steps are discussed separately below.

Step 1: The slope of the isobenefit contour at any price combination is $-Q_1/Q_2$, *where* Q_1 *and* Q_2 *are the quantities demanded at that price combination. That is, the slope of the isobenefit contour at any point is the (negative) ratio of outputs demanded at that point.*

Let us demonstrate this fact. By definition, the slope of the isobenefit contour is the amount by which P_2 must drop in order for consumer surplus to remain constant when P_1 is raised by one unit (that is, the decrease in P_2 is required to keep consumers on the same isobenefit contour when P_1 is raised one unit). Consider a person who consumes quantities Q_1 and Q_2 at given prices. Suppose P_1 increases by \$1. For the consumer to continue consuming quantity Q_1 of the good, the consumer must pay \$$Q_1$ more: \$1 more for each unit consumed.

For the person to be able to still afford Q_1 and Q_2, the price of good two must decline. Each \$1 decrease in P_2 saves \$$Q_2$; or, stated equivalently, each (\$1/Q_2) decrease in P_2 saves \$1. To get back \$$Q_1$, there must be a \$$Q_1(1/Q_2)$ decrease in P_2. That is, for the consumer to remain unaffected by the rise in price of good one, the price of good two must be lowered by \$$Q_1/Q_2$.

This fact can be illustrated with a concrete example. Suppose a person buys ten shirts and five pairs of jeans per year. If the price of shirts goes up by \$1, the consumer would have to pay \$10 extra for the ten shirts. To make up this \$10, the price of jeans would have to drop by \$2 such that the consumer would have to pay \$10 less for the five pairs of jeans. The \$2 is simply the quantity of shirts divided by the quantity of jeans.

The change in P_2 that allows the person to continue buying the same consumption bundle in the face of a \$1 increase in P_1 is, as we have discussed, $-Q_1/Q_2$, where the negative sign indicates that P_2 must drop. Because the person is consuming the same quantities and paying the same amount in total, the person's consumer surplus is the same. Consequently, $-Q_1/Q_2$ is the slope of the isobenefit contour, namely, it is the drop in P_2 that is necessary to keep consumer surplus constant when P_1 is raised one unit.

Perceptive readers will point out that the consumer will not choose to consume the same quantities of the two goods when their prices change, but rather will respond to the new prices by increasing consumption of good two (whose price has dropped) and less of good one (whose price has risen). This observation is correct for sufficiently large changes in prices. However, for sufficiently small changes in prices, the consumer will not change consumption levels. If a \$1 change in P_1 would induce the consumer to change consumption levels, then the units can be changed to consider, say, a 1 cent change in P_1. The analysis is the same: P_2 must drop by Q_1/Q_2¢ to compensate for a 1 cent increase in P_1. Technically, the slope of the isobenefit contour, as all slopes, is defined for infinitesimally small changes, under which consumption levels do not change.

Step 2: The slope of the zero-profit contour is

$$-\frac{Q_1 + (P_1 - MC_1)s_1}{Q_2 + (P_2 - MC_2)s_2},$$

where s_1 is the slope of the demand function for good one, and analogously for good two.

We demonstrate this fact as follows. The slope of the zero-profit contour is, by definition, the amount by which P_2 must change for profits to remain zero when P_1 is raised by one unit. If P_1 is raised by \$1, two things occur. First, the firm earns an extra dollar of revenue on each unit that it sells, such that its profits increase by $\$Q_1$. Second, the quantity demanded decreases when the price increases, and the firm loses the profits that it earned on these units. This loss is the difference between the revenues it earns per unit (P_1) and the marginal cost of each unit (MC_1) multiplied by the number of units by which demand decreases (s_1, where s_1 is the slope of the demand function, with the demand function giving quantity demanded as a function of price).[6] Summing these two effects, the change in profits that results from a \$1 increase in P_1 is $Q_1 + (P_1 - MC_1)s_1$. Label this quantity $\Delta\pi_1$. Similarly, a \$1 decrease in P_2 changes profits by $-(Q_2 + (P_2 - MC_2)s_2)$, which we label $-\Delta\pi_2$.

For profits to remain constant when P_1 rises by \$1, P_2 must drop by an amount that exactly offsets the gain in profits attributable to the rise in P_1. Profits rise by $\Delta\pi_1$ when P_1 increases by \$1. Each \$1 decrease in P_2 reduces profit by $\Delta\pi_2$, or, stated equivalently, each $\$(1/\Delta\pi_2)$ decrease in P_2 reduces profit by \$1. Therefore, to reduce profit by $\Delta\pi_1$, P_2 must be reduced by $\Delta\pi_1/\Delta\pi_2$.[7]

Substituting in the terms for $\Delta\pi_1$ and $\Delta\pi_2$, we know that the change in P_2 that is necessary to maintain constant profits when P_1 is raised \$1 is

$$-\frac{Q_1 + (P_1 - MC_1)s_1}{Q_2 + (P_2 - MC_2)s_2}.$$

This is the slope of the zero-profit contour.

Step 3: Equate the slopes and rearrange for the Ramsey rule.

At Ramsey prices, the slope of the isobenefit contour equals the slope of the zero-profit contour. Setting the expressions for these slopes equal to each other, we have

---

6. Demand is often represented with price being a function of quantity. For example, demand is usually graphed with quantity on the x-axis and price on the y-axis, such that the relation is price as a function of quantity. In this case, s is the inverse of the slope of the demand curve. In either case, s is the same quantity, namely, the decrease in output that results from an increase in price.

7. For example, suppose raising P_1 by \$1 increased profits by \$100 and lowering P_2 by \$1 decreased profits by \$50. It would be necessary to lower P_2 by \$2 (i.e., \$100/\$50) for profits to stay constant when P_1 is raised by \$1.

$$-\frac{Q_1+(P_1-MC_1)s_1}{Q_2+(P_2-MC_2)s_2}=-\frac{Q_1}{Q_2}.$$

Rearranging:

$$(Q_1+(P_1-MC_1)s_1)\,/\,Q_1=(Q_2+(P_2-MC_2)s_2)\,/\,Q_2$$

or

$$1+(P_1-MC_1)(s_1/Q_1)=1+(P_2-MC_2)(s_2/Q_2).$$

Subtracting one from both sides:

$$(P_1-MC_1)(s_1/Q_1)=(P_2-MC_2)(s_2/Q_2). \tag{4.3}$$

Multiplying the left-hand side by (P_1/P_1) and the right by (P_2/P_2) does not change the equation because these quantities are simply one:

$$((P_1-MC_1)/P_1)s_1\cdot(P_1/Q_1)=((P_2-MC_2)/P_2)s_2\cdot(P_2/Q_2).$$

Note that $s_1(P_1/Q_1)$ is the elasticity of demand for good one, which is labeled ϵ_1; and similarly for good two.[8] Using this fact, the equation then becomes

$$\frac{(P_1-MC_1)}{P_1}\epsilon_1=\frac{(P_2-MC_2)}{P_2}\epsilon_2,$$

which is equation (4.2), the inverse elasticity rule. Thus we have shown that at Ramsey prices, the inverse elasticity rule holds.

We now proceed to demonstrate equation (4.1), namely, that at Ramsey prices, the quantity of each good is reduced by the same proportion below its marginal-cost level. The quantity demanded of each good is lower at Ramsey prices than when each good is priced at its marginal cost; label this reduction in demand for good one as ΔQ_1, and analogously for good two. Because demand is linear, the amount by which demand for good one is reduced is equal to the amount by which price is raised above marginal cost (namely, P_1-MC_1) multiplied by the slope of the demand function (s_1, which is the change in output for each one-unit change in price). That is, $\Delta Q_1=(P_1-MC_1)s_1$, and similarly for good two. Substitute this relation into equation (4.3) to obtain

---

8. The elasticity is, by definition, the percent change in quantity that results from a percent change in price: $\epsilon=(\Delta Q/Q)/(\Delta P/P)$. This term can be arranged as $\epsilon=(\Delta Q/\Delta P)(P/Q)$. The slope of the demand curve is $s=\Delta Q/\Delta P$, such that $\epsilon=s(P/Q)$, which is the term that appears in the expression above.

$\Delta Q_1/Q_1 = \Delta Q_2/Q_2$,

which is equation (4.1), stating that the percent change in output from its marginal-cost level is the same for both goods.

4.4   Finding the Ramsey Prices

The Ramsey rule describes relations that must hold at the second-best prices. For example, equation (4.2) states that, at the Ramsey prices, the elasticity of demand times the percent by which price exceeds marginal cost is the same for all goods. It is important to note, however, that the Ramsey rule can be used to *find* the Ramsey prices, as well as characterize events that occur at the prices once they are found.

To find the Ramsey prices, we start by setting price equal to marginal cost for each good. If these prices result in the firm earning zero or positive profits, we retain these prices and obtain first-best optimality. However, if marginal-cost pricing results in negative profits (as we have assumed as the motivation for this chapter), then prices must be raised to allow the firm to remain solvent.

According to equation (4.2) of the Ramsey rule, prices must be raised in such a way that the elasticity of demand times the percent deviation of price from marginal cost is the same for all goods. Note that this equation holds at the marginal-cost prices: because price equals marginal cost, the percent deviation of price from marginal cost is zero for both goods, and the product of this deviation with the elasticity is also zero for each good, independent of the size of the elasticity. In fact, the equation holds for a whole set of prices, not just the Ramsey and marginal cost prices. The Ramsey prices are unique in that they are the only prices at which equation (4.2) holds *and* the firm makes zero profits. Other price combinations that satisfy equation (4.2) result in either negative or strictly positive profits. This fact is the key to finding the Ramsey prices.

Consider figure 4.10. The upward-sloping curve denotes the set of price combinations for which equation (4.2) holds. The Ramsey prices and marginal-cost prices are necessarily on this curve. To find the Ramsey prices, prices are first set equal to marginal cost. Then prices are raised slightly and in such a way that Equation (4.2) holds; this moves the prices from F to a point, say B, somewhat further up on the curve. This change in prices increases the firm's profit (i.e., decreases its loss); however, for a small-enough change in prices, the firm will still be losing money. Prices are therefore raised again, making sure that equation (4.2) holds. This process is continued until prices are raised sufficiently that the firm breaks even. Stated succinctly: prices are raised by successively larger amounts, always in such a way that equation (4.2) holds, until prices are found that allow the firm to break even. Graphically, prices are moved up the curve in figure 4.10 until the zero-profit contour is reached; the intersection of the curve with the zero-profit contour is the Ramsey prices.

Ramsey prices can also be found using equation (4.1). This equation states that at the Ramsey prices, the output of each good is reduced by the same proportion from its level under marginal-cost pricing. Note that while this equation says that the proportionate reduction is the *same* for each good, it does not state what this proportion is. Each output could be reduced by 1%, 5%, 10%, or whatever, and equation (4.1) would hold. The percent reduction that results in zero profit is the appropriate one. This fact provides a procedure for finding the Ramsey output levels: start at the quantities demanded under marginal-cost pricing and then reduce output for each good by successively larger proportions until the firm breaks even.

Figure 4.11 depicts the situation. Note that the axes on this graph are the quantities of output for the two goods, rather than prices as in previous figures. Each point on the graph represents an output combination for the two goods. The zero-profit contour depicts the set of output combinations that result in zero profit. Any output combination that is outside of this contour results in negative profits, while

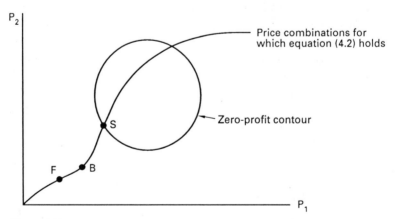

Figure 4.10
Using equation (4.2) to find Ramsey prices

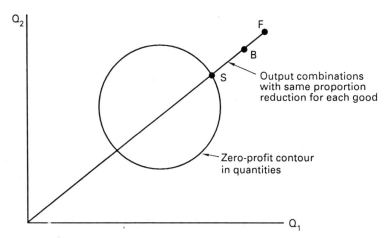

Figure 4.11
Using equation (4.1) to find Ramsey prices

a combination inside the contour provides positive profits. At marginal-cost pricing, output combination F is demanded. At this output combination, the firm is presumably losing money (and hence is located outside the zero-profit contour). For the firm to break even, output must be reduced (that is, prices must be raised). The ray from the origin through point F is the set of output combinations that are obtained by reducing the quantity of each output by the same proportion. Reducing each output by zero proportion is equivalent to no change, and so point F is on the ray. Reducing each output by 100% is equivalent to producing no output, such that the origin is on the ray. Any other point on the ray is obtained by reducing both outputs by some proportion between zero and 100%.

To find the Ramsey output levels (that is, the outputs that would result from Ramsey prices), we start at point F, the outputs obtained under marginal cost pricing, and reduce both outputs by some small proportion, adjusting the price of each good appropriately to obtain this equal-proportion reduction. This reduction moves the firm from point F inward on the ray to, say, point B. The firm loses less money as a result of this reduction in output (and the corresponding increase in price), but it is still losing money. Each output is therefore decreased again, by a larger proportion. This process is continued, reducing both outputs by an increasing large proportion until the firm breaks even.

Note that the two methods for finding Ramsey prices are equivalent, in that they result in the same prices and output. That is: if outputs are reduced proportionately until the firm breaks even, the prices that result in these output levels being demanded are the same prices that would be obtained if prices were raised in accordance with equation (4.2) until the firm breaks even; and vice versa. This correspondence is simply a reflection of the fact that equations (4.1) and (4.2) are alternative and equivalent ways of stating the same result. Equation (4.1) is expressed in terms of output, with prices being implicit; equation (4.2) is expressed in terms of price, with output being implicit.

Finally, it is important to note that these methods for finding Ramsey prices are not meant to be applied to a regulated firm in real time. That is, it is not being suggested that the regulator set prices at marginal cost, observe the firm's loss, and then slowly raise prices appropriately until the firm is observed to break even. Rather, the methods are meant to be used as a means for calculating Ramsey prices given information about the firm's costs and demand. An application of the use of the methods in a real-world setting is provided in section 4.6.

4.5 Relaxation of Assumptions

Two assumptions that have been maintained in the discussion so far can be relaxed for a more general statement of the Ramsey rule. These assumptions are: (1) there are no cross-elasticities of demand, such that the price of one good does not affect the demand for the other, and (2) the demand curve for each good is linear. These assumptions simplify the analysis considerably and allow a clearer view of the meaning and purpose of the Ramsey rule. However, in most situations they do not hold. For example, energy utilities often sell both natural gas and electricity. Because either of these power sources can be used for heating, one would expect that if the price of electricity is raised, some consumers who use electric heaters would, over time at least, switch to gas heating. As a result, the demand for gas would increase in response to the higher price for electricity, contrary to the assumption of no cross-elasticity. Similarly, the assumption about linear demand is probably unrealistic in many if not most settings.

The Ramsey rule can be generalized to allow for situations in which these two assumptions do not hold. The more general rule is derived in a way that is analogous to our derivation in the previous section, but with more cumbersome notation. We simply state the more general rule and explain its meaning intuitively. Interested readers can work through the algebra themselves.

Consider first a situation with cross-elasticities of demand. The more general version of equation (4.2), which allows for cross-elasticities, is the following (Dreze 1964):

$$\frac{(P_1 - MC_1)}{P_1}(\epsilon_1 - \epsilon_{21}) = \frac{(P_2 - MC_2)}{P_2}(\epsilon_2 - \epsilon_{12}), \tag{4.2'}$$

where ϵ_{21} is the elasticity of demand for good two with respect to the price of good one, and analogously for ϵ_{12}.[9] This equation is essentially the same in meaning as the original version. However, in this more general version, the cross-elasticities are subtracted from the own-price elasticities. This subtraction gives, in a sense, a "net" elasticity: the effect of one good's price on the demand for that good itself *net* of the effect on the demand for the other good. Note that if the cross-elasticities are zero, then this more general statement of the Ramsey rule reduces to the original statement (that is, becomes equation 4.2).

Equation (4.2') holds whether demand is linear or nonlinear. As such, it is a fully general statement of the Ramsey rule, applicable with zero or nonzero cross-elasticities and with linear or nonlinear demand curves.

Equation (4.1), which states that each output is reduced by the same proportion, still applies without modification if there are cross-elasticities of demand. However, if demand is nonlinear, it holds only approximately. Recall that the demonstration of equation (4.1) uses the fact that ΔQ_1 is equal to $(P_1 - MC_1)s_1$, because demand is assumed linear. That is, the amount by which output changes from its marginal-cost level is equal to the slope of the demand function, s_1, times the amount by which price is raised above marginal cost. If demand is not linear, then the slope is not constant; rather, the slope changes as one moves along the demand curve. With nonlinear demand, ΔQ_1 must be calculated using the *average* slope of the demand function between P_1 and MC_1. The slope of a nonlinear demand function at the Ramsey prices is only approximately the same as this average slope. Consequently, with nonlinear demand, ΔQ_1 is only approxi-

---

9. That is, ϵ_{21} is the percent change in demand for good two that results from a 1% change in the price of good one; and analogously for ϵ_{12}. To be perfectly accurate, the elasticities for this formulation are taken on the compensated demand curve rather than uncompensated demand.

mately equal to $(P_1 - MC_1)s_1$, where s_1 is the slope at the Ramsey prices. The general statement of equation (4.1), which allows for non-linear demand, is therefore

$$\Delta Q_1/Q_1 \cong \Delta Q_2/Q_2, \tag{4.1'}$$

where an approximately equal sign replaces the equal sign.

For small deviations from marginal cost, the average slope (averaged over the part of the demand curve between marginal cost and the Ramsey prices) is nearly the same as the slope at the Ramsey prices. Consequently, the approximation (equation 4.1') is better for smaller deviations from marginal-cost prices (that is, when the Ramsey prices are fairly close to marginal cost). Furthermore, the approximation is better for demand curves that are more nearly linear, becoming exact when demand is perfectly linear in the relevant region.

These generalizations of the Ramsey rule, while perhaps adding complications conceptually, do not introduce difficulties from a practical perspective. Equation (4.2') is nearly as easy to apply as its more restricted version (equation 4.2). In either case, the researcher or regulator uses information on demand and costs.[10] Furthermore, equation (4.1) can often be applied as a strict equality without undue concern about the approximation. That is, while demand might not be linear throughout the entire demand curve, the part of demand between marginal cost and the Ramsey prices might be sufficiently linear, and/or marginal cost and Ramsey prices might be sufficiently close, such that reducing each output by exactly the same proportion will not result in unreasonable errors. The following section provides an application of the Ramsey rule in a real-world situation.

4.6   An Application of the Ramsey Rule: Transit Pricing

The East Bay area of the San Francisco Bay region includes Berkeley, Oakland, Walnut Creek, and numerous other cities, plus some unincorporated areas. Two forms of public transit are provided in this area: bus service by the Alameda-Contra Costa (AC) Transit Company and rail service by the Bay Area Rapid Transit (BART) system. A regional transportation agency, the Metropolitan Transportation

---

10. Information on cross-elasticities is required for application of equation (4.2'), whereas they are assumed to be zero for equation (4.2). However, given information on same-price and cross-elasticities, Ramsey prices are as easy to calculate from equation (4.2') as from equation (4.2).

Commission (MTC), coordinates service among the various transit agencies in the San Francisco Bay region and exercises considerable oversight of each agency's fares.

As with most public transit providers, AC Transit and BART are natural monopolies in that their marginal cost is below their average cost over the relevant range of output. Consequently, pricing each service at its marginal cost would result in the two agencies losing money. Given the authority of MTC, the possibility of Ramsey pricing is feasible in this situation. The two transit providers can be considered one for the purpose of pricing and covering costs. Ramsey prices for the two services are those that provide the greatest surplus for travelers while allowing the combined revenues for the two agencies to cover their combined costs. MTC could administer any cross-subsidization that is required at the Ramsey prices.[11]

Ramsey prices for AC Transit and BART have been calculated by Train (1977) using demand functions estimated by McFadden (1975) and cost functions estimated by Lee (1974) for AC Transit, and Merewitz and Pozdena (1974) for BART. For the demand functions, travelers are assumed to choose among bus, rail, and auto for each of their trips and to make this choice on the basis (at least partially) of the cost and time of taking the trip by each mode. The demand for each mode therefore depends on the price for that mode as well as the price for other modes. This characteristic of the demand functions reflects the fact that, if bus fares rise, some bus patrons will switch to rail, and similarly for rail fares. Because cross-elasticities are explicitly incorporated in the demand relations, the calculation of Ramsey prices utilizes the generalized version of the inverse elasticity rule, equation (4.2′).

In the current context, equation (4.2′) takes the following form:

$$\frac{(P_r - MC_r)}{P_r}(\epsilon_r - \epsilon_{br}) = \frac{(P_b - MC_b)}{P_b}(\epsilon_b - \epsilon_{rb}), \tag{4.4}$$

where r denotes rail and b denotes bus. In addition to satisfying this equation, Ramsey prices allow the providers to break even. In the

---

11. Each provider's individual revenues will not necessarily exactly cover the costs for that service. If each provider priced separately, at average cost, each service's revenues would cover its own costs. The value of Ramsey pricing in this situation is that it allows greater surplus because it involves only one constraint on prices (namely, that combined revenues cover combined costs) rather than two constraints (namely, that each of the two provider's revenues cover its own costs).

context of AC Transit and BART, breaking even takes a slightly different meaning. BART is required by law to cover its operating costs, but its capital costs are paid through a regional sales tax. AC Transit is assumed to be required to cover all of its costs. Therefore, for the two agencies in combination to break even, bus and rail revenues must be sufficient to cover the operating costs of BART and all of AC Transit's costs.[12] This break-even constraint is expressed as

$$P_r Q_r + P_b Q_b = OC_r + TC_b,$$ (4.5)

where Q is quantity, OC is operating cost, and TC is total cost. Because fares for AC Transit and BART are distance-based, quantity is expressed in passenger-miles (that is, the sum over passengers of the number of miles traveled by each passenger). Price is correspondingly expressed in cents per mile of travel.

Ramsey prices for AC Transit and BART are those that satisfy both equations (4.4) and (4.5). The most straightforward way to determine the Ramsey prices in this context is to consider each possible price combination, use the demand and cost functions to calculate the terms in equations (4.4) and (4.5), and observe whether the equations hold at these prices.

Consider the break-even constraint first (that is, equation 4.5). At any price combination (that is, at any price for bus travel and price for rail travel), the demand functions determine the quantity of travel on each mode (i.e., Q_r and Q_b). Quantities times prices gives revenues. The cost function for AC Transit is then used to determine the total cost of providing Q_b passenger-miles of travel on bus, and the cost function for BART determines the operating cost of providing Q_r. Total revenues are compared with the sum of BART operating cost and AC Transit total cost to determine whether the combined transit provider, AC Transit/BART, breaks even.

The price combinations at which combined revenues equal combined costs are charted as curve A in figure 4.12. This curve is the relevant portion of the zero-profit contour. If the axes on the graph were extended (that is, if higher prices were represented on the graph), the curve would extend to form a circular contour (as in figure 4.10).

Consider now equation (4.4). This equation states that the percent by which price deviates from marginal cost, multiplied by the "net" elasticity, is the same for both rail and bus. At each price combina-

---

12. In actuality, AC Transit is subsidized through state funds. However, the amount of subsidy is not fixed and varies from year to year. For any given level of subsidy, the same method can be employed to calculate alternative, lower Ramsey prices.

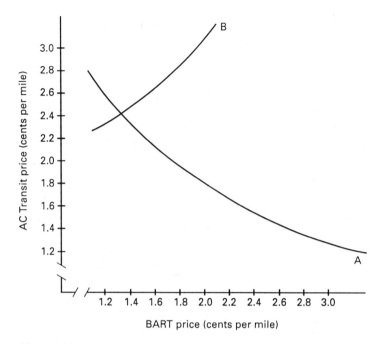

Figure 4.12
Ramsey prices for AC Transit and BART

tion, the demand functions are used to calculate elasticities. Marginal
costs are determined from the cost functions. For each mode, the percent deviation of price from marginal cost is multiplied by the "net"
elasticity. Curve B charts the price combinations at which these products are the same for bus and rail.

The intersection of curves A and B is the Ramsey price combination, because both equations (4.4) and (4.5) are satisfied at this point.
The Ramsey prices are 2.42 cents per mile for bus and 1.28 cents per
mile for rail. For comparison, the average cost of bus travel is 2.0 cents
per passenger-mile, and the average operating cost for rail is 1.78 cents.
Because the Ramsey price for bus exceeds the average cost of bus
service, while the rail price is less than BART's average operating cost,
bus service in this case would be subsidizing rail.[13] This subsidy is in

---

13. In many applications of Ramsey prices, some costs are shared jointly in the production of the goods. For example, the same generation capacity is used for the production of electricity for residential and commercial customers, even though the two
groups are charged different prices. In these cases, it is not possible to calculate average
cost of each service separately. However, in the case of AC Transit and BART, no costs
are shared, such that the average cost of each service can be calculated.

addition to the subsidy that covers BART's capital cost (this latter being already reflected in the fact that BART's price is compared to its average *operating* cost, whereas the bus price is compared to its average of all costs).

This subsidy from bus patrons to rail patrons raises some important issues regarding the advisability of Ramsey prices. In the East Bay area, the average income of bus riders is considerably lower than that of BART patrons. This difference in income is partially the result of the routes provided by each service. For example, people who live in suburban areas can easily ride BART into the the financial and commercial centers of the area. In fact, BART is faster and in many ways easier than driving for these trips. Consequently, many of its riders are people who work at relatively high-paying jobs in the city and live in relatively high-income neighborhoods in the suburbs; they often own a car but choose to take BART to work because BART is faster. AC Transit, on the other hand, provides more short-haul trips, especially within the more central areas. A larger percentage of its patrons live in inner-city, lower-income neighborhoods and use AC Transit for travel within the city. Many of the riders do not have cars and take AC Transit not because it is faster than driving but because they do not have the option of driving.

The Ramsey prices, if implemented, would require that the lower-income riders of the bus subsidize the higher-income riders of BART. From an equity perspective, this arrangement would seem unsuitable.

The issue of equity in this application elucidates an important characteristic of Ramsey prices. By construction, Ramsey prices are those that provide the greatest *total* consumer surplus, while allowing the provider to break even. The distribution of this surplus among consumers is not considered. And, in fact, the distribution that results from Ramsey prices might very well, as in this application, seem inequitable.

If total surplus is as high as possible, then there is, theoretically at least, some way that this surplus can be redistributed such that all people are better off than at any other price combination. If the regulator can accomplish this redistribution, then the issue of equity can be resolved. However, generally the regulator cannot effectively implement a redistribution of surplus. In these cases, the regulator needs to consider the equity impacts of Ramsey prices when deciding whether to implement them.

In the current application, Ramsey prices imply that lower-income consumers would subsidize higher-income households. This result is not entirely a coincidence and in some sense is inherent in the concept of Ramsey pricing. Recall that the Ramsey rule is often called the inverse elasticity rule, because Ramsey pricing requires that price be raised further above marginal cost for goods with lower elasticities. A low elasticity of demand means that the consumers of that good are relatively insensitive to price: they will largely continue to buy the good even if its price is raised. When people do not have options and consumption of the good or service is necessary, then people will not be price-responsive: they will, of necessity, buy the good at the higher price. In the case of bus and rail, the BART riders generally own cars that they can drive to work if the cost of BART becomes too high. However, the lower-income patrons of AC Transit often do not own cars, precisely because they have less income, and consequently cannot choose to drive instead of paying a higher bus fare. Furthermore, BART is usually not a viable option for these people, because BART does not serve the inner-city residential neighborhoods as well as the bus. The primary option that these bus riders have to respond to a higher bus fare is not to travel, which for the commute to work would end up costing the person more in lost wages than the extra bus fare.

The basic point is: insofar as lower-income consumers have fewer options, their demands will tend to be less elastic. Application of the Ramsey rule will, in these cases, result in their facing higher prices relative to consumers with more options and hence higher elasticities.

A similar consequence occurs when comparing demands for different goods. Necessities, such as medical care, have very low elasticities of demand because people will largely continue to buy them even when price is raised substantially. The Ramsey rule would imply that prices be raised more on these goods than on goods with more elastic demands. However, it does not seem appropriate for people who become sick or injured to bear an even greater burden through higher prices for care.

These examples point out that the application of Ramsey pricing should be tempered with an appreciation for the distributional consequences of such pricing in any particular situation. The fact that Ramsey prices obtain the greatest total surplus does not guarantee that they are "best" or even "good" by other social criteria that the regulator might consider relevant.

5   The Vogelsang-Finsinger Mechanism

5.1   Introduction

Vogelsang and Finsinger (1979) have suggested a regulatory mechanism that induces the regulated firm to move, over time, to Ramsey prices and outputs. This mechanism is intriguing for several reasons. First, it is very simple, both conceptually and in implementation. Given the complex nature of the Ramsey rule (namely, that the percent deviation of price from marginal cost multiplied by the "net" elasticity is the same for all goods), the simplicity of the mechanism that attains these prices is surprising. Second, the mechanism explicitly accounts for the asymmetry in information that necessarily exists in regulatory settings—namely, that the firm knows more about its operations than does the regulator. The regulator using the Vogelsang and Finsinger (or V-F) mechanism need not know the firm's demand or cost functions, which the firm itself knows. Nor does the regulator need to know beforehand what the Ramsey prices and outputs are. The mechanism will induce the firm to move to them even without the regulator knowing what they are. A large literature has arisen on the issue of optimal regulation under different forms of asymmetric information. The V-F model serves as an excellent introduction to this literature. Third, the mechanism is dynamic, in that actions of the firm in one time period determine the options that the regulator allows the firm in the following period. More precisely, the information revealed to the regulator through the firm's actions in one period is used by the regulator to constrain the firm in the following period. This sequence of revealed information followed by a constraint based on that information leads, in the situation described by Vogelsang and Finsinger, to the Ramsey outcome. A large literature has arisen on dynamic regulation of this kind. The V-F model, and especially comments on the model by Sappington (1980), elucidate some of the fundamental issues within this literature—including the important issue of when the firm will have an incentive to "reveal" incorrect information.

Section 5.2 describes the mechanism proposed by Vogelsang and Finsinger. Sections 5.3 and 5.4 demonstrate that the mechanism induces the regulated firm to choose, in equilibrium, the second-best prices in one-good and multi-good situations, respectively. Section 5.5 delineates conditions under which the firm has an incentive, under this mechanism, to inflate its actual or reported costs.

The chapter can be summarized as follows. Under V-F regulation, the firm's prices, output, and costs in one period determine the prices that the regulator allows the firm to charge in the next period. In particular, the firm is able to charge any prices in the next period, as long as those prices, when multiplied by the firm's output in the *current* period, do not exceed the firm's costs in the *current* period. Successive application of this constraint over several periods results in second-best pricing. In particular, the one-output firm prices at average cost in equilibrium, and the multi-output firm charges Ramsey prices.

Under V-F regulation, the firm might have an incentive to report costs that are higher than those actually incurred (i.e., misreport costs) and/or to incur costs in excess of the minimum required for production (i.e., waste). In both cases, the firm is allowed to charge higher prices in the next period because its reported costs are higher in the current period. Both of these possibilities are explored.

To prevent, or reduce, misreporting, the regulator can audit the firm's cost. If the regulator is able (legally) to levy a sufficiently high penalty for misreporting, the firm can be induced to report costs truthfully. The regulator performs audits very infrequently, but does not tell the firm when the audit will occur. To avoid risking the large penalty, the firm reports truthfully in *each* period. Furthermore, the cost of auditing is essentially zero because very few audits are actually performed. (With a high enough penalty, the frequency of audits can be reduced nearly to zero and still induce the firm to be honest.) If audits are not able perfectly to determine the true costs of the firm, there is a chance that the firm will be levied a penalty even if it reports truthfully (i.e., if the audit "finds," incorrectly, that costs are lower than reported). However, this chance is nearly zero because the frequency of audits is nearly zero and the probability of an incorrect penalty, given an audit, is low because the firm reports truthfully.

If the maximum size of the penalty is limited, the frequency of audits cannot be nearly zero and still induce honesty. A higher frequency of audits is required. In this case, the cost of auditing and the chance of an incorrect penalty are not nearly zero, but rather are nonnegligibly positive.

When the firm is audited appropriately, it will not misreport costs. However, it might waste. We show that, if the firm knows beforehand that V-F regulation will be imposed, it might waste in one period so as to be allowed higher prices in the next period. This waste might occur for several periods. However, the firm will not waste in equilibrium. Furthermore, if the firm does *not* know beforehand that V-F regulation will be imposed, it will not waste either in the movement toward, or in, equilibrium.

5.2   The V-F Mechanism

The process can be started in any time period, with a time period being a year, month, or whatever is feasible. In the first period of regulation, the regulated firm charges some price for each good, sells some quantity of each good, and incurs some cost in producing these outputs. The regulator observes these prices, outputs, and costs. The regulator uses this information to constrain the firm in its choice of prices in the second period. In particular, the regulator tells the firm that the firm can charge whatever prices it wants in the next period—so long as the next period's prices, when multiplied by the first period's quantities, do not exceed the first period's costs. For example, suppose the firm produces only one good and in the first period prices the good at $10, sells 150 units, and incurs costs of $1,200 (thereby earning a profit of $300 in the current period). The regulator tells the firm that it can charge any price in the second period that, when multiplied by 150, does not exceed $1,200. Clearly, the first-period price is not permissible for the next period: $10 times 150 equals $1,500, which exceeds $1,200. However, $6 is permissible, because $6 times 150 is $900, which is less than $1,200. A price of $8 dollars is also permissible for the next period, because $8 times 150 is $1,200, which does not *exceed* the first period's costs of $1,200.

In the second period, after the firm has chosen its new prices within the regulator's constraint, the firm will sell a different quantity of each good (because the demand depends on price) and will incur a different level of costs (because cost depends on quantities sold). The regulator observes these figures and places the same type of constraint on the third period's prices, using the new figures. For example, suppose our one-output firm chose a price of $8, which was permissible as described above. At this price, suppose the firm sells 180 units (because a lower price increases quantity demanded) and incurs costs of $1,400 in producing this output (because costs rise with quantity), earning a profit of $40. The regulator observes the price, quantity, and costs and tells the firm that now, in the third period, it can only charge a price that, when multiplied by 180, does not exceed $1,400. A price of $7 is permissible in the third period, as is a price of $7.50 or $7.77; however, the price of $8 is no longer permissible.

This process continues from period to period, eventually inducing the firm (as shown below) to charge the second-best price.

The mechanism operates analogously with two or more goods. Suppose a two-output firm in the first period charges a price of $4 for good A and $6 for good B, sells 100 units of good A and 50 units of good B, and incurs costs of $600. In the second period, the firm would be allowed to charge, say, $3 for good A and $5 for good B [because ($3 \cdot 100$) + ($5 \cdot 50$) = $550, which is less than $600]. Prices of $3.25 and $5.50 would also be permissible, as would many other price combinations. The current prices of $4 and $6, respectively, would, however, not be permissible [because (4×100) + (6×50) = $700 > $600]. After the firm chose its prices for the second period, the regulator would observe the quantities it sells at these new prices and its costs for producing these outputs. The regulator would then require that for the third period, the firm adjust its prices to meet the constraint based on these second-period quantities and costs.

The regulatory mechanism can be stated algebraically. Given the output and cost of the firm in any period t, the firm must choose prices in the next period, period $t + 1$, that satisfy the following constraint. For one-output firms, the constraint is

$$P^{t+1}Q^t \leq C^t. \tag{5.1}$$

That is, the price in the next period, P^{t+1}, when multiplied by current-period output, Q^t, cannot exceed current-period costs, C^t. For two-output firms

$$P_a^{t+1}Q_a^t + P_b^{t+1}Q_b^t \le C^t, \tag{5.2}$$

where a and b denote the two goods. The constraint is defined analogously for firms with more than two outputs. In each case the constraint is applied repeatedly, period after period. Eventually, as shown below, the constraint induces the firm to choose the second-best prices.

Before demonstrating the outcome of this process, two notes are important. First, the quantity $P^{t+1}Q^t$ (and its counterpart in the two-good case) appears to be a revenue calculation because it takes the form of price times quantity. However, this product is not revenues in either period t or in period $t+1$. In period t, revenue is period t's price times period t's quantity (that is, P^tQ^t); and revenue in period $t+1$ is price in period $t + 1$ times the quantity that is demanded in period $t + 1$ (that is, $P^{t+1}Q^{t+1}$). The quantity $P^{t+1}Q^t$ is price in period $t + 1$ multiplied by the quantity in period t, which is neither period's revenues. Rather, it is a calculation that the regulator defines in order to implement the regulatory mechanism; because it takes the form of price times quantity (though with price taken from one period and quantity from another) it is often called "pseudorevenue" for period $t + 1$. It is the revenues that the firm would earn in the next period under a new price if demand remained the same as under the old price. However, with price-sensitive consumers, a change in price from one period to another induces a change in quantity demanded, such that pseudorevenue in period $t + 1$ does not generally equal the actual revenues in period $t + 1$.

The second aspect of the mechanism that requires note is the informational requirements of the mechanism. To specify the constraint on the firm, the regulator must, in each period, observe the prices, quantities, and costs of the firm in that period. This information can reasonably be assumed to be available to the regulator, because the prices and quantities sold can be observed from the bills sent by the firm to its customers, and the costs that are actually incurred can be observed from wage payments, invoices for expenses, and capital accounting. The regulator does *not* need to know the demand and cost functions of the firm. That is, the regulator must be able to observe the demand and costs that actually occur in each period, but does not need to know the demand and cost curves. This is important because cost and demand relations are generally inaccessible to the regulator.

5.3   Demonstration for a One-Good Firm

Consider the situation depicted in figure 5.1. The firm is assumed to be a natural monopoly, such that its average cost curve is downward sloping. Suppose in the first time period the firm charges a price of P^1 and sells quantity Q^1 (how the firm arrived at this point is not relevant). At this quantity of output, the firm's average costs are AC^1, such that its total costs are AC^1Q^1.

The regulator observes price, quantity, and total costs. It then tells the firm that in the next period (period two) the firm can charge any price as long as the new price, when multiplied by Q^{1}, does not exceed AC^1Q^1:

$$P^2Q^1 \leq AC^1Q^1. \tag{5.3}$$

In a one-good situation, this constraint can be expressed more readily in terms of average cost. Dividing both sides of equation (5.3) by Q^1 gives

$$P^2 \leq AC^1.$$

That is, the firm can charge any price in period two as long as that price does not exceed period one's average cost.

The firm will choose the highest price that it is allowed to charge in

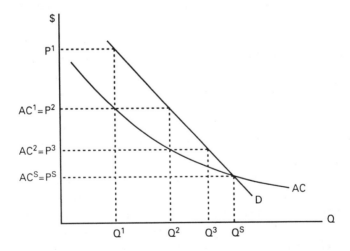

Figure 5.1
V-F regulation with one good

period two.[1] Consequently, the firm will charge a price in period two that is equal to its average cost in period one. This price is represented as P^2 on the graph.

At its new price, the firm sells a higher level of output: Q^2. Its average cost drops to AC^2 (with total costs becoming AC^2Q^2.) The regulator observes in period two the firm's price, quantity, and costs. The regulator then tells the firm that, in period three, the firm can only charge a price that is no greater than the firm's average cost in period two. In response to this directive, the firm lowers its price to AC^2, which is the highest permissible price for period three.

This process continues, with the firm lowering its price and increasing its output in successive period until it reaches P^S and Q^S, which are the second-best price and output. When this outcome is reached, the regulatory mechanism induces the firm to continue choosing this price rather than changing its price any further. The regulator requires that the firm charge in the next period a price no higher than AC^S. However, since the firm is already charging a price equal to AC^S, its current price is the highest permissible price. The firm chooses not to change its price, staying at P^S.

The optimal outcome is reached even if the firm starts out charging a price below average cost, that is, if the firm starts out earning negative profits. Figure 5.2 depicts the situation. In period one, the firm charges price P^1, sells output Q^1, and incurs average cost of AC^1, which exceeds price. The regulator tells the firm that it can charge any price in the second period as long as the new price is below AC^1. The firm raises its price in period two to AC^1. Quantity demanded drops in period two and average cost rises, such that the firm loses money in the second period as well (though its losses are smaller). This process continues until price becomes P^S, the optimal outcome consistent with nonnegative profits.

It is interesting to note that the mechanism can also identify whether marginal cost pricing is feasible. Recall that the first-best price is mar-

---

1. The firm will charge the highest permissible price if marginal revenue is negative, such that raising price and reducing output increases revenues. More generally, the firm will choose the permissible price that provides the greatest profit. If marginal revenue is positive, this price might be the highest permissible price. However, the firm will still be pushed toward the optimal price in the same way as under the assumption that the firm chooses the highest permissible price. The assumption allows a less cluttered graph and a more intuitive explanation of the movement toward optimality.

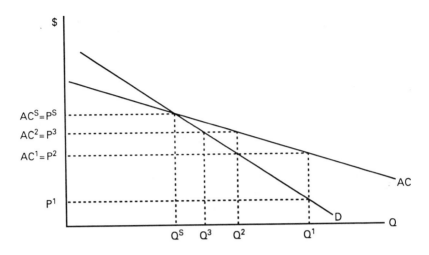

Figure 5.2
V-F regulation with one good and price starting below average cost

ginal cost. If average cost is decreasing, as in figures 5.1 and 5.2, then
marginal cost is below average cost, and pricing at marginal cost would
result in negative profits. However, if average cost is increasing in the
relevant range, marginal-cost pricing is feasible. In this case, V-F regulation will still induce the firm to price at average cost; however, the
movement toward average-cost pricing will provide information that
allows the regulator to observe that marginal-cost pricing would be
feasible. Consider figure 5.3. Note that the firm could operate at the
intersection of the marginal cost and demand curves, because price at
this point is above average cost. Suppose, however, that the regulator
did not know this fact (because the regulator does not know the demand and cost curves of the firm) and applies V-F regulation to the
firm. The firm starts at, say, P^1, where it is earning a positive profit.
The regulator requires that its price in period two not exceed AC^1.
The firm therefore sets price in period two equal to AC^1. Its demand
increases to Q^2 and, since its average cost is upward sloping in the
relevant range, its average cost increases to AC^2. Because P^2 is below
AC^2, the firm loses money in period two. The regulator continues to
apply V-F regulation, requiring that the price in period three not exceed AC^2. Because average cost in period two is greater than that in
period one, this new constraint is less stringent than the previous one
and allows the firm to *raise* its price in period three, to AC^2. In period

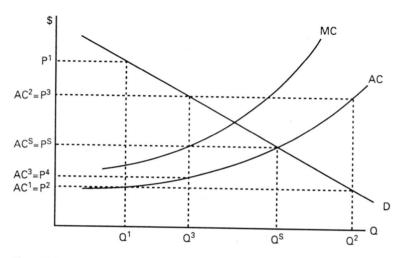

Figure 5.3
V-F regulation with upward-sloping AC

three, the firm earns positive profit. This process continues until the firm reaches P^S and Q^S, where price equals average cost. Notice, however, that the process results in cyclical movements of price and profits. That is, price is alternately raised and lowered by the firm in successive periods, and profits are alternately positive and negative. This pattern occurs because average cost is upward sloping. When average cost is downward sloping, prices and profits move continuously in one direction over time.

The regulator can use this information to determine whether marginal-cost pricing is possible, without needing to know the firm's demand and cost functions. If the regulator implements V-F regulation and observes that the firm's price and profit move continuously in one direction over time, the regulator can infer that the firm's average-cost curve is downward sloping. In this case, marginal-cost pricing would result in negative profits, such that average-cost pricing is the optimal feasible outcome. The V-F regulation will induce the firm eventually to move to this second-best outcome. If, however, the regulator observes that prices moves up and down over time, and profits are alternatively positive and negative in successive periods, the regulator can infer that average cost is upward sloping. Marginal-cost pricing is therefore feasible and should be pursued. In this case, the regulator should discontinue the V-F regulation, because it induces the firm to move to average-cost pricing instead of marginal-cost pricing.[2]

5.4 Demonstration for a Two-Good Firm

In a one-good situation, only one price results in zero profit, namely, price equaling average cost. The second-best price is therefore attained simply by pushing the firm toward zero profit, as the V-F mechanism does. With two or more goods, many price combinations result in zero profit. Consequently, pushing the firm to zero profit is not sufficient to attain the second-best prices. A demonstration of V-F regulation with two goods is therefore not a trivial generalization of the one-good case. Rather, it introduces concepts that are critical to the meaning and function of the mechanism.

In any period t, the firm has a price for each good, sells a certain quantity of each good, and incurs certain costs. The regulator observes these amounts and constrains the firm's choice of prices for period $t + 1$. The constraint takes the form

$$P_a^{t+1}Q_a^t + P_b^{t+1}Q_b^t \leq C^t, \tag{5.4}$$

where a and b denote the two goods.

The price combinations that meet this constraint can be depicted graphically. Consider figure 5.4. Suppose that in period t, the firm is charging the price combination designated by point X in the graph. The question to be addressed is: what price combinations is the firm permitted to charge in period $t + 1$? The permissible price combinations can be depicted on the graph using three pieces of information, each of which is discussed in detail below: (1) the permissible price combinations form a line in the graph, (2) the slope of this line is the same as the slope of the isobenefit contour at X, and (3) the y-intercept of this line is an identifiable point. With the shape, slope, and intercept determined, the set of permissible prices can be located on the graph.

---

2. Two caveats are required, however. First, if the firm's profits fluctuate between positive and negative levels in the movement to equilibrium, it is possible that the present value of the stream of profits is negative. In this case, the firm would choose to shut down rather than submit to V-F regulation. Second, suppose the firm knows that the regulator will discontinue V-F regulation if prices fluctuate. The firm would perhaps have an incentive, then, to alternately raise and lower its price as a means of eliminating V-F regulation. This strategic behavior is separate from that described in section 5.5. (I thank David Sappington for pointing out these caveats.)

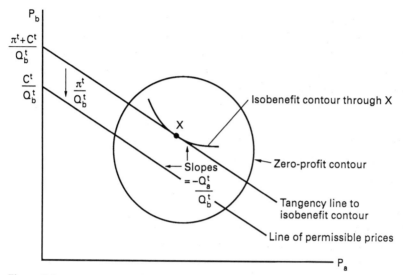

Figure 5.4
Permissible prices for two goods

1. *The permissible price combinations form a line.*

The graph in figure 5.4 places the price of good A on the x-axis and the price of good B on the y-axis. Inequality (5.4) is rearranged such that P_b^{t+1} is expressed as a function of P_a^{t+1}:

$$P_b^{t+1} \leq C^t/Q_b^t - (Q_a^t/Q_b^t)P_a^{t+1} \tag{5.5}$$

That is, the highest price for good B that is permissible in period $t + 1$ depends on the price that is charged for good A in period $t + 1$. The equality part of equation (5.5) is a line with slope $-(Q_a^t/Q_b^t)$ and y-intercept C^t/Q_b^t. The graphical interpretation of this slope and intercept is given below.

2. *The slope of this line is the same as the slope of the isobenefit curve at X.*

As indicated by equation (5.5), the line that designates the permissible prices for period $t + 1$ has slope equal to the ratio of outputs in period t. This fact is convenient, because it relates to the isobenefit contour at X. Recall from chapter 4 that an isobenefit contour is a set of price combinations that result in the same level of consumer surplus. The slope of an isobenefit contour at any point (that is, at any price combination) is the ratio of outputs that are demanded at that price combination. This fact was established in section 4.3. For example, suppose that, at given prices, demand for good A is 100 and demand for good B is 50. Then, if the price of good A is raised by \$1, then the price of good B must be lowered by \$2 (that is, $-100/50$) in order for the person to afford the original consumption levels and hence to attain the same surplus.

Point X in figure 5.4 is the price combination the firm charges in period t. The isobenefit contour through this point is drawn in the graph. The slope of the isobenefit contour at price combination X is the ratio of outputs that are consumed in period t, namely:

$-Q_a^t/Q_b^t.$

The line designating the permissible prices in period $t + 1$ also has this slope. Consequently, the line of permissible prices must be parallel to the tangency line of the isobenefit contour at X.

We know that the line of permissible prices is parallel to the tangency line of the isobenefit contour at X. However, we do not yet know the location of this parallel line. By determining its y-intercept, its location is established.

3. *The y-intercept of this line is an identifiable point.*

By the equality part of equation (5.5), the line of permissible prices has a y-intercept of

$C^t/Q_b^t.$

The question is: where is this y-intercept relative to the intercept of the tangency line of the isobenefit contour? Consider the tangency line of the isobenefit contour through X. This line has slope

$-Q_a^t/Q_b^t,$

as described above. It therefore takes the form

$$P_b = k - (Q_a^t/Q_b^t)P_a. \tag{5.6}$$

The value of k, the y-intercept, can be determined by knowing that the line passes through point X. The profits of the firm in period t are, by definition,

$\pi^t = P_b^t Q_b^t + P_a^t Q_a^t - C^t.$

Rearranging:

$$P_b^t = (\pi^t + C^t)/Q_b^t - (Q_a^t/Q_b^t)P_a^t. \tag{5.7}$$

Because equation (5.6) holds for all points on the tangency line, and equation (5.7) holds at point X, which is on the tangency line, then k in equation (5.6) must be equal to

$(\pi^t + C^t)/Q_b^t$.

That is, the y-intercept of the tangency line is

$(\pi^t + C^t)/Q_b^t$.

This fact is important because it allows us to locate the line of permissible prices. The y-intercept of the line of permissible prices is C^t/Q_b^t, while the y-intercept of the tangency line is $(\pi^t + C^t)/Q_b^t$. That is, the y-intercept of the line of permissible prices is π^t/Q_b^t lower than the y-intercept of the tangency line. Therefore, by starting at the y-intercept for the tangency line and moving down an amount equal to the profits in period t divided by the quantity of good B sold in period t, the y-intercept of the line of permissible prices is located.

In summary, the permissible price combinations for period $t + 1$ form a line that is parallel of the tangency line of the isobenefit contour at the price combination charged in period t, and yet is lower than the tangency line by the amount of profits earned in period t divided by the quantity of good B sold. This line is given in figure 5.4. Taking into account the "less than" part of equation (5.5), any price combination on or *below* this line is permissible in period $t + 1$.

In period $t + 1$, the firm will choose the permissible price combination that provides the greatest profit. That is, the firm will choose the point on or below the permissible line that provides the greatest profits. The regulator will then use the prices, output, and costs in period $t + 1$ to establish permissible prices for period $t + 2$. And so on, until equilibrium is reached.

A sequence of two price changes is depicted in figure 5.5. The firm starts at price combination X in period t. The set of permissible prices for period $t + 1$ is denoted by the lower solid line. The firm chooses the profit-maximizing point on or below this line; say this is point Y. With the firm charging price combination Y in period $t + 1$, the regulator places a constraint on the prices that the firm can charge in period $t + 2$ based on the quantities and costs in period $t + 1$. The set of permissible prices for period $t + 2$ is denoted by the lower dotted line. The firm chooses the profit-maximizing price combination on or below this dotted line, say, point Z. And the process continues.

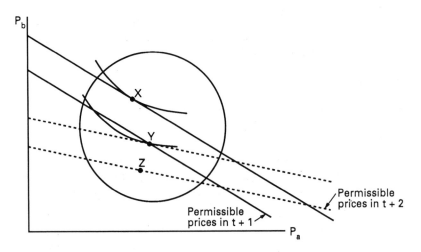

Figure 5.5
Sequence of price combinations

Note that the lower dotted line is not parallel to the lower solid line. That is, the line of permissible prices in one period does not have the same slope as the line of permissible prices in the next period. This is because the quantities of goods sold changes from one period to the next as the firm changes its prices. The line of permissible prices for period $t + 1$ has a slope equal to the ratio of outputs sold in period t — that is, Q_a^t/Q_b^t. However, the line of permissible prices for period $t + 2$ has a slope equal to the ratio of outputs sold in period $t + 1$, not t (that is, Q_a^{t+1}/Q_b^{t+1}). Because prices are different at X than Y, the ratio of outputs is generally different.

Note also that the line of permissible prices for each period is below the tangency line of the isobenefit curve by an amount that depends on the profits of the firm in the previous period. That is, the lower solid line is below the higher one by an amount that is the profits earned in period t divided by the quantity of B sold in period t, π^t/Q_b^t. And the lower dotted line is below the higher one by the profits earned in period $t + 1$ divided by the quantity of good B sold in period $t + 1$, π^{t+1}/Q_b^{t+1}. Because profits and quantities sold change when prices change, the amount by which the line of permissible prices is below the tangency line changes from period to period.

As suggested in figure 5.5, the regulatory process pushes the firm closer and closer to the zero-profit contour. (This occurs because the line of permissible prices is lowered each period whenever profits are

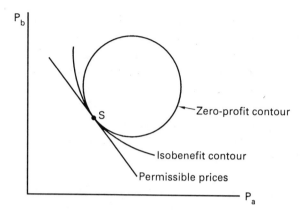

Figure 5.6
Isobenefit contour tangent to zero-profit contour

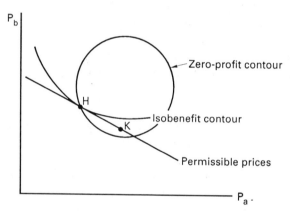

Figure 5.7
Isobenefit contour not tangent to zero-profit contour

positive.) The process continues until the firm earns zero profit—that is, until the firm's chosen price combination is on its zero-profit contour. When this occurs, one of two situations must arise. Either (1) the isobenefit contour through the firm's chosen price combination is tangent to the firm's zero-profit contour, as in figure 5.6, or (2) the isobenefit contour is *not* tangent to the zero-profit contour, as in figure 5.7. In the first case, as demonstrated below, the firm is charging Ramsey prices and will continue to do so indefinitely. In the second case, the firm will change its price, eventually moving to a situation like that in figure 5.6, that is, to Ramsey prices.

In figure 5.6 the firm is charging price combination S, at which the isobenefit contour is tangent to the zero-profit contour. This point is the Ramsey price combination. Recall from chapter 4, and especially figure 4.9, that Ramsey prices are those at which the isobenefit contour is tangent to the zero-profit contour (such that the highest possible level of consumer surplus is attained consistent with non-negative profits). The firm in figure 5.6 is therefore charging Ramsey prices.

Once at Ramsey prices, the firm will continue to charge these prices indefinitely over time. This fact can be demonstrated in two steps.

Step One
Consider the set of permissible prices for the following period, given that the firm is charging price combination S in the current period. The line of permissible prices is parallel to the tangency line of the isobenefit contour and is lower by the amount of profits earned by the firm divided by the quantity of good B sold. Note, however, that at S, the firm earns zero profits. The line of permissible prices is therefore lower than the tangency line by zero. Because it is parallel to and the same level as the tangency line, the line of permissible prices is the same as the tangency line.

Step Two
Since the isobenefit contour is tangent to the zero-profit contour, the tangency line, and hence the line of permissible prices, touches but does not cut the zero-profit contour. This means that the line of permissible prices is outside the zero-profit contour at all points except S, where it is on the zero-profit contour. Of all the points on the line of permissible prices, the firm chooses S, because at S it earns zero profit, whereas at any other permissible point it earns negative profit.

Stated succinctly, once the firm is charging Ramsey prices in one period, the V-F mechanism will induce it to continue doing so in the next period. The firm will therefore stay indefinitely at Ramsey prices once it has reached them.

Consider now the possibility that the firm reaches the zero-profit contour at a point where the isobenefit contour is not tangent to the zero-profit contour, as point H in figure 5.7. In this case the firm will move away from point H in the following period. Given that the firm is at H, the line of permissible prices for the following period is the line of tangency of the isobenefit contour at H, for reasons discussed in relation to figure 5.6. Because the isobenefit contour is not tangent to the zero-profit contour, the line of permissible prices cuts the zero-profit contour. A range of permissible prices lies inside the zero-profit contour. In the following period, the firm will choose one of the points inside the zero-profit contour, say K, because these result in positive profits, rather than staying at H earning zero profits.

Once the firm moves to K, the situation becomes as before, with the line of permissible prices being lowered in each successive period until the firm is back on the zero-profit contour. If, this time around, the firm is at Ramsey prices, it will remain there. If, however, the firm is at prices that provide zero profits but are not Ramsey, then it will move in the next period, once again, to prices that result in positive profits. The process continues until the firm is at Ramsey prices. Stated another way, the process of price changes only stops when Ramsey prices are attained; consequently, Ramsey prices are the equilibrium of the V-F mechanism.

There are two fundamental reasons why the V-F mechanism results in Ramsey prices. First, the mechanism pushes the firm toward zero profits by lowering the prices that are permissible in the next period whenever positive profits are being made in the current period. Second (and this is the more subtle and more significant reason), the mechanism induces the firm to operate under a trade-off between prices that is the same trade-off that consumers are willing to undergo. Consider the consumer's perspective. When one price is raised, the other price must be lowered for consumer surplus to remain unchanged. As discussed, the amount that this other price must be lowered is equal to the ratio of quantities consumed at the original prices. That is, consumers are willing to "trade" a rise in one price for a lowering of another, as long as the rate of this trade is the ratio of quantities consumed. Under V-F regulation, the firm is induced to take the same perspective. From any permissible price combination, the firm can move to another permissible price by raising one price and lowering the other, thereby staying on the line of permissible prices. The slope of the permissible price line determines the amount by which the price of a second good must be lowered when the first price is raised. Under V-F regulation, this slope is the ratio of quantities consumed. That is, the firm is permitted to "trade" a rise in one price for a lowering of another, as long as the rate of this trade is at the ratio of quantities. Because the rate at which the firm is permitted to trade off price increases and decreases is the same as the rate at which consumers are willing to trade off such increases and decreases, consistency is established between the choices of the firm and the surplus of consumers. As in the discussions of chapters 1 and 2, the establishment of such consistency leads to optimality.

5.5 Strategic Issues in V-F Regulation

A firm subject to V-F regulation might have an incentive to inflate its costs of production. This incentive arises from the fact that, when reported costs are higher in one period, the regulator allows the firm to charge higher prices in the next period. This inflation of costs can take either of two forms. First, the firm can simply report costs to the regulator that it does not actually incur; that is, it can lie about its costs. Alternatively, the firm can incur unnecessary costs. In this latter case, the firm reports its incurred costs accurately, but engages in some form of waste to increase its costs above that minimally needed for production.

Each of these actions is a type of strategic response to V-F regulation: the firm engages in the activity for the *purpose* of affecting the decisions of the regulator. The potential for strategic behavior by the firm arises in any regulatory mechanism in which the regulator determines the constraints it places on the firm on the basis, at least partially, of the firm's actions. In the case of V-F regulation, the regulator bases its constraint (that is, determines the permissible prices) on the basis of the costs the firm reports for the previous period. The firm knows that the regulator behaves in this way and takes this fact into consideration when deciding what costs to incur and report.

Regulators often, if not always, base their decisions on actions of the firms they are regulating, and especially on the basis of information reported by the firms. Because the potential for strategic behavior is present in these contexts, it is important to determine whether (or, more precisely, under what conditions) the firm will indeed choose to engage in strategic behavior that is not consistent with the goals of the regulator. In the paragraphs below, we address this issue in the context of V-F regulation, and, in particular, with respect to two forms of strategic behavior: misrepresentation of costs and purposeful waste. The discussion, however, is intended to serve a more general purpose as an illustration of the need and procedure for examining these issues under any regulatory mechanism.

5.5.1 Misreporting of Costs

If the firm is able to deceive the regulator as to its costs, then, under V-F regulation, the firm will clearly find it advantageous to do so. Any costs the firm reports but does not actually incur can be retained as profit. Overstatement of costs can slow the movement toward equilibrium: the regulator will think that the firm is earning less profit in each period than it actually is and consequently will require a smaller reduction in prices in the following period. More important, equilibrium can occur at a price above the true average cost, with the firm earning positive profits indefinitely. If the firm's reported profits are zero (based on its reported costs), the regulator will not require that the firm change its prices in the following period. Thus, by reporting costs that exceed actual costs by exactly the amount of profit the firm is earning, the firm can continue earning those profits indefinitely.

The incentive for misreporting of costs is pervasive in regulatory settings. A way for the regulator to prevent the practice is to audit the firm periodically and levy a penalty if the firm's actual costs are less than its reported costs. If audits are costless and, when performed, are able perfectly to determine the firm's true costs, optimality can easily be achieved. The regulator can simply audit the firm's costs each period. Because the firm knows that its true costs will be discovered, it has no incentive to misreport; in fact, it has a clear incentive to report truthfully to avoid the penalty it would have to pay when any untruth is (inevitably) discovered. Furthermore, because the audits are costless, society incurs no additional cost from this component of regulation.

In reality, audits do entail cost and, when performed, are not able to assess the firm's true costs perfectly. Because audits are not free, a trade-off exists between the benefits that audits induce, through more truthful reporting, and the costs of the audits themselves. Since audits are not perfectly accurate, uncertainty enters the process in a way that can hurt both the public and the firm. The firm could misreport costs and the regulator not discover it; or the firm could report its costs truthfully and yet be penalized when an audit "finds" (incorrectly) that the firm overstated its costs.

Townsend (1979) has examined the issue of audits being costly, abstracting from the issue of uncertainty. That is, Townsend assumed that audits cost but are perfectly accurate. Within this context, his analysis suggests that the regulator can conduct audits in a particular way to obtain an outcome that is essentially the same as if audits were free. That is, the regulator can induce the firm to report its costs truthfully while incurring essentially no auditing costs. The procedure consists of auditing the firm very infrequently (that is, in only a few periods over a span of many periods), not letting the firm know beforehand whether or not it will be audited in a particular period, and levying a very high penalty if the firm is found to have misreported its costs. Auditing costs are maintained at a very low level because audits are seldom performed.

However, with a sufficiently high penalty, the firm is induced to report truthfully, even though the chance of an audit in any given period is low.[3] Because the firm does not know when an audit will be performed, it is induced to report truthfully *each* period in anticipation of an audit perhaps being performed in that period.

The fact that this procedure can obtain an outcome that is essentially the same as with free audits depends on there being very few audits, such that auditing costs are very low (essentially zero, as in the case with free audits). A very small number of audits can induce honesty when the penalty is sufficiently large. In many situations, however, there is a limit on the size of penalty that the regulator can impose. For example, the penalty might not be able to exceed the limits of corporate liability, under which a corporation cannot be held liable for more than its net assets. Or, the regulator might be bound to treat the firm "reasonably and fairly," which might be interpreted to mean that any penalty cannot be incommensurate with the mag-

---

3. The expected cost to the firm of not reporting truthfully is the probability of an audit times the penalty that is levied if any audit is performed and the untruth discovered. Even if the probability of an audit is low, the expected cost of misreporting can be high if the penalty is sufficiently high. In fact, the penalty can be set high enough such that the firm will always find the expected cost of misreporting to exceed the expected benefit it would obtain (in the form of higher prices) from any misreporting.

nitude of the offense (such that a misreporting of, say, $1 million cannot result in a $100 million penalty).

If there is a limit on the penalty, then the procedure does not necessarily result in the same outcome as with free audits. Specifically, auditing costs will not be essentially zero. The reason here should be clear. If the penalty is unlimited, the number of audits performed over a span of many periods can be reduced to nearly none: the firm can still be induced to report truthfully by raising the penalty sufficiently and not letting the firm know which period will be audited. Stated in probabilistic terms, the probability of an audit can be reduced arbitrarily close to zero if the penalty is raised sufficiently such that the expected loss of misreporting in each period is maintained at a high enough level to induce the firm to be truthful. If there is a limit on the magnitude of the penalty, the number of audits cannot necessarily be reduced nearly to none, since the penalty cannot necessarily be raised sufficiently to induce the firm to be truthful. In fact, the probability of an audit might need to be fairly high given the limited size of the penalty. The cost of auditing might therefore be significant, instead of essentially zero as in the case of a limitless penalty. As a result, there is a social cost involved in regulating when audits are not free and the penalty is limited.

In addition to being costly, audits are not perfect instruments for assessing the true costs of the firm. Because an audit provides only an estimate of true costs, a discrepancy between the audited cost and the costs that the firm reported does not necessarily mean that the firm was untruthful: the audit estimate could be incorrect while the firm's report is correct. The regulator needs to decide, therefore, how large a discrepancy between the audit's estimated costs and the firm's reported costs is enough to warrant a penalty (or, more generally, the regulator must determine a relation between the size of the penalty and the magnitude of the discrepancy). Errors can be made in either direction. If a small discrepancy results in a penalty, the firm could often be penalized even though it reports its costs truthfully. In fact, if a small enough discrepancy results in a penalty, the firm will have little incentive to be truthful, because it realizes that it will probably be penalized even if it is truthful. However, if the regulator requires that the discrepancy be large before assessing a penalty, the firm can misrepresent its costs without substantial risk of discovery.

Baron and Besanko (1984) derive pricing and auditing procedures for the regulator when audits are costly and not perfectly accurate in determining the firm's true costs.[4] They demonstrate an important result, namely, if there is no limit on the size of the penalty the regulator can levy, auditing procedures can be established that attain the same outcome as with costless and perfect audits, even though audits are costly and imperfect. The firm is levied a penalty whenever the costs estimated by the audit are below the firm's reported costs. This penalty is levied even though the firm might have reported its costs accurately and the audit simply underestimated the true costs. (This procedure does not hurt the firm for reasons to be described shortly.) Audits are performed very infrequently, but without the firm knowing when. If an audit is performed and costs are estimated to be lower than reported, a very large penalty is levied.

With a high enough penalty, the firm is induced to report its costs truthfully, because doing so minimizes its chance of being penalized (even though it could still be penalized when reporting truthfully). The number of audits is reduced to practically none by raising the penalty sufficiently to assure that the firm remains truthful in the face of fewer audits. With practically no audits, essentially no costs are expended on auditing. Furthermore, the firm's chance of being assessed a penalty even though it is reporting truthfully is essentially nil: hardly any audits are performed, and the chance of the firm being penalized, if audited, is as low as possible since the firm's report is honest.

If there is a limit on the size of the penalty, Baron and Besanko show that a loss is incurred compared to a situation with perfectly accurate and free audits. In particular, some (not arbitrarily low) cost will be expended on auditing, and the firm will face a (not arbitrarily

---

4. Technically, Baron and Besanko structure their analysis somewhat differently than described in the text; however, the substantive conclusions are the same. Baron and Besanko assume that costs depend on random factors (such as equipment failures). At the beginning of the period, the firm submits to the regulator information on the distribution of possible costs (e.g., the historical average number of breakdowns). The regulator sets prices for the upcoming period based on this information. During the period, some costs are actually incurred (e.g., some number of breakdowns actually occur). If the regulator audits the firm, the regulator is assumed to be able to determine accurately the costs the firm actually incurred. However, this information does not perfectly determine whether the firm's original report on the distribution of costs was accurate. The regulator calculates an estimate of the cost-distribution information on the basis of the costs observed in the audit. The regulator compares this estimate with the firm's original report to determine whether to assess a penalty. That is, the firm's report is compared with an estimate of the same information derived from an audit. In this sense, Baron and Besanko's model has implications for situations in which audits provide only an estimate of the firm's costs rather than perfectly assess the incurred costs.

low) chance of being assessed a penalty even while reporting its costs truthfully.

5.5.2   Purposeful Waste

If the regulator monitors costs appropriately, the firm will not be able to misrepresent its costs. However, the firm will still be able to affect the prices it is permitted to charge in future periods. In particular, rather than reporting costs that are not incurred, the firm can actually *incur* higher costs. This purposeful incurring of unnecessary costs can take many forms: an inefficient input mix (i.e., using a mix of inputs that is not cost minimizing), more inputs than minimally required (such as large offices and fancy boardrooms), paying more than necessary for inputs, excessive research and development efforts (such as research on topics with little chance of fruition or small potential benefit), and various other forms. For the purpose of discussion, all of these manifestations are collectively called "waste."

A firm under V-F regulation will engage in waste in some circumstances and not in others. The most critical factor is whether the firm knows in advance (that is, prior to being regulated) that V-F regulation will be imposed. As shown below, the firm could find it profitable to waste in some periods if it knows in advance that V-F regulation will be imposed. However, if there is no advance notice, the firm will not find it profitable to waste. The two situations are described separately below, with the analysis based largely on concepts of Sappington (1980).

1.   Firm with Advance Notice
Consider first the situation in which the firm knows that V-F regulation will be imposed in the following period. Consider a one-output firm, depicted in figure 5.8, which is charging P^1 in period one and knows that V-F regulation will be imposed in period two. To focus on the central issues, average cost is assumed to be constant. (This assumption is not necessary for the results.) The question to be addressed is: will the firm waste in period one?

Without waste, the firm incurs costs of $AC \cdot Q^1$ in period one. Its profits are denoted by the rectangle $ABCJ$. When V-F regulation is imposed in period two, the firm must lower its price to P^2_n, equal to its average cost in period one. Its profits in the second period are therefore zero; and because price equals average cost in the second

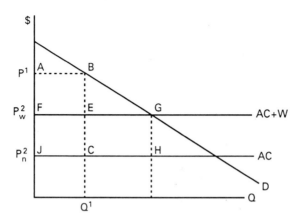

Figure 5.8
Firm wastes in period 1

period, the firm is in equilibrium and earns zero profits in all future periods. Its total profits from period one through all future periods is therefore the rectangle $ABCJ$.

Suppose now that the firm wastes an amount W for each unit produced in the first period. Its profits in the first period are then $ABEF$, which is less than if the firm did not waste. When V-F regulation is imposed, however, the regulator does not see the waste; the regulator only observes actual costs, which include both needed and unneeded expenses. The regulator therefore requires that the firm lower its price in the second period to $P_w^2 = AC + W$, which is higher than would be permitted if the firm did not waste in the first period. With the higher price, the firm has an opportunity to earn profits in the second period. In particular, suppose the firm does *not* waste in period two. Without wasting, it earns profits of $FGHJ$ in the second period: the difference between price and average cost, over the number of units sold. In the third period, the firm is required to lower its price to the average cost incurred in the second period: $P_w^3 = AC$. The firm earns zero profit in the third and all subsequent periods. The total profits of the firm, over all periods, is therefore the area $ABEF$ plus area $FGHJ$. Because these areas combined exceed area $ABCJ$ (the firm's profits without waste), the total profits of the firm are greater if it wastes in the first period than if it operates efficiently. The firm therefore chooses to waste.

The driving force behind this waste is clear: by incurring unnecessarily high costs in one period, the firm is able to charge higher prices in the subsequent period. The firm foregoes some profit in one period in order to earn greater profits in the next. Because demand is downward sloping, the extra profits earned in the next period exceed the reduction in profits in the first period.

The waste can be seen from an informational perspective as well. Essentially, the firm is providing incorrect information to the regulator in an effort to affect the regulator's decisions. If the regulator knew the minimum cost for producing the firm's output, the regulator would set each period's price equal to the minimum average cost in the previous period. In such a case, the firm would have no incentive to waste because doing so would only reduce its profits in the current period without raising its price in subsequent periods. Unfortunately, the regulator generally does not know the minimum cost of producing a given output and only observes the actual costs of the firm, which might include waste. By wasting, the firm induces the regulator to think that average cost is actually higher than it minimally need be. The regulator sets prices in the next period on the basis of this misinformation and thereby inadvertently allows the firm to earn greater profits than it would have if the regulator had known the true average costs.

Two important details have been omitted from the discussion thus far. First, when considering a stream of profits over time, a firm will discount (value less highly) profits earned in future years compared to profits earned in the current year. A dollar today is worth more than a dollar next year, because, among other reasons, a dollar obtained today can be invested to earn more money over the year. The standard way to represent this fact in the decisionmaking of firms is to calculate the "present value" of a stream on profits over time. Denote the discount rate as d, with $0 < d < 1$, to capture the fact that future-year profits are valued less than current-year profits. The present value of profits π_1 in year one, π_2 in year two, π_3 in year three and so on is

$$\pi_1 + d\pi_2 + d^2\pi_3 + \ldots ,$$

where the discount rate reduces the value of each future year's profits relative to the current year, with the reduction being greater the further in the future the profits accrue. For example, at a discount rate of .9 (meaning that future profits are valued at 10% less than current profits), the present value of a profit stream of $100 each year for two years is *not* $200; rather, it is $100 + .9 · $100 = $190. Similarly, if the profit stream is $100 for *three* years and zero thereafter, the present value is $100 + .9 · $100 + .9 · .9 · $100 = $271.

Because future profits are valued less highly than current profits, the firm that knows that V-F regulation will be imposed will not *necessarily* choose to waste. Consider again figure 5.8. If the firm wastes, its profits in the first period are lower by *FECJ* (compared to the case in which it did not waste), but its profits in the second period are higher by *FGHJ*. If profits in each period were valued equally, the firm would always choose to waste because area *FGHJ* exceeds area *FECJ*. However, the firm generally discounts future profits. That is, it compares the *discounted* value of the extra profits it will earn in the second period with the *undiscounted* reduction in profits in the first period. It is possible that the discounted value of area *FGHJ* is less than the undiscounted value of area *FECJ*. If so, the firm will choose not to waste.[5] Stated generally, the firm that anticipates the imposition of V-F regulation will waste if the discounted value of the gains in the future period exceeds the reduction in current-period profits, and otherwise it will not waste.

Second, the firm will not necessarily waste in only one period. Our example has shown that the firm could make more profit by wasting in the first period and not wasting in the second period than by not wasting in either period. Similar logic can be used to show that the firm might make more profit by wasting in the first *and* second periods and not wasting in the third period than by wasting in only the first period and not in the second or third periods. And so on for subsequent periods.

The firm will never, however, choose to waste in equilibrium. Consider an equilibrium in which the firm is wasting. We can show that such an equilibrium is impossible. Suppose a firm is charging P^* and wasting an amount W per unit of output. The minimal average cost plus the amount of waste equals the price the firm charges, such that the firm is permitted to continue charging this price in each subsequent period. That is, the firm can choose to remain in equilibrium at this point if it so chooses. The situation is depicted in figure 5.9.

If the firm continues to charge P^* and waste W per unit, then its

---

5. For example, suppose a firm that has a discount rate of .9 would earn $100 less profits in the first period from wasting and then would obtain $108 extra profit in the next period. This firm would choose not to waste since the present value of its gain in the second period (.9 · $108 = 97.20) is less than the $100 reduction in profits in the first period.

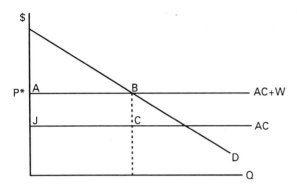

Figure 5.9
Firm does not waste in equilibrium

profits are zero in the current and all subsequent time periods. However, the firm can make positive profits by not wasting. In particular, if the firm chose not to waste in the current period, it would earn profits of *ABCJ*. It would then, of course, be required to lower its price to average cost and would earn zero profits in all subsequent periods. However, earning *ABCJ* in the first period and zero thereafter is clearly preferable to earning zero profits in the first period as well as thereafter. The firm will choose not to waste rather than remain in an equilibrium with waste. Eventually, the firm will move to an equilibrium with no waste at optimal prices. That is, the firm might waste on the way to equilibrium, but will not waste at equilibrium.

2.   Firm without Advance Notice

Consider now the possibility that the regulator imposes V-F regulation without the firm knowing beforehand. In period one, the firm is unregulated and does not anticipate regulation. It charges, say, P^1 and maximizes profits by minimizing the cost of producing the output demanded at that price. That is, the firm does not waste in the first period. In the second period, V-F regulation is imposed on the firm. The regulator observes the firm's true average cost in the first period and requires that the firm reduce its price in the second period to this average cost. Because the firm did not know that the regulation would be imposed, it had no reason to incur waste in the first period to falsify its cost situation in anticipation of being permitted a higher price in the second period.

The question now is: will the firm choose to waste in the second period, after V-F regulation has been imposed? The answer is no.

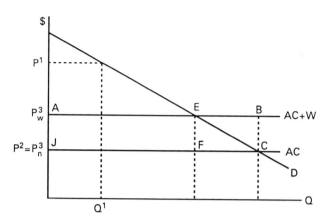

Figure 5.10
Firm without advance notice

Consider figure 5.10. The firm charges $P^2 = AC$ in the second period, because the regulator observed the firm's true costs in the first period. If the firm continues not to waste, it will earn zero profits in the second and all subsequent periods. The firm could, however, waste in the second period. If the firm wasted W per unit of output, it would earn negative profits in the second period: its losses would be area $ABCJ$. However, with higher costs in the second period, the regulator would allow the firm to charge a higher price in the third period. In particular, the firm, if it wasted in the second period, would be able to charge P_w^3 in the third period. Then, by not wasting in this third period, the firm could use its higher price to earn positive profits; in particular, its profits would be area $AEFJ$.

Note, however, that this gain in the third period is less than the loss in the second period: the firm would lose more than it would gain by wasting. The underlying reason is clear. Output is lower in the third period than in the second since price is higher. The price increase in the third period is applied to the lower third-period output. However, the inflated average cost in the second period is applied to the higher second-period output. The gain in the third period is therefore necessarily less than the loss in the second period. The firm would therefore choose not to waste.[6]

---

6. If demand is completely inelastic (that is, vertical), then area $ABCJ$ is the same size as $AEFJ$. Even in this case, however, the firm would choose not to waste because the firm discounts future profits relative to current profits. The present value of the gain is smaller in magnitude than the present value of the loss, since the gain occurs after the loss.

The findings regarding waste can be summarized as follows. If the firm knows in advance that V-F regulation will be applied, it might have an incentive to waste so as to misinform the regulator as to the true costs of production, thereby inducing the regulator to permit higher prices in subsequent periods. Whether it is profitable for the firm in this situation to waste (that is, whether it does indeed waste) depends on a variety of factors, including the shapes of the demand and cost curves and the firm's discount rate. Waste, if it occurs, can continue over numerous periods while the firm is moving toward equilibrium. However, eventually the firm will reach equilibrium, at which it does not waste, and will charge optimal prices consistent with zero profits. Furthermore, if the regulation is imposed without the firm knowing in advance, the firm will not waste in its movement toward equilibrium or when it reaches equilibrium.

6   Surplus Subsidy Schemes

6.1   Introduction

Most of the regulatory mechanisms examined so far attempt to achieve the *second-best* outcome.[1] If the regulator is able to subsidize the firm, the first-best outcome is feasible. By subsidizing the firm for the losses it incurs at marginal-cost prices, the firm can remain solvent and continue to produce at these prices indefinitely. The question then becomes: what regulatory mechanisms can the regulator use to attain the first-best outcome, given that it is able to subsidize the firm?

Were the regulator able to know the firm's cost and demand curves, the task of regulation would be simple. The regulator would require the firm to set its prices at marginal cost and then subsidize the firm for the difference between revenues and the minimum cost of producing the output demanded. Unfortunately, the regulator seldom knows the cost and demand curves of the firm. Without knowing costs, the regulator cannot determine marginal costs and, just as important, does not know the minimum cost of producing a given output. If the regulator relied on the firm to report its costs, the firm would clearly have an incentive to misreport. By reporting a marginal cost that is higher than actual, the firm could keep prices above their first-best level. And by reporting higher-than-actual total costs, the firm could increase its subsidy and earn additional profits at any price level. Even if the regulator were able to audit the firm costlessly and accurately, the first-best outcome would still not be attained. Without knowing the firm's cost curves, the regulator would have to subsidize the firm on the basis of *incurred* costs, rather than minimum costs of

---

1. The one exception is price discrimination, which, as shown in chapter 2, attains first-best optimality.

production. The firm would have no incentive to produce efficiently, because it would earn zero profits whether it was efficient or wasteful. Total costs and marginal costs (and hence prices) would inevitably be above their first-best levels.

Several regulatory mechanisms have been proposed to induce the firm to price at marginal cost and produce efficiently without the regulator knowing the costs of the firm. Each of these procedures involves the regulator subsidizing the firm on the basis of the consumer surplus that the firm's pricing decisions generate. By letting the firm benefit (through the subsidy) whenever it acts in a way that benefits consumers (that is, increases consumer surplus), the regulator is able to induce the firm to act in accordance with social goals.

Three mechanisms are described in this chapter. Loeb and Magat (1979), who seem to have been the first to suggest this type of regulation, introduce the important concept that transferring consumer surplus to the firm induces the firm to behave optimally. Sappington and Sibley (1988) propose a mechanism that transfers to the firm only the period-to-period *change* in consumer surplus. This procedure, in addition to inducing first-best prices and efficient production, provides the firm with only zero profits in equilibrium, rather than positive profits as under Loeb and Magat's procedure.[2] Both the L-M and S-S procedures require that the regulator have information about the firm's demand curve, at least in the vicinity of optimal prices. Finsinger and Vogelsang (1981, 1982, 1985) have developed a procedure that can be implemented without this information, that is, without knowledge of *either* the demand or cost curves. This procedure uses an *approximation* to the period-to-period change in consumer surplus. Because the subsidy is based on an approximation rather than the actual change in consumer surplus, equilibrium is attained more slowly than under the other procedures. However, once attained, equilibrium consists of the first-best outcome.[3]

---

2. The L-M procedure can also result in zero profits if there are many potential producers and the regulator can auction the right to be the monopoly among these potential producers. See section 6.2.

3. Chronologically, Sappington and Sibley's analysis developed from issues raised by the earlier work of Finsinger and Vogelsang. Finsinger and Vogelsang suggested the use of the period-to-period change in surplus and developed an approximation to this change that does not require information on demand curves. Sappington and Sibley, responding to the fact that the F-V mechanism can take many periods to attain equilibrium, proposed a means of using information on the demand curve to attain equilibrium more quickly. It is pedagogically useful to present the procedures in the reverse

6.2   Loeb and Magat

Loeb and Magat have proposed a mechanism that induces the firm to charge the optimal price and produce efficiently even when the regulator does not know the firm's costs. Under this mechanism, the regulator allows the firm to chose its price without constraint. Given the firm's price, the regulator subsidizes the firm by the amount of consumer surplus that is generated at that price. To calculate this quantity, the regulator must possess information on the firm's demand curve, but not its costs. (Recall that consumer surplus is the area under the demand curve and above the price: the shaded area in figure 6.1 for price P_0. The size of this area depends on the demand curve but not on costs.)

The firm's total profits with this subsidy are the sum of the producer's surplus (that is, its profits without the subsidy) and consumer surplus. The mechanism therefore gives all surplus to the firm. Because all surplus accrues to the firm, it chooses the price that provides the greatest total surplus, which by definition is the first-best outcome. Stated alternatively: because total surplus is greatest when price is set at marginal cost, and because the firm's profit with the subsidy

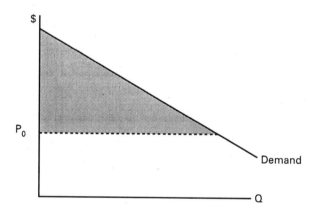

Figure 6.1
Subsidy under L-M: consumer surplus

order. The L-M procedure shows the value of transferring consumer surplus to the firm. The S-S procedure illustrates that the same effect can be obtained by transferring the period-to-period change in surplus. Then, the F-V procedure shows that the period-to-period change in surplus can be approximated when the regulator does not know the demand curve, with the only loss being the speed at which the first-best outcome is attained.

consists of the total surplus, the firm maximizes its own profits by pricing at marginal cost.

The result is the same with many products as with one: the multi-product firm maximizes its profit (which consists under the subsidy of total surplus) by setting all prices equal to their marginal costs. Furthermore, the firm produces efficiently. Any reduction in costs translates into an increase in surplus, which the firm keeps; the firm therefore makes the most profit by producing at the least possible cost.

The L-M procedure is an extreme, and thereby illuminating, example of the general principle that optimality is attained by creating consistency between the goals of the firm and the goals of the regulator. The goal of the regulator is to maximize total surplus, and the goal of the firm is to maximize profits. The L-M procedure makes these two goals consistent by giving all surplus to the firm, such that the firm's profits *are* the total surplus. The firm, in maximizing its own profits, maximizes total surplus.

This way of attaining consistency results in an outcome that, while efficient, might not be considered equitable. The firm obtains all the surplus, and consumers obtain none.[4] Loeb and Magat suggest two

---

4. If the regulator considers it inequitable for the firm to obtain all the surplus, the regulator's goal is apparently more complex than simply maximizing total surplus. Suppose the regulator's goal is to maximize the *weighted* sum of consumer and producer surplus rather than the simple sum, with the weights representing the relative importance the regulator places on surplus for the two parties. Baron and Myerson (1982), Sappington (1983), and Laffont and Tirole (1986) derive optimal pricing and subsidy policies under this more general goal, along with the assumption, as in L-M, that the regulator knows demand but not costs. When consumer and producer surplus are weighted equally (that is, the regulator maximizes total surplus), the L-M mechanism is of course optimal: the firm is subsidized by the amount of consumer surplus, sets price equal to marginal cost, and minimizes costs. However, when the producer's profit is weighted less than consumer surplus, these studies indicate that the regulator's goal is better met by having a smaller subsidy and a price above marginal cost. The reason for these results hinges on the fact that the subsidy is a transfer from consumers to the producer. This transfer, in itself, reduces the regulator's welfare measure when the producer (who receives the transfer) is weighted less than consumers (who provide the transfer). The purpose of a subsidy is to induce the firm to price closer to marginal cost, which generates additional surplus. A subsidy is justified if the surplus gained from pricing nearer marginal cost is greater than the loss incurred by the transfer from consumers to producers. There comes a point, however, as the subsidy is raised and prices move closer to marginal cost, that an additional subsidy generates a greater loss due to the transfer than a gain due to pricing nearer marginal cost. That is, the regulator's welfare measure is higher by not subsidizing as much and allowing the firm to price somewhat above marginal cost. (Of course, when consumer and producer

methods for correcting this inequity. First, the monopoly could be auctioned. That is, different firms could bid for the right to be the monopoly producer of the good, with the regulator choosing the firm with the highest bid. Supposedly, each firm would be willing to bid up to the maximum surplus that can be obtained in the market, because, under the terms of the regulation, the firm knows that it will be able to earn that much if it wins the auction and becomes the monopoly. The highest bid will therefore be essentially equal to the total surplus that is attainable in the market.[5] When the winning firm becomes the monopolist, it will earn a profit, including subsidy, that is the same as the amount it paid to become the monopolist. On net, the firm will earn zero profits (profits including subsidy and minus auction bid), and all surplus will accrue to consumers.

Second, the regulator can subsidize the firm by a *portion* of consumer surplus rather than the entire amount. Suppose, for example, that the regulator knows that the firm will not choose a price over P_a. The regulator can then subsidize the firm for the portion of consumer surplus between P_a and the price the firm actually charges. This subsidy is the shaded area in figure 6.2, where P_b is the price that the firm charges. Stated alternatively, the subsidy is the consumer surplus at the firm's chosen price P_b minus the consumer surplus at P_a.

---

surplus are weighted equally, the transfer of surplus from consumers to the producer has no effect, in itself, on the welfare measure. As a result, there is no loss from raising the subsidy as high as necessary to induce the firm to price exactly at marginal cost.)

It is important to note that the optimality results obtained by these studies apply to situations in which regulation occurs entirely in one period. When the regulator can use information in one period to determine prices and/or subsidy in the next, other mechanisms can be utilized that bring prices to marginal cost in equilibrium with a subsidy that is the minimum necessary to keep the firm in business. (The S-S and F-V mechanisms, described in the following sections, are examples.) Total surplus is maximized under these mechanisms, because price equals marginal cost. And since profits are the minimum feasible (zero, through subsidy), consumer surplus is also as great as possible. With total surplus and consumer surplus both as high as possible, the regulator's welfare measure (in equilibrium) is necessarily as high as possible no matter what weights the regulator places on consumer and producer surplus (provided of course that producer surplus is not weighted more than consumer surplus). Stated succinctly: with multiperiod regulation, the first-best outcome with unequal weighting of consumer and producer surplus is the same as the first-best outcome with the weights being equal. In either case, prices are set at marginal cost and the firm is subsidized sufficiently to just break even.

5. The winning bid will equal the entire surplus if each producer faces the same costs or if there are many bidders, each of whom has an independent assessment of costs. Riordan and Sappington (1989) derive optimal methods for awarding the monopoly franchise under more general conditions.

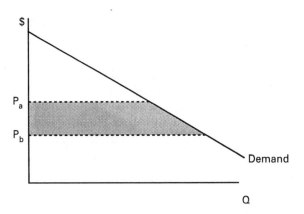

Figure 6.2
Subsidy as portion of consumer surplus

Subtracting a fixed amount from the firm's profits does not change the firm's *relative* profits at each outcome: the firm's profits including subsidy are still highest when total surplus is highest. The firm will again choose the surplus-maximizing (that is, first-best) price and will produce with cost-minimizing inputs. And yet, because the firm obtains only a portion of consumer surplus, some surplus is retained by consumers.

The difficulty with this approach is that the regulator does not generally know how high to set P_a. P_a must be sufficiently above the first-best price to provide enough subsidy to the firm for it to break even. Otherwise, the firm will choose to stop production rather than produce at a loss. However, because the regulator does not know the firm's costs, it does not know how high P_a must be. The regulator, in making sure that P_a is sufficiently high, could easily establish a subsidy that is far larger than needed to induce the firm to behave optimally. This difficulty is the motivation for the S-S and F-V procedures described below.

6.3 Sappington and Sibley: The Incremental Subsidy Surplus (ISS) Scheme

Sappington and Sibley have introduced a multiperiod regulation mechanism in which the regulator uses information on the firm's prices, revenues, and expenditures in one period to determine the subsidy the firm obtains in the next period. The mechanism is based on the concept that the firm need not receive the *entire* surplus in order to choose first-best outcomes. Rather, in each period, the firm can be allocated the improvement, or gain, in surplus that its actions in that period generate. Under this subsidy, the firm will, in each period, choose to provide the greatest possible *improvement* in surplus. This period-to-period improvement leads over time (and in fact very quickly) to surplus being as great as possible.

Suppose the firm in period t is charging P^t and selling the quantity Q^t demanded at that price. The consumer surplus generated at this price is CS^t, which is the area under the demand curve and above P^t. The firm expends E^t producing the output. Expenditures E^t are perhaps higher than the minimum cost of producing the output due to inefficiency. (We show below that the firm will not waste in equilibrium, such that E^t actually does equal minimum cost in equilibrium.) The firm earns profit from its operation, called operating profit, of $O^t = P^t Q^t - E^t$, that is, revenue minus expenditures. This operating profit includes any waste the firm incurs in its operations and excludes any subsidy it receives. By definition, total surplus is the sum of consumer surplus and operating profit.

The regulator allows the firm to choose its price and expenditures in each period. The regulator subsidizes the firm on the basis of the *extra* consumer surplus it generates each period. In particular, the regulator provides the following subsidy in period t:

$$S^t = (CS^t - CS^{t-1}) - O^{t-1}.$$

The first term is the change in consumer surplus from the previous period to the current period; that is, it is the improvement in consumer surplus that the firm generates in the current period. Visually, this quantity is the area $ABCE$ in figure 6.3 for a firm that charges P^0 in one period and P^1 in the next. The second term is the firm's operating profit in the previous period. Taken together, the subsidy is therefore the improvement in consumer surplus minus the previous period's operating profit.

The reason this subsidy is effective becomes clear when the subsidy is added to the firm's operating profit in each period. Under this subsidy, the firm's *total* profit in each period is its operating profits plus the subsidy

$$\pi^t = O^t + S^t.$$

Substituting in the formula for the subsidy, total profit is

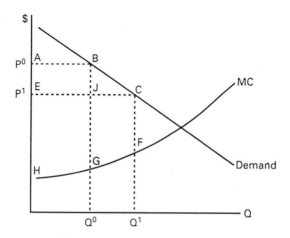

Figure 6.3
Effects of price reduction

$$\pi^t = O^t + (CS^t - CS^{t-1}) - O^{t-1}.$$

Rearranging:

$$\pi^t = (O^t - O^{t-1}) + (CS^t - CS^{t-1}).$$

That is, the firm's total profit in each period is the change in operating profit and consumer surplus from the last period. Because total surplus is the sum of operating profit (producer surplus) and consumer surplus, the firm's total profit in each period under this subsidy is the change in total surplus since the last period. Visually, and ignoring the possibility of waste, the firm's total profit in figure 6.3 is area $BCFG$, the increase in total surplus.[6]

Given that the firm's profit is the change in total surplus, the firm maximizes its profit by generating the greatest possible improvement in surplus in each period. No matter where the firm starts out, the greatest improvement in surplus is attained by the firm moving to the first-best outcome, namely, to marginal-cost prices with no waste. In

6. When price is reduced from P^0 to P^1, consumer surplus increases by $ABCE$. Operating profit in period zero is area $ABGH$ (the difference between price and marginal cost for each unit sold). The firm's subsidy in period one is therefore area $ABCE$ minus area $ABGH$. Operating profit in period one is area $ECFH$. The firm's total profit in period one is its operating profit in that period plus its subsidy: $ECFH + (ABCE - ABGH)$, which is area $BCFG$. Note that area $BCFG$ is the increase in total surplus that results from the price reduction from P^0 to P^1: it is the difference between the value of each unit to consumers (as denoted by the demand curve) and the marginal cost of each unit, summed over all the extra units sold.

fact, because future profit is discounted relative to current profit, the firm will want to obtain the largest improvement in surplus *as soon as possible*. Therefore, the firm will move to the first-best outcome in the first period after this subsidy mechanism has been established.

This fact can be demonstrated visually. Recall that if the firm lowered its price in period one from P^0 to P^1, then its profit, including subsidy, in period one is area $BCFG$ in figure 6.3. The firm will therefore choose the price in period one (that is, will choose P^1) in such a way as to make area $BCFG$ as large as possible. As P^1 is lowered, points C and F move out, such that area $BCFG$ increases in size. The area is as large as possible when P^1 is lowered to the level shown in figure 6.4, namely to marginal cost. That is, the firm maximizes its profit in period one by setting its price in period one at the first-best level.

Under the S-S scheme, the firm's profit changes over time in a particular way. Before regulation is imposed, the firm earns some profits, which can be denoted π^0. The firm does not choose the first-best outcome prior to regulation; in fact, this is the reason to impose regulation. Two types of losses occur relative to the first-best outcome. First, the firm might waste. Second, a "deadweight loss" occurs because price is above marginal cost. This deadweight loss is the difference between the surplus attained at marginal cost prices and the surplus attained at the prices the firm charges, independent of any waste. Visually, it is the shaded area in figure 6.5 given that the firm is pricing at $P^{0.}$

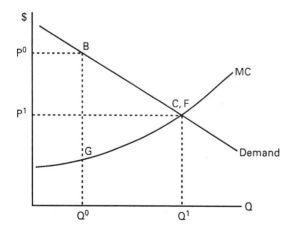

Figure 6.4
Period 1 price change for firm under S-S regulation

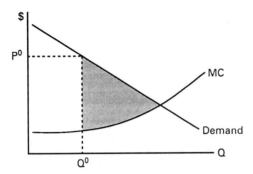

Figure 6.5
Deadweight loss due to pricing above marginal cost

The subsidy scheme is imposed in period one. The firm's total profit in period one is equal to the improvement in surplus that the firm generates in period one. The firm moves to the first-best outcome in period one to generate the maximum possible improvement in surplus (which, under the scheme, translates into maximum profit for the firm). The firm's profit in this period is therefore equal to the deadweight loss and waste that the firm incurred prior to regulation.

In period two the firm remains at the first-best outcome, because no further improvement in surplus is possible.[7] Because consumer surplus does not increase, the subsidy to the firm is $S^2 = -O^1$. That is, the firm is subsidized by the amount of operating profits of the firm in period one. Because the firm was at the first-best outcome in period one with prices equal to marginal cost, the firm, being a natural monopoly, incurred negative operating profit. The subsidy in period one is therefore equal to the operating loss that the firm incurs at the first-best outcome. The firm's total profit in period two is the sum of its operating profit and its subsidy: $\pi^2 = O^2 + S^2 = O^2 - O^1$, which equals zero since the firm operates at the first-best outcome in both periods one and two such that $O^1 = O^2$.[8]

---

7. The firm will not move away from the first-best outcome after it has reached it because doing so would result in the firm's total profits in that period being negative. The firm would be able to make up the loss in the following period by moving back to the first-best outcome (being subsidized for the improvement); however, because the firm discounts future profit relative to current profit, it will not choose to incur a loss in one period that is just made up in the next period.
8. The firm's profit in period two can be derived more directly. With the subsidy, total profit in any period is the additional surplus the firm generates in that period. Since the firm remains at the first-best outcome in period two, surplus does not change and total profit, including subsidy, is therefore zero.

All subsequent periods are the same: the firm stays at the first-best outcome, charging marginal cost prices and not wasting, and receives a subsidy that allows it to just break even.

In short, in the first period of regulation, the firm moves to the first-best outcome. Its profit in this period, including subsidy, is equal to the amount of waste and the deadweight loss that the firm incurred prior to regulation. In the second and subsequent periods, the firm stays at the first-best outcome and its profit, including subsidy, is zero.

6.4 Finsinger and Vogelsang: An Approximate Incremental Surplus Subsidy (AISS) Scheme

To implement the subsidy scheme proposed by Sappington and Sibley, the regulator needs to know the shape of the demand curve, at least in the region between the firm's price prior to regulation and the optimal price.[9] Finsinger and Vogelsang have proposed a mechanism that is conceptually similar to that of Sappington and Sibley, but does not utilize information on the demand curve. Rather than providing a subsidy to the firm on the basis of the exact improvement in consumer surplus, F-V subsidizes the firm on the basis of an approximation to this improvement. The approximation is calculated on the basis of information that the regulator can observe directly, namely, the prices and quantities sold in each period.

Under the F-V scheme, the firm receives a subsidy each period equal to

$$S^t = Q^{t-1}(P^{t-1} - P^t) - O^{t-1}.$$

The first term is the approximate improvement in consumer surplus. It is area $ABJE$ in figure 6.3: the change in price multiplied by the

---

9. Sappington and Sibley point out that their mechanism can be used even when the regulator does not know the demand curve exactly, provided that the regulator possesses the same information as the firm regarding the unknown demand curve. For example, demand might vary and its realization in each period be unknown to both the firm and the regulator prior to the setting of prices. If the regulator and firm both know the distribution of demand, the S-S procedure will induce the firm to price at expected marginal cost (that is, marginal cost of the output demanded at that price, averaged over all possible levels of demand). Similarly, demand might be fixed though unknown. If the regulator and firm have the same a priori concepts about the probability that demand is at a certain level, the procedure will induce the firm to choose prices that are optimal given the regulator's concepts of demand. However, if the regulator and firm are not symmetrically informed about demand, the procedure does not necessarily lead to the first-best outcome.

quantity sold in the previous period. The exact improvement in consumer surplus is area *ABCE*, which enters in the subsidy under the S-S procedure. The F-V scheme differs from the S-S scheme in that the subsidy to the firm for a given price change is less by the amount *BCJ*. The second term is the operating profit in the previous period, which, as in S-S, is subtracted from the improvement in consumer surplus.

The total profit of the firm in each period is the operating profit in that period plus the subsidy:

$$\pi^t = O^t + S^t$$

$$= O^t + Q^{t-1}(P^{t-1} - P^t) - O^{t-1}$$

$$= (O^t - O^{t-1}) + Q^{t-1}(P^{t-1} - P^t).$$

Total profit is therefore the change in operating profit since the last period plus the approximate improvement in consumer surplus. That is, total profit in each period is the approximate improvement in total surplus for the period.

It is useful to visualize this approximate improvement in total surplus. In figure 6.3, the *exact* increase in total surplus is area *BCFG*. Under the S-S procedure, this area is the total profit (operating profit plus subsidy) that the firm would obtain in the period. Under the F-V procedure, the firm's total profit in each period is not equal to this exact improvement in surplus, but rather to an approximation. The firm's subsidy is less than the true change in consumer surplus by the amount *BCJ*. Total profit under F-V regulation is therefore area *JCFG*, which is less than the exact improvement in surplus by area *BCJ*.

Consider now the behavior of the firm under the F-V scheme. Suppose first that the firm does not discount future profits relative to current profits. Then it would change prices each period to obtain the largest possible sum of profits over time. The firm can obtain essentially all the deadweight loss as profits if it takes many very small price reductions over time. Figure 6.6 depicts this fact. The original deadweight loss (that is, the deadweight loss at price P^0) is *AJG* in either graph. This is the amount of total profit that the firm would receive under the S-S scheme, under which the firm receives exactly all the improvement in surplus. Under the F-V scheme, suppose the firm took two steps, reducing price from P^0 to P^1 in the first period and then from P^1 to P^2 in the second period. Its total profit over both periods would be the shaded area in panel (a): *CBFG* in the first period plus *EJF* in the second period. Because of the approximation in

(a) Two-layer steps   (b) Many small steps

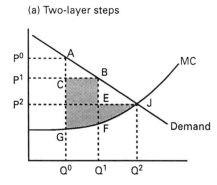 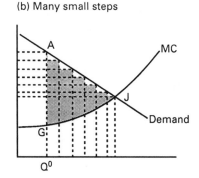

Figure 6.6
Total profit over time under F-V scheme

the F-V scheme, the firm would lose the areas *ABC* and *BJE*. However, suppose the firm took small price reductions over many periods. Its total profit over time in this case would be the shaded area in panel (b). As this graph suggests, the firm can obtain essentially all the surplus improvement, just as in the S-S scheme, if it takes sufficiently many small steps.

If the firm does not discount future profits, the F-V scheme is the same as the S-S scheme in that the firm obtains (essentially) all the improvement in surplus that it generates. The firm therefore maximizes the total improvement in surplus, moving eventually, as under the S-S scheme, to the first-best outcome. The only difference is that under F-V regulation the firm chooses to move very slowly to the first-best outcome, taking very small steps along the way.

In actuality, the firm discounts future relative to current profit. The firm therefore does not simply try to maximize the simple sum of profit over time; rather, it maximizes the sum of *discounted* profit over time, with future profit discounted more than current profit. As a result, the firm does not necessarily choose to take many small steps, because doing so means that much of its profit would be deferred far into the future. The firm does better by making larger price reductions early, incurring some loss due to the approximation, but gaining by receiving the profits earlier. The firm can therefore be expected to move toward the first-best outcome more quickly than would occur if the firm did not discount future profits.

The speed of the movement to the first-best prices is still not as great as under the S-S procedure: the firm will generally not move to the first-best outcome in one step. The reason is most easily discernible when marginal cost is constant, as in figure 6.7. If the firm were

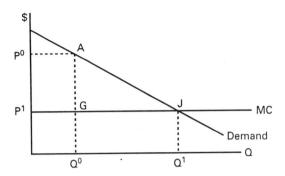

Figure 6.7
Constant marginal cost and one step to optimality

to decrease price to marginal cost in the first period after regulation is imposed, its profits in that period (and all future periods) would be zero. The move generates extra surplus in the amount of area AJG. However, the area AJG is also the amount that the approximation under the F-V scheme falls short of the true surplus gain: it is the part of the surplus gain that the firm does not receive because of the approximation. The firm therefore receives nothing in the first period. And because the firm stays at the first-best outcome once it reaches it, profit is zero in each subsequent period. Clearly, the firm would be better off, whatever its discount rate, by taking more than one period to reach the first-best outcome, because its profits would be greater than zero in each period along the way.

The conclusions can now be summarized. The F-V scheme can be implemented without the regulator having information on the demand curve of the firm. In equilibrium the firm chooses the first-best outcome, setting the price of each good at its marginal cost and producing at minimum cost. However, the firm may take many periods before it reaches the first-best outcome. This slowness is the "cost" the regulator incurs, relative to the S-S scheme, for not knowing the firm's demand curve.

The issue of speed can be fairly important. In an environment in which costs or demand shift over time, the outcome that constitutes first-best changes. For example, the price at which the demand curve intersects the marginal cost curve changes when either curve shifts. Under F-V regulation, the firm might move toward the first-best outcome more slowly than the first-best outcome itself moves, such that optimality is never achieved. In a changing environment, therefore, the speed of the S-S mechanism becomes more attractive.

7   Multipart Tariffs

7.1 Introduction and Definitions

A tariff is an algorithm for determining the bill to the customer for consumption of a firm's products. In the trivial case of one good with one price, the tariff is simply that price: the customer's bill is the price times the quantity consumed. This is called a one-part tariff.[1] For many regulated firms, tariffs are more complex, consisting of several billing components. For example, many local phone companies charge a monthly fee for service plus a charge for each call. The tariff in this case consists of the monthly fee and the per-call charge. Similarly, electricity providers often charge one price for consumption up to a certain number of kilowatt-hours during a month and then charge a different price for consumption beyond this amount. The tariff consists of the two prices and the consumption level, called the threshold, at which the price changes. Tariffs with several billing components are called multipart.

Multipart tariffs have important welfare implications. Perhaps the most relevant is the fact that a regulator, by applying an appropriately designed multipart tariff, can induce a natural monopolist to operate closer to the first-best outcome than would be possible with only one price. In fact, in some cases the first-best outcome can be attained exactly. These findings are demonstrated in the sections to follow. But first, some definitions, distinguishing various types of multipart tariffs, are required.

A *usage/access tariff* consists of a fixed fee that does not depend on level of consumption (called the access charge) and a per-unit price

---

1. The term "one-part tariff" is seldom used, because it is simply a price. The terminology serves to distinguish multipart tariffs.

for consumption (called the usage charge). Local phone service is usually subject to a usage/access tariff: the monthly fixed fee is the access charge and the price per call is the usage charge. The fixed monthly fee is called an "access fee" because by paying this fee, the consumer has access to the phone network. In a sense, the access fee is charged for the right to make phone calls (that is, for potential calls), and the usage fee is for actual calls.

With local phone service, a distinction is often made between *flat* and *measured* rates. Under flat-rate service, the consumer pays a fixed monthly fee and is not charged for local calls, while under measured service the consumer pays a monthly fee and is also charged for each local call. It is important to note that both flat and measured rates are types of access/usage tariffs. They differ only in whether the usage charge is zero or strictly positive.

Block rates are tariffs under which the price for each additional unit of consumption changes when the total level of consumption reaches certain thresholds. Electricity is usually charged in this way. One such tariff is represented in figure 7.1 and consists of: 7 cents per kilowatt-hour for up to (and including) 1,000 kWhs in a month, 5 cents for each kWh between 1,000 and 2,500 in the month, and 4 cents for each kWh over 2,500. Under this tariff, a consumer who uses 1,500 kWhs of electricity in a month is charged $95 ($70 for the first 1,000 kWhs, which are priced at 7 cents apiece, plus $25 for the 500 kWhs over 1,000, which are priced at 5 cents each).[2] The term "block rates" arises from the fact that the pricing algorithm, when graphed as in figure 7.1, looks like a series of blocks. The consumption interval under which one price applies (that is, from one threshold to the next) is called a *block.* The tariff in figure 7.1 therefore consists of three blocks: zero to 1,000, 1,000 to 2,500, and 2,500 and over.

Block rates can be *declining* or *inverted,* depending on whether the price for additional units decreases or increases as total consumption

---

2. Note that each price applies only for the portion of consumption within the range for that price. That is, when consumption is 1,500, the 5 cent price applies only to the kWhs over 1,000, not to the entire 1,500. It is possible to define a tariff that consists of charging one price for all units of consumption, with that price depending on the total level of consumption. If the same prices and thresholds are used as in figure 7.1, then, under this alternative definition, the consumer of 1,500 kWhs would be billed $75 (5 cents for each of the 1,500 kWhs). However, this type of tariff has the peculiar feature that, at the thresholds, the consumer's bill can decrease when consumption increases. In our example, consumption of 1,000 kWhs costs $75 (1,000 times 7 cents each), while consumption of 1,001 kWhs costs $50.05 (1,001 times 5 cents each).

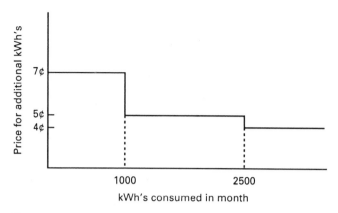

Figure 7.1
A block-rate tariff: declining blocks

increases. Figure 7.1 depicts declining blocks. An example of an inverted blocks tariff is given in figure 7.2, consisting of a charge of 3 cents per kWh for up to 800 kWhs, 5 cents for each kWh between 800 and 3,000, and 10 cents for kWhs over 3,000.

When discussing an individual consumer under a block-rates tariff, a distinction is made between *marginal* and *inframarginal* prices. The marginal price is the price the consumer pays for additional consumption given the total consumption of the consumer, and inframarginal prices are the prices that apply to lower levels of consumption. For example, a customer that consumes 1,500 kWhs under the tariff in figure 7.1 faces a marginal price of 5 cents and an inframarginal price of 7 cents. If, instead, this customer had used 2,600 kWhs, then the marginal price would be 4 cents and there would be two inframarginal prices: 7 and 5 cents.

Because the consumer is paying different prices for different units, a distinction between average and marginal prices is also necessary. Average price is the total dollar outlay of the consumer divided by the total consumption. (In the case of the consumer of 1,500 kWhs, this average price is 6⅓ cents: $95 divided by 1,500.) If total consumption does not exceed the first block, average and marginal price are the same. However, for total consumption beyond the first block, marginal price is below average price under declining block rates (because price declines as consumption increases) and above average price under inverted block rates (because price increases with consumption).

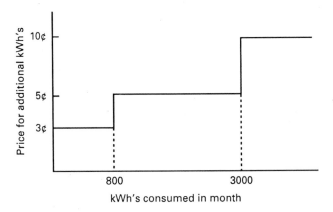

Figure 7.2
An inverted block-rate tariff

Block-rate tariffs and access/usage tariffs are not mutually exclusive concepts. In particular, the usage charge under access/usage tariffs can consist of block rates. In this case, a fixed monthly fee is charged and usage is priced in blocks. Local phone service is sometimes billed in this way. For example, it is increasingly common for local phone companies to charge a fixed monthly fee, allow a certain number of local calls per month (called an allowance) at no extra charge, and then levy a fee for each call above this allowance. In this case, usage is charged in inverted blocks, with the price in the first block being zero.

In much of the theoretical literature on multipart tariffs, an access/usage tariff is considered to be a type of block-rate tariff. Because the consumer cannot consume any of the product unless the access fee is paid, the price of the first unit of consumption can be viewed as the access fee plus the usage charge for one unit. For example, a tariff that consists of a $10 access fee and 5 cent usage charge can be viewed as a block-rate tariff with a charge of $10.05 for the first unit of consumption and 5 cents for each unit over one. This tariff is depicted in figure 7.3.

This equivalence between an access/usage fee and a block-rate tariff with two blocks is meaningful as long as the consumer would never choose to have access without consuming any units. Under an access/usage tariff the consumer is charged the access fee even if consumption is zero, while under a block-rate tariff the bill for zero consumption is necessarily zero. This distinction is important, for example, in

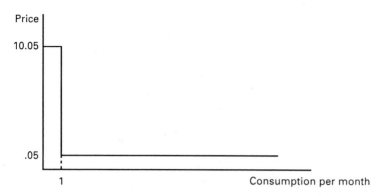

Figure 7.3
Access/usage tariff represented as a block-rate tariff

the case of phone service. A person might choose to have phone service (purchase access) and yet not make any calls. Any of several reasons could explain this choice: (1) having phone service allows the customer to receive incoming calls, even though no outgoing calls are made; (2) the customer might not know, when deciding to obtain service, whether it will want to make any calls during the upcoming period; (3) the customer might know that it will make no calls in the upcoming month (for example, the household might be going on vacation), but the cost of discontinuing service and then reconnecting after service is needed again is sufficiently high (in terms of time and any connect/disconnect charges that the phone company might levy) to prevent the customer from taking such action.

Generalizing from these reasons allows us to determine the conditions under which an access/usage tariff is equivalent to a block-rate tariff. The first reason given above for obtaining phone service without placing any calls is a simple case of externalities: the phone service provides an unpriced benefit, namely incoming calls. The second reason consists of the customer not knowing its demand; if the customer knew that its demand would be zero, it would (aside from the other reasons) choose not to have service and save the access fee. The third reason reflects transaction costs; if connecting and disconnecting were costless and effortless, then the customer that knew its demand and did not care about the externalities would choose service only for those periods when it knew it would use the service. The theoretical literature on multipart tariffs usually assumes (consistent with standard economic theory) that there are no externalities or transaction costs and that the customer knows its demand. Under these conditions, an access/usage tariff is behaviorally the same as a block-rate tariff. The fact that a consumer with access but no usage would be billed the access fee under the access/usage tariff and not billed at all under the block-rate tariff is irrelevant under these conditions, because no consumer would do such a thing. However, in situations in which any of these conditions does not hold, an access/usage tariff differs from a block-rate tariff: a consumer could reasonably choose access without having any usage in a period.

The following sections describe the welfare gains that can be obtained with multipart tariffs, the optimal prices under these tariffs, and regulatory mechanisms that induce the firm to charge these prices. Some concepts and results are more evident or relevant for access/usage tariffs, and others for block-rate tariffs. To exploit this fact, the two types of tariffs are discussed separately. Similarities, which are numerous and illuminating, are identified along the way.

The findings of the chapter can be summarized as follows:

1. When access demand is fixed, the optimal access/usage tariff consists of a usage charge equal to the marginal cost of usage and an access fee that is sufficiently high to allow the firm to break even. First-best optimality is achieved. This is called the "Coase result."

2. When access demand is fixed, the surplus subsidy schemes of chapter 6 can be used to attain first-best optimality through an access/usage tariff without direct subsidy. The firm is allowed to choose the usage price. The regulator sets an access fee based on the surplus the firm generates at that price. Essentially, the access fee becomes the method by which the regulator subsidizes the firm. Over time, the firm moves to a usage price equal to marginal cost, and the access fee is set to allow the firm to break even.

3. When access demand is price sensitive, the optimal access/usage fees are determined by the Ramsey rule. Usage is priced above its marginal cost (except in very rare circumstances), and the access fee is lower than it would be if access demand were fixed. Second-best optimality is attained.

4. With price-sensitive demand for access, the V-F mechanism described in chapter 5 can be used to attain the optimal access/usage tariff.

5. Under traditional assumptions about consumer behavior, the con-

sumer acquires access only if the surplus from usage exceeds the access fee.

6. For any N block tariff with prices in excess of marginal cost, an $N + 1$ block tariff can be designed that Pareto dominates the N block tariff. (An N block tariff is a tariff that consists of N number of blocks, such as a two-block tariff or a three-block tariff.)

7. The optimal (second-best) $N + 1$ block tariff attains greater surplus than the optimal (second-best) N block tariff if prices under the N block tariff exceed marginal cost. This result implies that surplus can be increased by increasing the number of blocks in the tariff until first-best optimality is attained.

8. Except in very rare circumstances, the optimal (second-best) block-rate tariff consists of declining blocks.

7.2   Access/Usage Tariffs

7.2.1   Fixed Access Demand: The Coase Result

Consider first a situation in which demand for access is fixed independent of the access fee (at least within the range of possible fees under consideration). For example, all households in a region might choose to have phone lines at any of the prices that the local phone company and its regulator are considering. In this case, the optimal access and usage charges are easy to determine. Recall that the first-best outcome results from pricing at marginal cost and subsidizing the firm for whatever losses it incurs at these prices when producing efficiently. Coase pointed out in 1946 that an access/usage tariff can be designed that "mimics" this first-best pricing and subsidy scheme. In particular: charge a usage fee that equals the marginal cost for usage, and set the access fee at whatever level is needed for the firm to break even when it minimizes costs. With usage priced at marginal cost, the first-best consumption levels are attained. And the access fee provides sufficient revenue to the firm such that it breaks even when minimizing costs. Because the firm would lose money if it does not minimize costs, it chooses to produce efficiently.

To be concrete, consider, for example, a phone company that faces fixed costs of $1 million (to construct a phone network) and a constant marginal cost of 5 cents (to provide a call on the network). If the number of customers that obtain phone service is fixed at 100,000, the

Coase result states that the optimal access fee is $10 (the $1 million cost of the network divided by 100,000 customers) and the optimal usage charge is 5 cents. The access fee covers the cost of the network and the usage charge covers the cost of the calls on the network.[3]

This access/usage tariff is equivalent to charging marginal cost for usage and subsidizing the firm for its fixed costs. The access fee is the mechanism for providing this subsidy. With access demand fixed, the access fee is simply a transfer of funds with no consumption implications. The fact that the access fee does not affect consumption and therefore constitutes a pure transfer is the basic reason that first-best optimality can be attained.

7.2.2   Price-Sensitive Access Demand

Usually, access demand is not fixed, but rather varies, at least somewhat, on the basis of price. This fact is the basis for much of the pricing structure of telecommunication services, certainly prior to deregulation. Since the original establishment of the Bell system, one of the primary goals of local regulators has been to promote "universal service," which is expressed colloquially as "a phone in every home." This goal has been pursued through pricing strategies for local and long-distance service that maintain relatively low monthly charges for local access, so that as many households as possible are able and willing to purchase access.[4] Implicit in this approach is the idea that access demand is price sensitive: low monthly charges for access increases the number of households with phone service; conversely, raising the monthly charge reduces the demand for access.[5]

---

3. In the more general situation, marginal cost is not constant but varies with the level of production. In these cases, the optimal usage fee is the fee at which the marginal-cost curve intersects the demand curve for usage, and the optimal access fee is the firm's losses at this price divided by the number of customers.

4. Because of deregulation, the term "local access" has also been used to describe long-distance carriers' access to the local network. In this chapter, however, the term refers consistently to access from the customer's perspective, such that local access means acquiring of a phone line.

5. Given the importance of the concept of universal service in the regulation of local phone service, it is not surprising that a considerable body of empirical work has been directed toward determining the price elasticity of phone lines (that is, access). See for example the survey by Taylor (1980). Although the estimated elasticities vary over time and geographic regions (as one would expect), the general finding seems to be that price elasticity for access, while not zero, is fairly low. This result implies that, while

When access demand is not fixed, the access fee cannot be treated simply as a subsidy mechanism with no consumption implications. Raising the access charge involves a surplus loss because some consumers will be induced to forego phone service in the face of the higher price. This fact needs to be incorporated into the determination of optimal prices.

Identifying the optimal access and usage charges when access demand is price sensitive is actually quite straightforward. Instead of thinking of the firm as providing one good (e.g., phone service), we can think of the firm as providing two goods: access and usage. For example, in the case of local phone service, the phone company provides phone lines and calls on these phone lines. A person can choose whether or not to purchase a phone line and, given the line, whether or not to place calls. The two goods have separate, though interrelated, demands; and there is a marginal cost associated with each good separately. For example, the demand for phone lines is different from the demand for calls, though the two are related (because calls can be made only if a line is purchased and a line will be purchased more readily if the consumer anticipates making calls). From the company's perspective, there is a marginal cost for adding a phone line to the local phone network, and there is a marginal cost of providing a call on the network.

First-best optimality is attained by setting the access fee equal to the marginal cost of access and the usage fee equal to the marginal cost of usage. Generally, however, this would result in losses for the natural monopolist. The question becomes: what are the optimal access and usage fees when the firm is required to break even?

Chapter 4 identified the second-best prices for a two-good natural monopolist when the firm cannot be subsidized: Ramsey prices. The optimal access and usage fees that allow the firm to remain solvent are therefore those consistent with the Ramsey rule. Letting subscripts a denote access and u denote usage, the Ramsey rule in this situation becomes (see section 4.5)

$$\left(\frac{P_a - MC_a}{P_a}\right) \cdot (\epsilon_a - \epsilon_{ua}) = \left(\frac{P_u - MC_u}{P_u}\right) \cdot (\epsilon_u - \epsilon_{au}), \qquad (7.1)$$

where

---

in actuality access demand is price sensitive, treating access demand as fixed and using the Coase result for pricing might be acceptably accurate.

ϵ_a is the elasticity of access with respect to the access fee;
ϵ_{ua} is the elasticity of usage with respect to access fee;
ϵ_u is the elasticity of usage with respect to usage fee; and
ϵ_{ua} is the elasticity of access with respect to usage fee.[6]

The Ramsey rule in this situation states that the percent by which the access fee is raised above the marginal cost of access, multiplied by the "net" elasticity for the access fee, is the same as for the usage fee. This rule can be used to calculate the second-best access and usage fee, with the methods described in section 4.4.

In special situations, the Ramsey rule reduces to a simpler expression. For example, when access demand is fixed, the Ramsey rule reduces to the Coase result. That is, the Ramsey rule under this condition states that the optimal usage fee is the marginal cost of usage and the optimal access fee is whatever fee is necessary to allow the firm to break even. To see this, rewrite equation (7.1) with all the elasticities relating to access being zero, to represent the fact that access demand is fixed independent of price:[7]

$$((P_a - MC_a)/P_a)\cdot(0) = ((P_u - MC_u)/P_u)\cdot(\epsilon_u), \text{ or,}$$
$$0 = (P_u - MC_u)/P_u)\cdot(\epsilon_u). \tag{7.2}$$

The only way this equation can hold is for the percent increase in usage fee over its marginal cost to be zero; that is, for P_u to be set equal to MC_u. With the usage fee at marginal cost, the firm breaks even only if the access fee is raised sufficiently. Note that equation (7.2) holds no matter how high the access fee is raised, because the percent increase in the access fee is multiplied by zero. In short, the Ramsey rule implies the Coase result when access demand is fixed.

---

6. The cross-elasticities can be zero, but in general are not. For example, because calls can be made only if a phone line is acquired, the monthly charge (that is, access fee) indirectly affects the number of calls placed through its impact on the number of lines acquired. Similarly, with a high enough per-call charge, the customer might realize that it will make no calls and hence need not pay to acquire a phone line. Hence the usage fee can affect the demand for access.

7. The same-price elasticity ϵ_a is clearly zero. The cross-price elasticity ϵ_{ua} is also zero, because, if access demand is fixed, changes in the usage fee do not affect access demand. The fact that ϵ_{au} is also zero is less evident. Though it has not been stated so far, the elasticities in the Ramsey rule relate to compensated demand rather than uncompensated demand. A basic result from microeconomic theory is that cross-elasticities of the compensated demands for two goods are equal. Consequently, ϵ_{au} is necessarily zero if ϵ_{ua} is zero. This distinction between compensated and uncompensated demand has not been made in the text because it adds a layer of complication that we have found does not translate into sufficiently greater insight to warrant burdening readers.

When access demand is not fixed but rather is price sensitive, the Ramsey rule requires that (except in rare cases)[8] the usage fee be set above its marginal cost. With the usage fee above marginal cost, revenues from marginal usage exceed the cost of providing that usage; as a result, the additional revenues needed for the firm to break even are not entirely generated by the access fee. The access fee can therefore be lower than in the Coase situation. Stated succinctly: when access demand is price sensitive, the optimal access fee is lower and the optimal usage fee is higher than when access demand is fixed.

The first-best outcome is not attained when access demand is price sensitive and the firm is required to break even, unlike the situation with fixed access. The reason for this is clear. When access demand is price sensitive, the access fee cannot serve simply as a subsidy mechanism; it also affects access demand and, indirectly, usage. This fact gives additional insight to the Ramsey rule. Ramsey pricing results in the second-best outcome in general; this second-best outcome becomes the same as the first-best outcome when the demand for one good is fixed.

A result opposite to that of Coase is obtained when usage demand is fixed, rather than access demand. In this case, the Ramsey rule becomes

$$((P_a - MC_a)/P_a) \cdot \epsilon_a = 0. \tag{7.3}$$

This equation holds only if $P_a = MC_a$, that is, if the access fee is set equal to the marginal cost of access. The usage fee is then set sufficiently high to allow the firm to break even.

This result has some important implications. Regulated monopolists in many settings do not charge access fees; electricity and natural gas are examples. This practice of charging usage fees that allow the firm to break even but no access fee is optimal only if the demand for usage is fixed and the marginal cost of access is zero. However, usage demand can nearly always be expected to be more price sensitive than access demand, simply because usage is conditional on access. Surplus gains can therefore be expected from moving toward more reli-

---

8. It is interesting to note that the optimal usage price can actually be below marginal cost in particular circumstances. If $\epsilon_u - \epsilon_{au}$ has an opposite sign from $\epsilon_a - \epsilon_{ua}$, then equation (7.1) holds when $P_u - MC_u$ is negative. This event occurs if the cross-elasticity of demand between access and usage exceeds (in magnitude) the access elasticity but not the usage elasticity. This event is highly unlikely in reality.

ance on access fees, a practice that is starting, for commercial and industrial customers at least, in electricity sales.[9]

7.2.3 Regulatory Mechanisms for Optimal Access/Usage Tariffs

Chapter 5 identified a regulatory mechanism that induces the firm to charge Ramsey prices in equilibrium, namely, Vogelsang-Finsinger (V-F) regulation. Because the second-best access and usage fees are simply the Ramsey prices for these two goods, V-F regulation can be imposed to induce the firm to charge these access and usage fees in equilibrium. The regulation takes the form of allowing the firm in each period to charge whatever usage and access fees it chooses as long as these fees, when multiplied by the past period's access and usage quantities, equal the last period's costs. That is, in period t, the firm is allowed to charge any access and usage fees that satisfy

$$P_a^t \, Q_a^{t-1} + P_u^t \, Q_u^{t-1} \le C^{t-1}, \tag{7.4}$$

where Q_a is the quantity of access (for example, number of phone lines), Q_u is the quantity of usage (for example, number of phone calls), and C is the cost of providing both access and usage.

As shown in chapter 5, the application of this type of regulation induces the firm to move over time to the second-best access and usage fees. While the firm might waste during its movement to equilibrium, once equilibrium has been reached the firm will produce efficiently at the second-best prices.

It is important to note that V-F regulation is applicable whether access demand is fixed or price sensitive. Recall that when access demand is fixed, the Ramsey rule implies the same prices as the Coase result, namely, usage priced at its marginal cost and access demand priced sufficiently high for the firm to break even. First-best optimality is attained, with the access fee providing the necessary subsidy for the firm. V-F regulation, which results in Ramsey prices in equilibrium, therefore achieves the Coase result and first-best optimality when access demand is fixed. When access demand is price sensitive, the Ramsey prices, and hence V-F regulation, attain second-best optimality.

---

9. Charging access fees for electricity might prevent some consumers from being able to purchase any electricity. While surplus will still increase, the hardship imposed on these consumers might be considered sufficiently inequitable to warrant foregoing these gains.

If access demand is fixed, other regulatory mechanisms can also be used by the regulator to induce the first-best outcome. In chapter 6, several surplus subsidy schemes are described that induce the first-best outcome in equilibrium. These procedures (at least those of Loeb/Magat and Sappington/Sibley) bring the firm to equilibrium more quickly than V-F regulation and with no waste on the way. With demand for access fixed, access/usage tariffs can provide a means for implementing these procedures.

Recall that under the surplus subsidy schemes, the regulator allows the firm to set its own price and then subsidizes the firm on the basis of the price that the firm charges. The need to subsidize the firm often constitutes a practical barrier to the implementation of these schemes. In particular, there is often no mechanism by which the regulator can subsidize a firm. Traditionally, regulators are not legally able to tax the population and use the generated revenues to subsidize public utilities. More fundamentally, if regulators were allowed to raise revenues for subsidies, they nevertheless would face the problem of how to generate revenues without distorting consumption patterns.

The dilemma can be solved by the use of access/usage tariffs. Recall that when access demand is fixed, the access fee serves simply as a transfer of funds from consumers to the firm, with no effect on consumption. The access fee can therefore provide the means by which the regulator subsidizes the firm for a surplus subsidy scheme.

In particular, the regulator can mandate that customers be billed under an access/usage tariff, with the firm free to choose the usage price in each period but not the access fee. Using the firm's chosen usage price, the regulator calculates the subsidy that the firm should be paid under whichever surplus subsidy scheme the regulator wishes to apply. The regulator can then set the access fee in each period to be this subsidy divided by the number of customers demanding access. The access fee generates the subsidy for the firm through the firm's bills to its customers, without the regulator needing to raise funds itself or pay a subsidy directly. That is, the regulator, within its traditionally defined role of approving tariffs, can institute a regulatory mechanism that is equivalent to subsidizing the firm.

When demand for access is fixed, this use of access fees to generate subsidies is appropriate, because the level of the access fee does not affect consumption patterns. If, however, access demand is not fixed, then the access fee does not constitute a pure transfer and the consumption implications of changing the access fee must be considered.

7.2.4   Behavior of Consumers under Classic Assumptions

In the previous sections, we state that access and usage can be considered two goods with separate but interrelated demands. Under certain conditions it is possible to describe more precisely the relation between the demand for access and the demand for usage. This analysis provides insight to the consumer's choice process even in situations in which the conditions do not hold.

Consider a situation in which the assumptions of traditional economic theory, mentioned in section 7.1, hold. In particular, assume that the customer knows its demand for usage and that there are no externalities or transaction costs involved in access. Our task is to determine, for any given usage and access fees, whether or not a customer will choose to acquire access and its level of usage conditional on this choice.

Figure 7.4 depicts a case in which the consumer's demand for calls is linear (to make the arithmetic simple). The y-intercept of the demand curve is 90 cents, meaning that, if calls were charged at 90 cents each, the consumer would choose not to make any calls. Suppose the phone company charges $15 per month (the access fee) and 10 cents per call. The question is: will the consumer choose to have a phone line and, if so, how many calls will be placed? Consider the two options available to the customer:

1.   Acquire Service
If the customer acquires a phone line, the customer will place 150 calls a month, as indicated by the demand curve at 10 cents per call. These calls provide surplus to the customer, because for all but the last call the customer is willing to pay more than 10 cents for the call. The total consumer surplus from the calls is the shaded area in the graph, which equals $60 ($150 \cdot (.9-.1) \cdot (1/2)$). The phone line costs $15 per month: the customer must pay this in order to make calls and receive the $60 of surplus from calling. On net, the customer would obtain surplus of $45 from acquiring a phone line (the $60 surplus from the calls minus the $15 cost of the phone line).

2.   Do Not Acquire Service
If the customer does not acquire a line, the customer will incur no costs but will also obtain no surplus, because no calls can be placed.

Given the choice of $45 extra surplus with a line and no gain with-

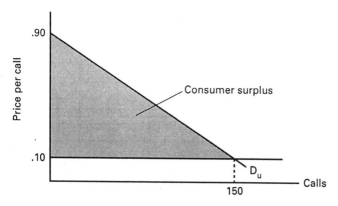

Figure 7.4
Interrelated demand for access and usage

out a line, the customer in this case will choose to acquire the line. Stated succinctly, the consumer acquires access if the surplus generated by usage, given the usage fee, exceeds the access fee, and foregoes access otherwise.

These concepts can be used to compare the behavior of consumers with different usage demands and to clarify the impacts of changes in access and usage fees. Consider, for example, a customer with lower demand, as depicted in figure 7.5. At 10 cents per call, this customer would make only forty calls in a month. The surplus from these calls would be only $12. Because the cost of acquiring a line ($15) is greater than the surplus the customer would obtain from making calls on the line, this customer will choose not to acquire a line.[10]

Consider now the impact of changes in usage and access fees on the demand for access and usage, using the customer depicted in figure 7.4 as illustration. If the access fee is raised, but not above the $60 of surplus the consumer obtains from calls, then the consumer continues to acquire service and place 150 calls. That is, usage is unaffected by a change in the access fee as long as the access fee is below the consumer's surplus from usage. The only effect of the access fee in this range is a transfer of funds from the customer to the

10. Recall that we have assumed that there are no externalities or transaction costs and that the customer knows its demand. If any of these assumptions does not hold, the consumer in this situation might nevertheless choose to acquire a line. For example, the consumer might expect to obtain more than $3 worth of benefit from incoming calls, such that the surplus from usage and the value of the externalities (incoming calls) exceeds the cost of acquiring the line.

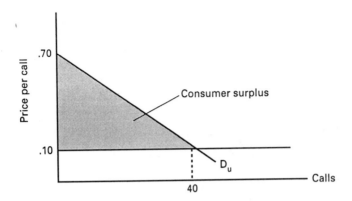

Figure 7.5
Consumer chooses not to acquire line

firm.[11] However, if the access fee is raised above $60, then the customer chooses to forego service and make no calls. Consumption drops to zero when the access fee exceeds the surplus obtained from usage.

The fact that the customer foregoes service when the access fee is too high creates a discontinuity in the relation between the access fee and the quantity of usage demand. Usage is positive and constant as long as the access fee is below the consumer's surplus from usage and is zero for any higher access fee. In our example, usage demand is 150 for access fees below $60 and zero for access fees above $60.

Consider now the usage fee. Raising the usage fee decreases, of course, the quantity of usage demanded. For example, as shown in figure 7.6, if the per-call charge is raised from 10 to 18 cents, then the customer will place only 135 calls instead of 150. The higher usage charge, however, also affects the surplus from usage and thereby can affect whether the customer acquires service. With a usage fee of 18 cents, the surplus from usage is $48.60 ($135 \cdot (.90 - .18)/2$). Because this surplus exceeds the access fee of $15, the customer will continue to acquire service when the usage charge is raised to 18 cents.

However, if the usage charge is raised high enough, the surplus from usage will shrink sufficiently that the customer will no longer choose to acquire service. At a per-call charge of 50 cents, the surplus that the customer obtains from usage is exactly $15 ($75 \cdot (.90 - .50)/2$).

11. Raising the access fee decreases the consumer's available income. If the consumer's usage demand depends on income, usage demand will be affected by the change in access fee. However, this is a second-order, and usually very small, effect.

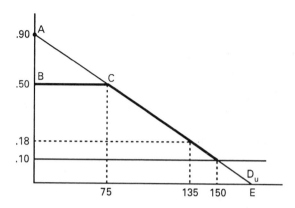

Figure 7.6
Impact of raising usage fee

Therefore, if the usage fee is raised above 50 cents, the customer will choose to forego service and make no calls. The demand for calls is therefore zero for any usage price above 50 cents.

Because of this phenomenon, two curves are relevant for the demand for usage. One curve is the demand for usage *conditional* on service being acquired. This curve is the line *ACE* in figure 7.6 and represents the quantity of usage that would be demanded at any usage fee provided the consumer chooses to acquire access. The other curve is the demand for usage given the consumer's choice process regarding access and the fee for access. This curve is the kinked line *ABCE*: zero for usage fees above 50 cents (because the consumer chooses not to acquire service when the usage fee is this high) and the same as the conditional demand curve for usage fees below 50 cents (because the consumer chooses to acquire service at these prices).

The situation of access demand being fixed can be viewed in the context of this discussion. Access demand is fixed only if surplus from usage is sufficiently large for each consumer that changes in access and usage fees (at least within the relevant range) do not induce any consumer to forego service. In this case, the access fee can be raised as much as necessary without the detrimental effects of consumers foregoing service. The optimal prices therefore consist of the usage fee at marginal cost and the access fee at the level needed for the firm to break even.

7.2.5   Empirical Example of Access and Usage Charges

Local phone companies have traditionally charged a fixed monthly fee for a phone line and allowed an unlimited number of local calls to be placed on the line at no extra charge. As stated in section 7.1, this type of access/usage tariff, under which the usage charge is zero, is called flat-rate service.

We know, however, that the optimal usage fee equals the marginal cost of usage if access demand is fixed, and (except in rare cases) exceeds marginal cost if access demand is price sensitive. Because the marginal cost of a local call is above zero, flat-rate service results in an inefficiently large amount of calling. With the price of a call below marginal cost, consumers make calls whose value is less than the marginal cost of the call. Furthermore, if access demand is price sensitive, flat-rate service results in fewer consumers obtaining phone lines than is optimal, because the price of access is higher than optimal.

Because of these and other considerations, local phone companies in many areas are introducing measured service, under which local calls are charged on a per-call and/or per-minute basis. The revenues generated by these usage charges allow the firm to provide service at a lower monthly access fee.

In considering flat-rate and measured service, the central issue is essentially empirical: does a shift from flat-rate to measured service actually increase consumer surplus, and, if so, by how much? Theory implies that surplus increases.[12] However, theory cannot determine the size of the gain. The gain might not be sufficiently large to warrant the disruption caused by the change in tariff.

Train (1989) investigated empirically the impact that a shift from flat-rate to measured service for local phone calls would have on consumer and producer surplus. Because both flat-rate and measured service are access/usage tariffs, the study is essentially an analysis of the surplus impact of moving from a usage fee of zero and a high access fee to the optimal usage and access charges. The investigation provides estimates of the potential surplus gains that can be obtained

---

12. If there are costs associated with measurement (for example, the cost to the phone company of keeping records on local calls to use in billing customers), surplus need not increase: the gains from pricing nearer marginal cost might be less than the cost of billing for usage.

from moving from zero to positive usage fees when the standard economic assumptions are satisfied.

Train's analysis is restricted in several ways. (1) The empirical demand model and calculation of surplus are specific to residential customers of the phone company in one particular area and are not necessarily generalizable to other areas. (2) The implementation of measured service requires that the phone company keep track of each customer's usage so that the customer can be billed appropriately. The company must incur costs for this accounting that it would not have to incur under flat-rate service. Train's analysis assumes that these costs are sufficiently small as not to affect the calculation of optimal prices under measured service. (3) Demand for access is considered fixed, such that the shift from flat-rate to measured service is assumed not to affect the number of consumers that acquire phone service. This assumption was necessitated by limitations of the empirical demand model, which predicts demand conditional on the consumer having a phone line and does not examine the choice of whether to acquire a line.

Because of these restrictions, the numerical results are not to be taken as prescriptions for particular rates. Rather, the analysis is useful in elucidating the types of trade-offs that need to be considered in a comparison of flat-rate and measured service in any setting, and in providing an indication of the orders of magnitude of the surplus losses and gains that are involved in these trade-offs.

For his analysis, Train borrowed a previously estimated model of the demand for calls (Train, McFadden, and Ben-Akiva 1987). He obtained cost information from the local phone company. With these data, he simulated the revenues, costs, and consumer surplus that would occur under various usage and access fees. Simulations were performed with a per call charge of zero cents (which represents flat-rate service), 1 cent, 2 cents, and so on up to 12 cents. At each usage charge, the access charge was derived that allows the phone company to break even.[13] Consumer surplus was then calculated.

The consumer surplus generated at each usage fee is given in the third column of table 7.1. A usage fee of zero constitutes flat-rate ser-

---

13. Because demand for phone lines was assumed to be fixed, the access charge was determined for each usage charge by: (1) determining the net operating profits (revenues from usage minus variable costs of providing usage), (2) subtracting these net operating profits from the portion of fixed costs that must be covered by residential local service, and (3) dividing this difference by the number of phone lines.

Table 7.1
Access/usage fees for local phone service

Usage price (cents per call)	Access fee that allows firm to break even (dollars per month)	Change in consumer surplus (dollars per household per month)	
		Under traditional assumption	With flat-rate bias
0	10.48	0[a]	0[a]
1	9.06	0.73	−1.17
2	7.97	1.25	−3.70
3	7.13	1.56	−5.84
4	6.46	1.77	−8.11
5	5.90	1.93	−10.43
6	5.13	2.02	−12.81
7	5.03	2.05	−15.23
8	4.67	2.07	−17.68
9	4.35	2.08	−20.16
10	4.06	2.07	−22.64
11	3.80	2.05	−25.15
12	3.55	2.02	−27.62

a. Flat-rate service is taken as base for comparison.

vice. The access fee associated with a zero usage fee is $10.48. This situation is taken as the base when comparing consumer surplus under measured rates (that is, under nonzero usage charges). The optimal usage fee (that is, the fee that provides the greatest consumer surplus) is about 9 cents per call. The access charge that allows the firm to cover its costs at this usage fee is $4.35. The cost information provided by the phone company indicates that a call of average duration costs about 9 cents to provide. The optimal prices therefore correspond to the Coase result, which states that when access demand is fixed, the optimal tariff consists of pricing usage at marginal cost (i.e., 9 cents) and setting the access fee sufficiently high to cover fixed costs.[14]

Consumer surplus was estimated to increase by an average of $2.08 per household at the 9 cent usage fee compared to flat-rate service. This is a fairly large increase, considering that households pay $10.48

14. The marginal cost of a call is probably lower than 9 cents in actuality. The analysis therefore probably overestimates the surplus benefits to be obtained from measured service.

per month under flat-rate service. It is interesting, however, that over half of these benefits are obtained at a usage price of 2 cents and over 90% are obtained at a price of 5 cents. These sharply declining returns suggest that a politically constrained regulator can implement "compromise prices" (that is, usage charges above zero but below marginal cost) and be assured that a large portion of the potential benefits are being obtained. More precisely, a compromise price that is a given percent of the marginal cost will obtain considerably more than that percent of the potential benefits.

The foregoing results were obtained under the standard economic assumptions regarding consumer behavior (namely, that demand is known and there are no externalities or transaction costs). There are reasons to believe, however, that consumers do not behave in accordance with these assumptions. In fact, the demand analysis of Train, McFadden, and Ben-Akiva (1987), which served as the basis for Train's work, suggests that consumers behave differently. In particular, these researchers found that consumers seem to value flat-rate service over measured service even when the bill that the consumer would receive under the two services, given the number of calls the consumer places, would be the same. This finding requires some elaboration. Suppose a consumer places a certain number of calls during a month. Under flat-rate service, the consumer is billed only the flat monthly fee for service. Suppose rates under measured service are set such that the consumer receives exactly the same bill as under flat-rate service. This measured service necessarily entails a lower fixed monthly fee to offset the usage charge, such that the total bill ends up the same. In this situation, the empirical analysis indicates that consumers strongly prefer the flat-rate service, even though the two cost the same. This phenomenon is called the "flat-rate bias," and has been found in many studies of local phone service.

The existence of this bias is problematical. Standard theory of consumer behavior does not incorporate it. According to this theory, if a consumer makes the same number of calls and pays the same bill under two different tariffs, the consumer's surplus is the same in both cases. (The benefits to the consumer are the same because the same number of calls are made, and the amount the consumer must pay to receive those benefits is the same. Therefore, the surplus, which is the difference between benefits and costs, is also the same.) However, empirically, consumers have been found to prefer flat-rate service over measured service in this situation, indicating that, contrary to theory, their welfare is higher under flat-rate service.

There are many possible explanations for this bias. The bias could reflect inertia. Flat-rate service is traditional, and consumers might prefer it simply because they are accustomed to it. Alternatively, the bias might reflect risk-avoidance. If the consumer does not know its demand exactly, then the consumer bears a risk under measured service that does not exist with flat-rate service. Under flat-rate service, the consumer's bill is fixed independent of how many calls are made. However, under measured service, the consumer does not know beforehand how large the phone bill will be. In fact, the bill will fluctuate from month to month depending on the number of calls made. A risk-avoiding consumer will therefore prefer flat-rate service over measured service even if on average the two cost the same.

The calculation of the impacts of a shift from flat-rate to measured service depends critically on how the bias toward flat-rate service is treated. If the bias is considered to result from inertia, such that it disappears in the long run when consumers eventually adjust to new circumstances, it can perhaps be ignored in the calculation of consumer surplus. This is the approach taken by Train for the results presented above. Alternatively, if the bias is considered to reflect risk avoidance, then it constitutes a legitimate aspect of consumer welfare and should be included in the calculations. A shift from flat-rate to measured service increases the risk that consumers bear, and this risk (in itself) reduces the welfare of consumers.

To investigate the impact of this bias on optimal prices, Train also simulated consumer surplus with the flat-rate bias included in the calculation of consumer surplus. The results are given in the fourth column of table 7.1. As the figures indicate, flat-rate service generates greater surplus than measured service under *any* strictly positive usage price. This implies that, if the bias that is evident in consumer's choices in the real world reflects risk-avoidance or some other factor that truly affects consumer welfare, a switch from flat-rate to measured service is not advisable. This conclusion runs counter to the standard concept that total surplus increases as prices move toward marginal costs. (It also suggests the importance of expanding pricing theory to explicitly account for the possibility of uncertainty in demand and risk avoidance by consumers.)

The overall conclusions of Train's study can be summarized. If the bias toward flat-rate service that is observed in consumers' choices is considered to constitute a real component of consumer surplus, a move from flat-rate to measured service would be inadvisable, because the evidence indicates that it will decrease consumer surplus, perhaps considerably. However, if the bias is considered not to be a real part of consumer surplus, then measured service offers the potential for significant gains for consumers. The gains rise at a sharply decreasing rate as the usage fee is raised toward marginal cost. As a result, a regulator can obtain a large share of the potential gains without raising price all the way to marginal cost.

7.3 Block Rates

Before describing the welfare implications of block rates, we first examine the behavior of customers under these tariffs.

7.3.1 Declining Block Rates: Outlay Schedule and Budget Constraint

The choice process of the consumer under declining block rates is, in the most basic characteristics, the same as in the standard situation of one price for each good, namely: the consumer maximizes utility subject to a budget constraint. The only difference is that with declining block rates the budget constraint is shaped differently than with one price.

To identify the budget constraint under declining block rates, consider, as a specific example, the tariff for electricity that was used in section 7.1: 7 cents per kWh for up to 1,000 kWhs per month, 5 cents for each kWh between 1,000 and 2,500 per month, and 4 cents for each kWh over 2,500. Panel (a) of figure 7.7 depicts the price schedule for this tariff. The bill that a consumer would receive for any level of consumption is computed directly from this price schedule. The relation between consumption and the bill a consumer would receive is called the "outlay schedule," because it represents the necessary "outlay" by the consumer for each level of consumption. Panel (b) gives the outlay schedule of this tariff. Outlay starts at zero for no consumption of electricity and increases at a rate of 7 cents per kWh up to 1,000 kWh. At this point, outlay is $70. After 1,000, outlay increases at the rate of 5 cents per kWh up to an outlay of $145 for 2,500 kWhs (which consists of $70 for the first 1,000 kWhs and $75 for the next 1,500 kWhs). After 2,500 kWhs, outlay increases at 4 cents per kWh.

The consumer's budget constraint is derived from the outlay sched-

Tariff: 7¢ for 0–1000 kWh's
          5¢ for 1000–2500 kWh's
          4¢ for 2500+ kWh's

(a) Price schedule

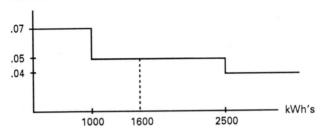

(b) Outlay schedule

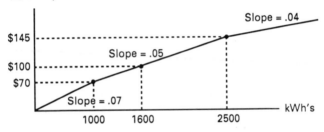

(c) Budget constraint

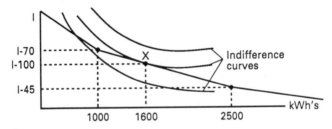

Figure 7.7
Schedule for a declining block tariff

ule. To allow the graph to be shown in two dimensions, suppose the consumer has a choice between two goods: electricity and a composite good called "other goods." The price of other goods is considered to be $1, by normalization. The budget constraint gives the combinations of electricity and other goods that the consumer can afford, given its income. If the consumer buys no electricity, then it can spend its entire income, denoted I, on other goods. The y-intercept of the budget constraint is therefore I units, because the price of other goods is $1. For consumption of electricity between zero and 1,000 kWhs, the consumer must forego 0.07 units of other goods to obtain 1 kWh of electricity. The slope of the budget constraint is therefore $-.07$ until electricity consumption reaches 1,000, at which point the consumer obtains only $I - 70$ units of other goods. For 1,000 to 2,500 kWhs of consumption, the consumer must forego 0.05 units of other goods to obtain one extra kWh, giving a slope of $-.05$ for the budget constraint in this range. And so on.

The consumer chooses the point on the budget constraint that provides the greatest utility. The consumer's preferences for electricity and other goods are, as usual, represented by the consumer's indifference mapping. The consumer chooses the point on the budget constraint that attains the highest possible indifference curve. Given the mapping shown in panel (c), the consumer chooses point X, which corresponds to 1,600 kWhs of electricity and $I - 100$ units of other goods. The consumer's electricity bill in this case is $100.

The consumer's decision process can also be represented in terms of demand curves. The most straightforward situation is depicted in panel (a) of figure 7.8. The price schedule is obtained directly from the tariff. The consumer's demand curve is derived from the indifference mapping.[15] The consumer purchases additional electricity until

---

15. To be completely accurate, it is necessary to assume that demand is independent of income, at least within the range of income that is relevant. By definition, the demand curve gives that quantity of electricity that the consumer would choose, given the consumer's income, at any particular level of the price for the good. As such, the demand curve is derived under the concept that there is one price for the good. With block-rate tariffs, there is more than one price. The difference between marginal and inframarginal prices under a block-rate tariff constitutes an income transfer from the consumer to the firm. This fact is demonstrated in the text to follow. It implies that a change in the marginal price changes the consumer's income, which, if demand is income sensitive, changes the demand curve. To maintain one demand curve in the graph, it is therefore necessary to assume that changes in income have no effect on the demand for electricity.

To avoid confusion, note that the change in income that results from a change in the

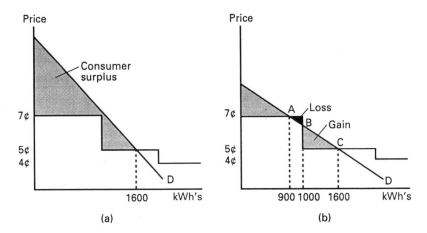

Figure 7.8
Demand curve and chosen consumption under declining block rates

the price for additional consumption, as given by the price schedule, equals the benefits of additional consumption, as given by the demand curve. This event occurs at 1,600 kWhs, consistent with the analysis based on indifference curve in figure 7.7. Consumer surplus is, by definition, the difference between the total benefits the consumer receives and the total amount the consumer pays. Total benefits is the area under the demand curve, and total outlay is the area under the price schedule. Consumer surplus is therefore the shaded area between the demand curve and the price schedule.

Because price declines as consumption rises, it is possible for the demand curve to intersect the price schedule at two or more points. Panel (b) of figure 7.8 is an example. Determining which point the consumer chooses in these situations requires an analysis of the surplus implications of the consumer's moving from one of these intersections to the next. Suppose the consumer is consuming at the first intersection, at 900 kWhs. The surplus at this level of consumption is the shaded area to the left of point *A*. The first question is: will the consumer's surplus increase or decrease by moving from *A* to the second intersection, *B*? The answer is clearly "decrease," because the

marginal price under a block-rate tariff occurs in addition to the standard income effect resulting from a price change in the standard one-price situation. The standard income effect represents a change in the buying power of a given nominal income. A change in the marginal price under a block-rate tariff results in a change in the nominal income itself.

value the consumer places on each kWh between A and B, as given by the demand curve, is less than the price that the consumer would have to pay for them, as given by the price schedule. Moving from A to B would decrease the consumer's surplus by the amount given in the deeply shaded area between these two points. The next question is: will the consumer's surplus increase or decrease by moving from A all the way to the third intersection, C? The consumer would lose the amount in the deeply shaded triangle by moving from A to B on the way to C. However, once the consumer reached the threshold for a lower price, additional consumption would be valued at more than this lower price and the consumer would obtain additional surplus. The lightly shaded area is the amount of additional surplus the consumer would obtain by moving to C once it had reached B. Moving from A to C would therefore entail a loss of the deeply shaded area and a gain of the lightly shaded area. Because, given the way the demand curve is drawn in this example, the gain exceeds the loss, the consumer would choose to consume at C instead of A (B is of course worse than either A or C).

Declining block tariffs have the peculiar characteristic that it is possible for the consumer to have two or more utility-maximizing consumption levels under these tariffs. Figure 7.9 illustrates this possibility. The consumer's indifference mapping could be such that the highest attainable indifference curve is tangent to the budget constraint at two points, as shown in panel (a). From a demand perspective, this phenomenon means that the demand curve intersects the price schedule at three points and that the the loss in moving from the first to the second intersection is the same in magnitude as the gain in moving from second to the third intersection. As a result, the first and third intersections provide exactly the same surplus.

It is interesting to note that a consumer with standard preferences would never choose to consume at a threshold of a declining block-rate tariff. Consider point T in panel (a) of figure 7.10. This point represents consumption at the threshold at which the price changes from 7 to 5 cents. For any smooth, convex (that is, inward-bending) indifference curves, point T could never be the point on the budget constraint that attains the highest indifference curve. Because indifference curves are smooth and the budget constraint is kinked at T, the indifference curve through T is necessarily below the budget constraint in some area around T. From T, the consumer could always move to a higher indifference curve by moving away from T. In the

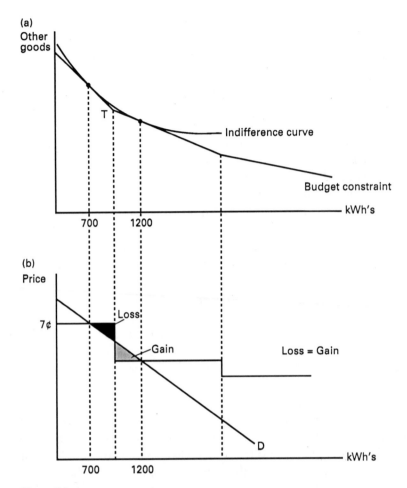

Figure 7.9
Two utility-maximizing consumption levels

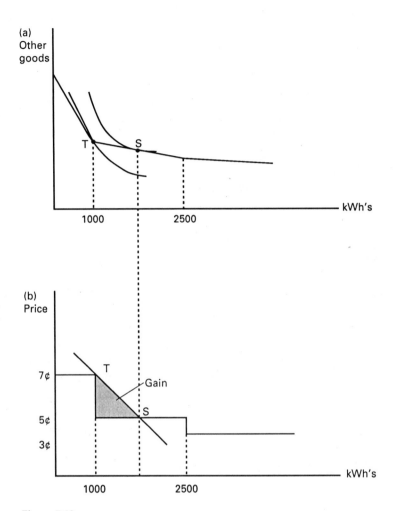

Figure 7.10
Consumer doesn't choose threshold

graph, for example, the consumer would move to S, at which an in-difference curve is tangent to the budget constraint.

Panel (b) depicts this situation in terms of the demand curve. If the demand curve intersects the price schedule at a threshold, such as point T, then it necessarily intersects at another point, such as S. Moving from the threshold to another intersection always entails an increase in surplus.

For each consumer, a block-rate tariff can be viewed as a access/usage tariff. That is, an access/usage tariff can be designed that provides the customer the same bill and the same marginal price as the block-rate tariff. Consider, as in figure 7.11, a consumer who consumes in the second block of a declining block tariff. Under the block-rate tariff, this person pays 7 cents for each of the first 1,000 kWhs and 5 cents for each additional kWh consumed in the second block. The total bill for 1,600 kWhs of electricity is $100 (.07 · 1,000 + .05 · 600). The marginal price the customer faces is 5 cents. An access/usage tariff can be designed under which the consumer would face the same bill and the same marginal price. Let the usage charge be the price in the second block (5 cents) to maintain the same marginal price for the consumer. Then set the access fee at the level necessary for the bill to be the same under the two tariffs. At 1,600 kWhs of consumption, the usage fee itself generates a bill of $80 (.05 · 1,600). Therefore an access fee of $20 provides the customer with a total bill of $100, the same as under the block rates. To summarize: a block-rate tariff with 7 cents for consumption up to 1,000 kWhs and 5 cents for consumption between 1,000 and 2,500 kWhs is "equivalent," for anyone consuming between 1,000 and 2,500 kWhs, to an access/usage tariff with an ac-

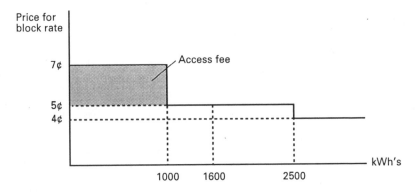

Figure 7.11
Relation of declining block rates to access/usage fees

cess fee of $20 and a usage charge of 5 cents. "Equivalent" in this context means that the customer faces the same bill and the same price at the margin.

The $20 access fee, which makes the two tariffs equivalent, can be visualized in figure 7.11. The first 1,000 kWhs are charged at 7 cents under the block-rate tariff and only 5 cents with the usage fee. The difference of 2 cents for each of the 1,000 kWhs gives the access fee of $20. That is, the access fee that makes the tariffs equivalent for this consumer is the difference between the inframarginal price (i.e., the price in the first block) and marginal price (in the second block) multiplied by the consumption in the first block.

For a consumer whose total consumption is in the third block, the equivalent access/usage tariff is different from that for a consumer in the second block, though it is calculated in the same way. The usage fee is the marginal price for the consumer, which is this case is the price in the third block: 4 cents. The access fee is the amount by which the first block price exceeds the marginal price (seven minus four) times consumption in this block (1,000 kWhs), plus the analogous amount for the second block $((.05 - .04) \cdot 1,500)$. That is, the access fee that makes the tariffs equivalent is $45.

For a consumer in the first block, the equivalent access/usage tariff consists of a usage fee of 7 cents and no access fee. Note that no one access/usage tariff is equivalent to a given block-rate tariff for all consumers. For those consumers whose consumption falls in the same block under the block-rate tariff, one access/usage tariff is equivalent. But for consumers in different blocks, the equivalent access/usage tariffs are different.

7.3.2   Inverted Block Rates

The choice process of consumers under inverted block rates is represented similarly to that for declining block rates. Figure 7.12 gives the price schedule, outlay schedule, and budget constraint for one such tariff. Opposite from declining blocks, each segment of the outlay schedule has a *greater* slope than the one before, reflecting the fact that the price increases with consumption. Similarly, each subsequent segment of the budget constraint is more steeply sloped. The consumer chooses the point on the budget constraint that attains the highest indifference curve.

Figure 7.13 depicts the choice process in terms of the demand curve. The consumer increases consumption whenever the value of addi-

Tariff: 3¢ for 0–800 kWh's
            5¢ for 800–3000 kWh's
            10¢ for 3000+ kWh's

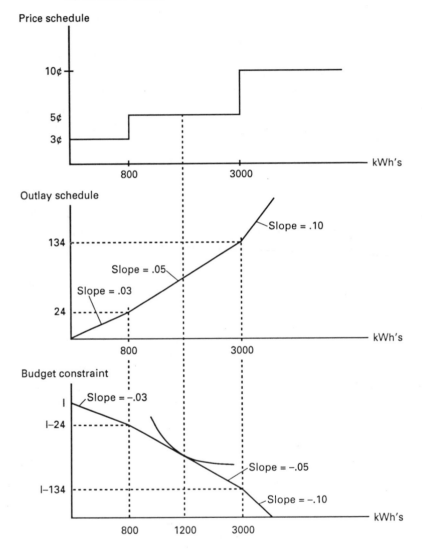

Figure 7.12
Schedules for an inverted block tariff

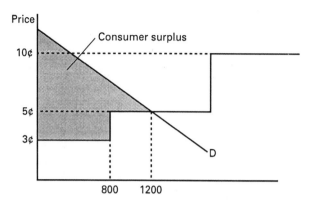

Figure 7.13
Demand curve and chosen consumption

tional consumption, as given by the demand curve, exceeds the price of additional consumption, as given by the price schedule. Consumer surplus is the area below the demand curve and above the price schedule.

While the choice process is essentially the same as for declining block rates, there are some important differences in implications. First, it is not possible under inverted block rates, unlike declining blocks, for utility to be maximized at two different points when indifference curves are convex. The budget constraint bends outward under inverted block rates (reflecting the fact that price becomes successively higher). It is not possible for an inward-bending indifference curve to be tangent to the outward-bending budget constraint at two different points. Visual inspection of panel (c) of figure 7.12 will verify this. The same conclusion can be drawn from the demand curve. Because the demand curve is downward sloping and the price schedule is upward sloping, they can intersect only once. Consequently, the situation depicted in figure 7.9 of multiple intersections under declining blocks cannot occur with inverted blocks.

Second, many consumers will choose to consume at a threshold under inverted blocks, unlike the situation with declining blocks, under which no consumer would choose a threshold. Figure 7.14 illustrates this fact. A consumer with demand curve D_1 will choose to consume 800 kWhs of electricity, which is the first threshold. A consumer with higher demand, at D_2, would also choose this threshold level of consumption. In a standard situation of one price for each

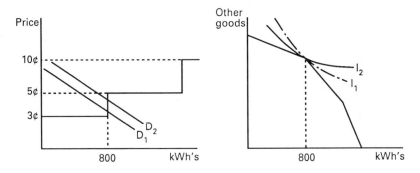

Figure 7.14
Consumer often chooses threshold: "collection point"

good, a consumer with greater demand will consume more of the good. However, the kink in the price schedule for inverted blocks creates a region in which demand can vary and yet consumption remains at the threshold level. As a result, in a population with heterogeneous demand, more consumers (in theory at least) consume at the threshold than at any single other level. In recognition of this phenomenon, the thresholds in inverted block tariffs are called "collection points," because consumers with different demands "collect" there.

The phenomenon can also be seen in terms of the budget constraint and indifference mapping. For any one consumer, the highest indifference curve can often be reached at a kink in the budget constraint, which corresponds to a threshold in the price schedule. Two consumers with different preferences, as represented by indifference curves I_1 and I_2, will both choose the threshold level of consumption. This result is contrary to the standard analysis with one price for each good, in which differences in preferences lead to different levels of consumption.

The third difference between inverted and declining block tariffs relates to their equivalence to access/usage tariffs. In some sense, access/usage tariffs cannot be constructed that are equivalent to inverted block tariffs. Because inframarginal prices are less than marginal prices under an inverted block tariff, the access fee would have to be negative for an access/usage tariff to be equivalent to an inverted block tariff. That is, the access fee would have to be a credit on the consumer's bill offsetting the charges for usage. If a negative access fee is considered infeasible or contrary to the definition of an access/usage tariff, then the equivalence that exists between declining block and access/usage tariffs does not carry over to inverted block tariffs.

7.3.3 Optimal Block-Rate Tariffs

In this section we first describe the optimal prices and thresholds for a block-rate tariff with a given number of blocks. We then show that increasing the number of blocks in a tariff has the potential to raise surplus in most situations. Because a uniform price (one price for all levels of consumption) is essentially a block-rate tariff with only one block, this result implies that surplus can usually be improved by moving from a uniform price to a block-rate tariff with two or more blocks. *Throughout this discussion, the optimal tariff is considered to be the tariff that provides the greatest consumer surplus while allowing the firm to break even.* For a natural monopolist, the optimal tariff defined in this way does not usually attain the first-best outcome because some price must exceed marginal cost for the firm to break even. We will show, however, that under some circumstances, even the first-best outcome can be achieved with block-rate tariffs.

1. The Optimal Two-Block Tariff
A two-block tariff consists of two prices (one for each block) and the threshold that identifies the consumption levels at which the price changes. Our task is to determine the optimal threshold and the optimal price in each block.

Given a threshold, the optimal prices for the two blocks are essentially Ramsey prices. Consumption up to the threshold and consumption beyond the threshold can be considered two different goods with interrelated demand. The inverse elasticity rule of Ramsey pricing states that price is raised more for the good with the lower elasticity of demand. One would usually expect the elasticity of demand for consumption in the first block to be lower than that in the second block for the following reason. For customers that consume in the second block, the first-block price is an inframarginal price that does not affect their consumption (at least as long as the first-block price is not raised too high). These customers demand the threshold amount of consumption in the first block for a wide range of first-block prices. The only response occurs when the price in the first block is raised so much that the consumer reduces consumption from the second to the first block. For example, the customer in figure 7.15 would consume

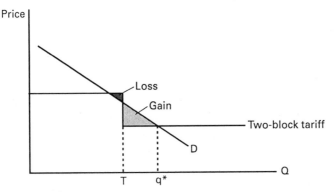

Price in first block must rise considerably for
consumer to reduce consumption from q* to
below T.

Figure 7.15
Customer in second block of two-block tariff

q^* in total and T (the threshold amount) in the first block until the
first-block price was raised so high that the area labeled "loss" increased to a size that exceeded the area labeled "gain." As long as
customers continue to consume in the second block, their price elasticity for consumption in the first block is zero. The total (market)
elasticity in the first block would therefore be comparatively small
because it incorporates the zero elasticities of customers in the second
block.

If elasticity is lower in the first block than the second, the inverse
elasticity rule suggests that the optimal price in the first block is higher
than that in the second block. With the optimal price being higher in
the first block, declining rather than inverted blocks are optimal.[16]

At least one price must exceed marginal cost for the natural monopoly to break even. If demand is price responsive in both blocks, then,
according to the Ramsey rule, both prices exceed marginal cost (though
by different amounts). If, however, demand in the first block is fixed
independent of price (at least within the relevant range of price), optimality is attained by setting the price in the second block to marginal

---

16. It is possible, in unusual circumstances, for the optimal block rates to be increasing
rather than declining. The reason is analogous to that described in footnote 8 for an
access fee below marginal cost. If the "net" elasticity (that is, the same minus cross-
elasticity) is greater in the first block than the second, the Ramsey rule suggests that
the optimal price in the first block is lower than that in the second.

cost and raising the price in the first block sufficiently that revenues cover total costs. In this case, first-best optimality is attained.[17]

The discussion so far has taken the threshold as given. The optimal threshold depends on a variety of factors, including the shape and distribution of individual demand curves. A general characterization of the optimal threshold is difficult and cannot, from a practical perspective, be implemented because information on individual demand curves is essentially unobtainable. However, the trade-off that occurs in choosing the threshold is meaningful, and knowing the factors that enter this trade-off can assist in setting the threshold even when the information needed to determine the exact optimum is unavailable.

For a declining block tariff with two blocks, consider the possibility of reducing the size of the first block, that is, reducing the threshold. Two countervailing impacts occur. First, more customers consume in the second block due to the reduction in the size of the first block per se. For example, a customer who consumes 90 units when the threshold is 100 would necessarily consume in the second block if the threshold is reduced below 90. With the price in the second block being closer to marginal cost than in the first block, these customers face a marginal price that is closer to marginal cost. A surplus gain occurs for these customers.

Second, a surplus loss occurs because of the requirement that the firm break even. Because the first-block price exceeds that in the second block, the firm loses revenues if the size of the first block is reduced but the price in each block remains the same.[18] To maintain zero profits, one or both of the prices must be raised. A loss is incurred because at least some customers face marginal prices that are further from marginal cost than with the larger threshold.

There is a trade-off, therefore, in the impacts on surplus from reducing the threshold: the gain from having more customers face the second-block price that is closer to marginal cost, versus the loss due

---

17. If an access/usage tariff is considered a two-block tariff with a threshold at the first unit of consumption, the optimal pricing rule for two-block tariffs are the same as those presented in section 7.2. In particular, when demand in the first block is fixed (that is, when access demand is fixed), the Coase result applies.

18. Revenues could conceivably increase due to a sufficiently large price response by those customers whose marginal consumption changes from the first to second block. Whenever such an event occurs, prices and the threshold can be adjusted such that consumers and the firm are all better off. At optimality, therefore, a shortening of the first block without a change in prices necessarily reduces revenues.

to one or both of the prices being raised further above marginal cost. If the gain exceeds the loss, the threshold should be reduced. At the optimal threshold, the gain equals the loss. Of course, the same impacts, though in the opposite directions, occur when the threshold is increased. The optimal threshold therefore occurs when the gains equal the losses for changes in the threshold in either direction.

2. Generalization to Three or More Blocks
If the number of blocks in a tariff is specified, the issues regarding optimal prices and thresholds for tariffs with three or more blocks are conceptually the same as with two-block tariffs. Given the thresholds, the Ramsey rule determines the optimal prices (taking into account the cross-elasticities among demand in different blocks). In choosing each threshold, the same trade-off arises as for two-block tariffs. However, the optimal thresholds are even more difficult to identify. With multiple thresholds, the trade-offs for the various thresholds are interrelated because the gains and losses from changing any one threshold depend on the positions of the other thresholds.

So far, we have taken the number of blocks in a tariff as given and examined issues related to the optimal prices and thresholds for those blocks. The question naturally arises: what is the optimal number of blocks? This is the topic of the next two sections.

7.3.4 Pareto-Dominating Block-Rate Tariffs

1. Background Concepts
Results regarding the implications of block-rate tariffs rest on the important distinction between Pareto improvements and surplus improvements. To facilitate this discussion, we first review the basic concepts of surplus and Pareto.

Total surplus is the sum over all consumers of each individual consumer's surplus, plus the profit of the firm (producer's surplus). A change that increases this sum is said to be surplus-improving. Optimal prices are those that provide the greatest possible surplus. A movement, therefore, from nonoptimal to optimal prices constitutes a surplus improvement. This improvement is the rationale for switching to optimal prices.

A change that increases total surplus can hurt some parties. In fact, most movements from nonoptimal prices to optimal prices hurt some parties. For example, a person who has low demand would be hurt by a switch from uniform pricing (i.e., one price) to the optimal two-block rates, because the optimal price in the first block would exceed the uniform price. A surplus improvement denotes simply that total surplus increases, not that each individual's surplus increases. Consequently, some individuals' surplus can decrease and there would still be an overall increase in surplus as long as other individuals' surplus rises sufficiently that their net sum increases.

By definition, a Pareto improvement is a change that benefits at least one party without hurting any other parties. Because at least one party gains and none loses, a Pareto improvement necessarily increases total surplus and hence is a surplus improvement. However, a surplus improvement need not constitute a Pareto improvement because, as stated above, some parties can be hurt by a change that increases total surplus.

Surplus-improving changes that are not Pareto improving are justified on theoretical grounds by the fact that the parties that benefit from the change could compensate the parties that are hurt such that all parties are better off. That is, any surplus improvement can, with compensations, be made into a Pareto improvement. From a practical perspective, however, the issue is more difficult. Although in theory one can consider lump-sum transfers that do not affect consumption, it is rare that a mechanism for compensation can be found that does not entail some distortion of prices and hence consumption. Furthermore, even if a compensation mechanism were possible, it is difficult to calculate the appropriate amount of transfer to and from each party. Each injured party has an incentive, of course, to overestimate the required compensation; and each party that benefits from a change has an incentive to pretend that the benefit is small or nonexistent. Because of these problems, compensations to accompany a surplus-improving change hardly ever occur in the real world.

Without compensations, it is difficult to justify the ethics of a surplus improvement that is not Pareto improving: how can one person's "happiness" be traded against another person's "pain?" Furthermore, in regulatory as well as other political settings, surplus-improving changes that are not Pareto improving can often be blocked by the parties that would be hurt. These might be the reasons that optimal pricing, which maximizes surplus without regard to which parties gain and lose, is observed in regulated settings with far less frequency than many economists would consider advisable.

Given the ethical and practical advantages of Pareto-improving changes, it is useful to identify tariffs that offer Pareto improvements over current tariffs. Such tariffs are called Pareto-dominating tariffs. One of the appeals of block-rate tariffs is that they can be designed to be Pareto dominating in certain situations. That is, in many circumstances, block-rate tariffs can be designed that benefit some parties without hurting others relative to an existing tariff. In fact, block-rate tariffs can be designed that benefit *all* parties, hurting none.

A block-rate tariff that provides Pareto improvements also, by definition, increases total surplus. However, the optimal block-rate tariff (that is, the tariff that generates the greatest total surplus without regard to who gains or loses) generally provides greater total surplus than any Pareto-improving block-rate tariff. Essentially, Pareto dominance is a constraint on surplus maximization when compensations are not possible: a tariff that maximizes total surplus under the constraint that no party be hurt relative to the current situation cannot provide greater surplus than the tariff that maximizes surplus without this constraint. There is, therefore, a "price," in terms of total surplus, to be paid for Pareto dominance. Whether the ethical and practical advantages of Pareto dominance are worth this price is an issue that regulators must consider.

2. Design of a Pareto Dominating Tariff

Willig (1978) and Panzar (1977) have demonstrated the following result.

Result 1: Given an N *block tariff with prices that exceed marginal cost, an* N + 1 *block tariff can be designed that Pareto dominates the* N *block tariff.*

Consider first what this result means. A uniform price is essentially a one-block tariff. The result states that if a uniform price is currently being charged and this price exceeds marginal cost (as required for a natural monopolist that is breaking even), it is possible to design a tariff with two blocks under which at least one party would be better off and no parties would be hurt. Similarly, given a two-block tariff with prices above marginal cost, a three-block tariff can be designed that benefits at least one customer and hurts no one. And so on for more and more blocks.

Willig and Panzar each demonstrated this result in a remarkably simple and intuitive fashion. We give the proof for a one-block tariff (uniform price), showing that a Pareto-dominating two-block tariff can be designed that Pareto dominates the uniform price. The generalization to tariffs with more blocks is straightforward.

Under a uniform price, each customer consumes the quantity of the good indicated by its demand curve evaluated at this price and obtains surplus from doing so. To design a Pareto-dominating two-part tariff, focus on the customer with the greatest demand. That is, identify the customer who, at the uniform price, consumes more of the good than any other customer. Label this customer L, the uniform price P_1, and the consumption of this highest-demand customer under the uniform price Q_1. Figure 7.16 depicts the demand curve of this customer, along with the firm's marginal cost curve (which for convenience is assumed to be constant).

Construct a two-block tariff as follows. Set the price in the first block to be the same as the original, uniform price, and make this price applicable for consumption up to the amount consumed by the largest-demand customer. That is, the first block in the tariff consists of price P_1 for consumption up to Q_1 units. For the second block, set price at any level between the price in the first block and marginal cost. Label this price P_2. A tariff constructed in this way is depicted as the heavy line in figure 7.16.

This two-block tariff Pareto dominates the uniform price. First note that no customer is hurt by this tariff relative to the uniform price. Because no customer consumes more than Q_1 under the uniform price, and this same price is applied under the two-block tariff to all consumption up to Q_1, each customer can consume the same amount under the two-block tariff as under the uniform price without a change in its bill or, hence, its surplus. Customers might change their con-

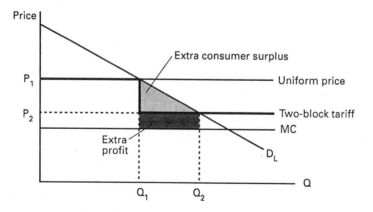

Figure 7.16
Pareto-dominating two-block tariff: customer with largest demand will increase consumption

sumption under the new tariff, but they will do so only if it benefits them. Each consumer therefore obtains either the same or greater surplus under the two-block tariff as under the uniform price.

To demonstrate Pareto dominance, at least one party must actually benefit (rather than staying the same). In fact, we can show that at least one customer *and* the firm benefit.

Consider the customer with the largest demand under the uniform price. This customer consumes Q_1 under the uniform price. Under the two-block tariff, this customer can continue to consume Q_1 with no change in outlay because the original price, P_1, applies for consumption up to Q_1. However, additional consumption can now be purchased by the customer at a lower price: at P_2 instead of P_1. The consumer will respond to the lower price by increasing consumption (given a downward-sloping demand curve), moving from Q_1 to Q_2 in figure 7.16. This additional consumption at the lower price provides the customer with extra surplus, represented by the lightly shaded area in the figure. The largest customer therefore benefits from the tariff.

Consider now the effect on the firm of this customer's increased consumption. The firm incurs the same costs and obtains the same revenues for the first Q_1 units of consumption as it did under the uniform price, because the price for this quantity of consumption is the same under the two-block tariff. For consumption beyond Q_1, the price, while lower, is still above marginal cost. Hence, any additional consumption generates additional profit for the firm. The extra profits generated by the increased consumption of the largest-demand customer are $(Q_2 - Q_1)(P_2 - MC)$, which is the darkly shaded area in the figure.

The largest-demand customer benefits from the two-block tariff, and the firm benefits from this customer's response. What about all the other customers? Clearly, as stated above, no customer is hurt by the two-block tariff because each customer can continue to consume the same quantity as under the uniform price and pay the same amount. It is possible, however, that some of these customers will choose to increase their consumption. For example, consider a customer with a demand curve as depicted in figure 7.17. Under the uniform price, the customer would purchase q_1 units, which is less than that of the largest-demand customer (that is, less than Q_1). Under the two-block tariff, the customer would increase consumption to q_2 because its sur-

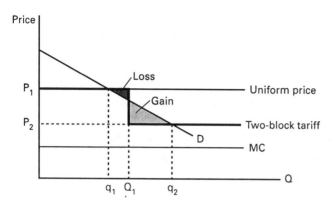

Figure 7.17
Pareto-dominating two-block tariff: a customer with lower demand might increase consumption

plus would increase by doing so. The change in surplus consists of the loss incurred from increasing consumption from q_1 to Q_1 (because the price exceeds the consumer's willingness to pay as indicated by the demand curve) and the gain obtained from increasing consumption from Q_1 to q_2. Because, given the way the demand curve is drawn, the gain exceeds the loss, the customer will choose to increase consumption from q_1 to q_2 to obtain this net gain in surplus.

Any customer that chooses to increase consumption under the two-block tariff necessarily gains from doing so (otherwise it would remain at its original level of consumption). Furthermore, because price exceeds marginal cost in both blocks of the two-block tariff, any increase in consumption generates additional profits for the firm.

In short: the two-block tariff that we constructed increases the surplus of the largest customer and the profits of the firm. It does not hurt any other customers and might, depending on the shapes of the individual demand curves, benefit some of them.

Actually, all customers can benefit from an appropriate two-block tariff. Because the firm earns extra profit under the two-block tariff described above, it is possible to lower the price in the first block and still have the firm as well off as under the uniform price. That is, the extra profit, or some portion of it, can be refunded to customers though a lower first-block price. If all the profit is refunded through this first-block price reduction (as would occur if the firm were required to earn no more than zero profit), then the change from a uniform price to the two-block tariff would benefit all consumers without hurting the firm. If a portion, but not all, of the extra profit is refunded, then all parties, including the firm, benefit from the switch to the two-block tariff. Stated in the strongest terms: given a uniform price that exceeds marginal cost, a two-block tariff can be designed that is better for all customers and the firm than the uniform price.

The same concepts can be applied to show that, given a two-block tariff with prices above marginal cost, a Pareto-dominating three-block tariff can be designed; and so on for more blocks. Figure 7.18 depicts a two-block tariff along with the demand curve for the customer whose consumption under the two-block tariff exceeds that of all other customers. Label the consumption of this largest-demand customer as Q_2. A Pareto-dominating three-block tariff is constructed as follows: the first block is the same as the first block of the two-block tariff; the second block has the same price as the second block of the two-block tariff, but instead of extending indefinitely, this block stops at Q_2; the third block starts at Q_2 and has a price that is closer to marginal cost than the price in the second block. Because prices are the same for consumption up to Q_2, no customer is hurt by this three-block tariff. The largest customer increases consumption under this new tariff, because the price of additional consumption for this customer is lower. This customer gains surplus and the firm earns extra profit, as designated by the shaded areas in the figure. Other customers might also increase consumption; if they do so, their surplus increases and the firm earns more profit. If the firm's extra profit is refunded through

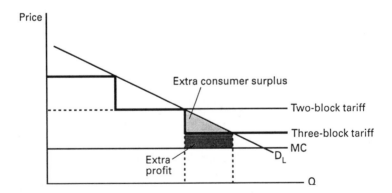

Figure 7.18
Pareto-dominating three-block tariff: the customer with largest demand will increase consumption

lower rates in the first and second blocks, all customers benefit by the change in tariff.

7.3.5 The Optimal Number of Blocks

Section 7.3.3 described, for a tariff with a *given* number of blocks, the optimal price in each block and the optimal thresholds between blocks. Result 1 in section 7.3.4 allows us to compare surplus under optimal tariffs with *different* numbers of blocks. As before, the term "optimal" is used throughout this section to refer to the tariff that provides the greatest surplus while allowing the firm to break even. In some cases, the optimal tariff attains first-best optimality (e.g., when demand in the first block is fixed). Otherwise, the optimal tariff attains second-best optimality.

Result 2: The optimal N + 1 *block tariff provides strictly greater surplus than the optimal* N *block tariff whenever prices exceed (do not equal) marginal cost under the optimal* N *block tariff.*

This result is one of the primary motivations for implementing block-rate tariffs. Consider first what it says. A uniform price (that is, one price for the good independent of consumption) is a one-block tariff; in a natural monopoly situation, the optimal uniform price is average cost, which exceeds marginal cost. The result states that greater surplus is obtained with the optimal two-block tariff than with this optimal uniform price. Similarly, optimal prices in a two-block tariff exceed marginal cost whenever demand in the first block is not fixed. The result states that in this situation, the optimal three-block tariff attains greater consumer surplus, while maintaining zero profits for the firm, than the optimal two-block tariff. And similarly for four-block tariffs compared to three-block, and so on.

Because of the difficulty of characterizing the optimal N block tariff, a heuristic proof of this result (that is, a proof that determines the optimal N block and $N + 1$ block tariffs and calculates surplus under each) has not been developed. Instead, the result is seen as a corollary to result 1. Consider first the optimal two-block tariff compared to the optimal uniform price (that is, one-block tariff). The optimal uniform price is average cost, which exceeds marginal cost if the firm is a natural monopolist. Because price exceeds marginal cost, result 1 states that a two-block tariff can be designed that Pareto dominates this optimal uniform price. This Pareto-dominating two-block tariff necessarily increases surplus. The optimal two-block tariff provides at least as much surplus as the Pareto-dominating tariff.[19] Consequently, the optimal two-block tariff provides strictly greater surplus than the optimal uniform price.

The same arguments apply in comparing the optimal two- and three-block tariffs. Under the optimal two-block tariff, both prices exceed marginal cost unless demand in the first block is fixed. When first-block demand is fixed, the optimal two-block tariff achieves the first-best outcome: price in the second block is set to marginal cost and the first-block price is set sufficiently high for the firm to break even. This means that, unless the first-best outcome is achieved by the two-block tariff, a three-block tariff can be designed that Pareto dominates the optimal two-block tariff. The optimal three-block tariff attains at least as much surplus as the Pareto-dominating three-block tariff and therefore provides greater surplus than the optimal two-block tariff. And so on for tariffs with more blocks. The basic finding is that, until the first-best outcome is achieved, surplus can be improved by adding more blocks to a block-rate tariff and adjusting the prices and thresholds accordingly.

7.3.6 Equity Considerations

The discussion of optimal and Pareto-dominating tariffs highlights the surplus advantages of having prices *decline* as consumption increases. The optimal block-rate tariff consists of declining blocks, and Pareto-dominating tariffs are constructed by adding a final block with

---

19. In fact, it is possible, and perhaps even likely, that the optimal two-block tariff provides considerably greater surplus than the Pareto-dominating two-block tariff. Given the way the Pareto-dominating tariff was designed, the only customer that is guaranteed to benefit is the customer with the largest demand under the uniform price. This surplus improvement might be very small, whereas the optimal two-block tariff (which is not constrained to be Pareto dominating) could provide a substantial surplus improvement. It is also important to note that other tariffs might exist that are Pareto-dominating and provide greater surplus than the tariff we constructed to guarantee Pareto dominance. In constructing our Pareto-dominating tariff, our goal was to prove that at least one Pareto-dominating tariff exists. Other Pareto-dominating tariffs might also exist, and these might, and probably will, provide greater surplus. Among the set of tariffs that Pareto dominate a given tariff, the tariff that provides the greatest total surplus is called the optimal Pareto-dominating tariff. An interesting area of research is to compare total surplus under the optimal tariff with that under the optimal Pareto-dominating tariff. The difference is, in a sense, the "price" of Pareto dominance, that is, the surplus that is potentially foregone in return for changing tariffs in a way that hurts no one.

a lower rate. From an equity perspective, however, *inverted* block rates might be preferable to declining blocks in many situations. Under declining block rates, customers with lower demand face relatively higher prices. Insofar as customers have low demand because their income is low, declining rates force lower-income customers to face higher prices. Inverted block rates, which are lower for small levels of consumption and increase for greater consumption, might be preferable from an equity perspective in cases like this.

Consumption does not always increase with income. For example, low-income housing units might be built with electric heating, rather than gas or oil heating, because electric heaters are less expensive to install. The households who occupy these units would demand more electricity in their attempts to stay warm than a higher-income household whose home has gas or oil heat. In cases like this, declining block rates can be advantageous from an equity as well as total surplus perspective.

8   Time-of-Use Prices and Riordan's Mechanism

8.1   Motivation

In many situations, demand varies over time more quickly than capacity can be adjusted. The classic example is an urban highway: demand is higher during rush hours than during other times of the day, and yet the size of the freeway cannot be adjusted hourly to accommodate these shifts.[1] Similarly, demand for electricity in many areas is greater in the afternoon, when people run their air conditioners, than during the morning and night; however, generation capacity is fixed, at least within the span of a day.

For many regulated firms facing demand that varies over the day, different prices are charged in different times of day. Telephone companies, especially long-distance carriers, charge higher rates during business hours than during evenings, nights, and weekends. Electric utilities often offer time-of-use rates, particularly for commercial and agricultural customers.

In situations such as these, important questions arise:

1. What is the first-best price to charge in each time period, given the available capacity? With a sufficiently low price, demand could exceed capacity, such that congestion occurs, or, in the case of electricity, possibly blackouts. However, with a sufficiently high price, demand could fall below capacity, such that the capacity is, in a sense, being wasted. Is the optimal price in each period the price that results in demand equaling capacity, such that there is no congestion or under-

---

1. Actually, many urban areas adjust highway capacity in each direction by moving the median barrier. This practice is an attempt to deal with the problem of fluctuating demand.

utilization; or is it perhaps optimal to have a degree of congestion and/or underutilization in certain periods?

2. Given the first-best price in each period, is there a mechanism that regulators can use to induce a firm with fixed capacity and time-varying demand to charge these prices? Riordan (1984) has proposed a mechanism that does just this.

3. Over time, capacity can be adjusted. What is the optimal capacity in situations where demand fluctuates? If sufficient capacity is constructed to handle the periods with high demand, then capacity in other periods will be underutilized. However, if less capacity is provided, there will be congestion in the periods with high demand. What is the optimal point in the trade-off between these two factors?

4. Finally, is there a mechanism regulators can use to induce the firm to provide the optimal level of capacity? Riordan's mechanism can, in certain circumstances, be used for this purpose as well as to induce optimal pricing.

These questions are addressed sequentially in the following sections. Section 8.2 identifies first-best prices given capacity. Section 8.3 describes Riordan's method for inducing these prices. Section 8.4 identifies the optimal capacity. And section 8.5 discusses the extent to which Riordan's method can induce optimal capacity.

The findings of this chapter can be summarized as follows:

• When demand fluctuates over time periods (e.g., rush and nonrush hours) and capacity is fixed, the first-best pricing rule is the following. In each period, price at marginal cost as long as doing so results in no more demand in that period than can be met with the available capacity. If demand exceeds capacity when price equals marginal cost, raise price until demand equals capacity.

• At these first-best prices with fixed capacity, there may be either excess capacity or congestion (i.e., insufficient capacity) in any period. That is, the existence of excess capacity and congestion are both consistent with first-best pricing under fixed capacity.

• The firm's profits may be positive or negative at the first-best prices with fixed capacity.

• Under Riordan's mechanism, the firm is subsidized on the basis of the price it charges in each period. The subsidy in each period consists of (1) the fixed costs of production in that period minus (2) the amount by which price exceeds marginal cost in the period times the capacity of the firm. With this subsidy, the firm earns zero profit at the first-best prices and negative profit at any other prices. The firm therefore chooses the first-best prices.

• The optimal capacity is the level at which the average amount that customers are willing to pay for extra capacity (averaged over all periods) equals the cost of extra capacity. With this optimal capacity, first-best prices are obtained by the same rule as when capacity is fixed.

• Under Riordan's mechanism, the firm is indifferent between choosing the optimal capacity and any other capacity: the firm earns zero profit at any capacity level. The firm therefore has no reason *not* to choose the optimal capacity. However, the mechanism does not *necessarily* induce the firm to choose this capacity.

• If the regulator knows the optimal capacity, the subsidy under Riordan's mechanism can be calculated on the basis of the optimal capacity rather than the firm's chosen capacity. With this subsidy, the firm will necessarily choose the optimal capacity. However, it is unlikely that the regulator knows the optimal capacity so as to implement this subsidy.

8.2 First-Best TOU Prices Given Capacity

Consider first a particular stylized situation.[2] Suppose a firm has a plant with fixed capacity K, which is the maximum number of units that can be produced per period of time (say, per hour.) The firm incurs a fixed cost, F, for the plant; this fixed cost is expressed as a flow of expenditures over time, that is, as dollars per period. The variable costs of production consist of a constant marginal cost, c, for each unit of output produced. An example might be an electric utility with a coal-powered electricity generating plant. The lease or mortgage on the plant, or the opportunity cost of funds tied up in the plant, is F per period. The cost of coal, labor, and other inputs for producing an extra kilowatt is c, and the plant is capable of producing

---

2. The framework of this analysis, and for the analysis of optimal capacity in section 8.4, follows most closely that of Williamson (1966). Riordan used this framework to describe his regulatory mechanism, which is one of the reasons for adopting it in this section. Issues of optimal pricing and capacity with fluctuating demand, often called peak-load pricing, have been examined extensively over the years; seminal studies include those by Steiner (1957), Houthakker (1958), Boiteux (1960), Mohring (1970), and Keeler and Small (1977).

up to K kilowatts per hour but no more. Figure 8.1 gives the marginal cost curve in this situation: MC is flat at c up to quantity K after which no more output can be produced.

Consider first a situation in which demand does not fluctuate over time. Setting price equal to marginal cost assures, as always, that customers buy units if and only if the the value of each unit to the customer is greater than or equal to the cost of producing the unit. With p set to c, two events can occur: either the quantity demanded in each period can be met with capacity K, or more units are demanded each period than can be produced. Panel (a) of figure 8.2 depicts the first case. At marginal-cost pricing, quantity $q^* < K$ is demanded. In this case, the first-best price is clearly c: if price were lowered, the additional output demanded at the lower price would be valued at less than the marginal cost of producing the additional output; and if price were raised, units that are valued above their cost would not be produced. Either way there would be a loss compared to marginal-cost pricing. Note that the first-best price in this situation results in "wasted" capacity, in the amount of $K - q^*$. In the short run, with K fixed, there is nothing that can be done about this extra capacity.[3] The second possibility is that demand exceeds capacity when price is set equal to marginal cost. This case is depicted in panel (b). At $p = c$, demand cannot be met, such that rationing is necessary. The issue therefore becomes: what is the most efficient basis on which to ration the K units that can be produced. With p maintained at c, rationing could occur in any number of ways: by customers queuing up, such that the customers who are most willing to spend time in line get the goods;

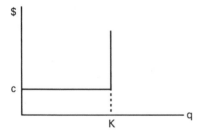

Figure 8.1
Marginal cost with fixed capacity

---

3. Lowering price in an effort to utilize a larger portion of capacity is counterproductive, because the additional units that are sold would be valued at less than the variable cost of producing them. Over time, the capacity of the plant should be reduced; this issue is addressed in section 8.4.

(a) At p=c, demand ≤ K

(b) At p=c, demand > K

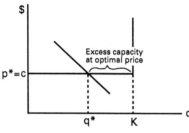

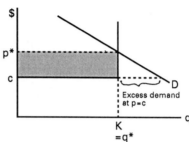

Figure 8.2
Optimal price with nonvarying demand

through a lottery; through force, such that the strongest customers obtain the units; and so on. An alternative form of rationing is to raise p until the quantity demanded drops to K; in the figure, this constitutes raising price to p^*. With price at p^*, customers that value the good at p^* or more obtain the good, and those that value it at less than p^* do not. That is, raising the price to p^* rations the K goods on the basis on customers' willingness to pay for the good. From an efficiency perspective, this basis for rationing is clearly optimal.[4]

The general rule for pricing under fixed capacity is: set price at marginal cost unless doing so results in more units being demanded than can be produced, in which case raise price until the quantity demanded drops to capacity.

Under this first-best pricing, the firm could end up making positive or negative profits. With price at marginal cost, the firm covers its variable costs but not its fixed costs, such that it incurs losses of F per period. When price is raised above marginal cost to eliminate excess demand, the firm obtains revenues in excess of its variable costs, de-

---

4. Under other forms of rationing, a customer that is willing to pay more that p^* for the good might not get the good, while another customer that values it at less than p^* might obtain it. Both of these customers would benefit from a transaction in which the customer with the higher value buys the good from the customer with the lower value at a price that is between their two values. Because mutually beneficial transactions are available after rationing on the basis of something other than price, nonprice rationing does not, by definition, provide an outcome that is Pareto optimal. This fact can be seen in another way. If any nonprice form of rationing were utilized and then followed by a series of voluntary, mutually benefiting barters among all customers, the customers that are willing to pay at least p^* would end up with the K units and those valuing it less would end up with payments but not the good. The result would be the same as pricing the good at p^* originally (except for transfers, which do not affect total surplus).

picted as the shaded area in the figure. Depending on how high price must be raised to equate quantity demanded with capacity, this extra revenue may exceed, fall short, or just cover the firm's fixed costs. In cases where the firm would lose money under the first-best prices, the firm must be subsidized to remain solvent. This subsidy can be provided in three ways: (1) directly, (2) by adding an access charge without changing the usage price, if access demand is fixed, or (3) by resorting to Ramsey prices.

These concepts can be readily translated to situations in which demand fluctuates over time periods. Suppose each day consists of two periods called peak and off-peak, with demand being greater in the peak. For convenience, suppose the two periods are the same length (twelve hours)[5] and that demand is constant over all the hours in each period.

Figure 8.3 depicts the three possibilities for the relation of demand in each period to capacity when price is at marginal cost. The subscript p refers to peak and the subscript o refers to off-peak. In panel (a), demand in each period can be met with existing capacity when price is set at marginal cost. In this case the first-best price is the same in both periods, namely marginal cost. The quantity demanded is q_p^* in the peak and q_o^* in the off-peak, for a total daily output of $q_p^* + q_o^*$. There is excess capacity throughout the day, and the firm loses money if it is not subsidized. In panel (b), the quantity demanded exceeds capacity in the peak but not in the off-peak when price is set at marginal cost. The optimal price in the off-peak is marginal cost, and the peak-period price must be raised, for optimality, until demand equals capacity in the peak. The firm earns revenues in excess of variable cost from the peak-period customers, but not from the off-peak customers. Hence, to the extent that fixed costs are covered, peak-period customers bear these costs. In panel (c), demand exceeds capacity in both periods when price equals marginal cost. For optimality, price is raised in each period until the excess demand is eliminated. Revenues in excess of variable costs are earned in each period. This excess is the rectangle HGJE in the peak and rectangle ABJE in the off-peak. Because the peak and off-peak are of equal length, the average revenue

---

5. This assumption is convenient for determining whether revenues in both periods cover fixed costs, because it allows average revenues per period to be the simple average of revenues over the two periods. With periods of unequal length, a weighted average is required, with the weights being proportional to the length of each period. The concepts are the same, but the notation and language is easier with equal lengths.

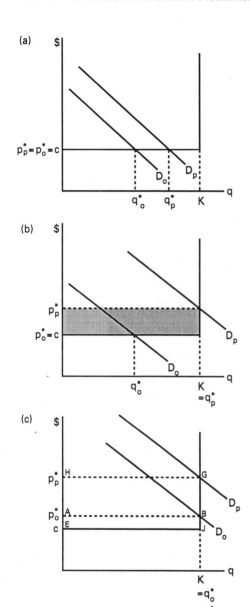

Figure 8.3
Optimal prices with fluctuating demand

per period in excess of variable cost is the average of these two areas; this average is compared to F, fixed costs per period, to determine whether the firm breaks even without subsidization.

As in the case of nonfluctuating demand, the first-best pricing rule with fixed capacity and fluctuating demand is: in each period, price at marginal cost unless doing so results in more quantity demanded in that period than can be met with the available capacity, in which case raise price until demand equals capacity.

As we have seen, this pricing rule can result in "wasted" capacity, the existence of which is not suboptimal in the short run when capacity is fixed. (It simply denotes the need to reduce capacity in the long run.) The rule can also result in congestion (as defined below), the existence of which is also not suboptimal.

This latter point requires elaboration. With fixed capacity, congestion usually occurs before output reaches full capacity. The classic example is freeway traffic. As more cars enter a freeway, traffic slows down. Such congestion imposes costs on drivers in terms of longer travel times. From a social perspective, the marginal cost of output includes both the cost to the firm of providing the output plus the extra cost borne by consumers through increased congestion.

The marginal cost curves in figures 8.1–8.3 do not, by their shape, permit congestion. In these graphs, marginal cost is constant until capacity is reached, at which point greater output is not possible. With congestion, marginal cost usually increases gradually as output approaches capacity. For example, it is not the case that traffic on a freeway flows at a constant speed as more and more cars are added and then immediately stops completely when the freeway's capacity is reached. The slowdown in traffic is more gradual, with speeds dropping as congestion gets worse and worse. Figure 8.4 contains a marginal cost curve for this type of situation. The marginal cost of one extra car, including the cost imposed on other drivers through the extra congestion this car produces, is constant for low levels of traffic (when there are so few cars that no congestion occurs) and increases gradually as more cars are added; eventually, capacity K is reached and no additional cars are possible. This curve is conceptually similar to that in the previous figures, except that the lower-right corner of the marginal cost curve in the previous figures is smoothed to allow a gradual increase in marginal cost as capacity is approached.

The concepts of optimal pricing given capacity are the same under

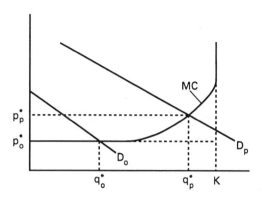

Figure 8.4
Optimal output can entail congestion

this marginal cost curve: the first-best price is marginal cost unless this price results in demand exceeding capacity, in which case price is raised to equate demand with capacity. In the off-peak, the first-best price is p_o^* and there is no congestion. In the peak, the first-best price is p_p^*, which results in some congestion. While the absolute capacity K has not been reached, the marginal-cost curve has started to rise indicating, in the case of a freeway, that there is congestion and that each additional driver is making the congestion worse. This example shows that the first-best prices can result in congestion when capacity is fixed.

8.3 Riordan's Mechanism for Inducing First-Best TOU Prices with Fixed Capacity

To describe Riordan's proposal, we return to the more stark cost situation where marginal cost is constant at c up to capacity K, beyond which extra output is impossible. Suppose the regulator observes c and K, but does not know the demand curves that the firm faces in the peak and off-peak and consequently does not know the optimal prices. Riordan has devised a subsidy mechanism that the regulator can impose on the firm under which the firm is induced, through its pursuit of profit, to charge the first-best price and sell the first-best output in each period. The mechanism consists of the following. In *each* period, the regulator pays the firm a subsidy $S(p)$ that depends on the price that the firm charges in that period. The particular form of the subsidy is:

$$S(p) = \begin{cases} F - (p-c)K & \text{if } p \geq c \\ 0 & \text{if } p < c. \end{cases}$$

That is, if the firm prices below marginal cost c in the period, the regulator pays the firm nothing. If the firm prices at or above marginal cost in the period, the regulator pays the firm its fixed costs of capacity (F) minus the amount by which price exceeds marginal cost for each unit of output that can be produced *at capacity*.[6] For example, if the firm has a capacity of 5,000 units and prices at $6 when its marginal cost is $4, the regulator pays the firm its fixed costs minus $10,000 (that is, $(6-4) \cdot 5,000$).

To calculate this subsidy, the regulator needs to know the fixed and marginal costs of the firm, its capacity, and the price it charges in the period. Demand information is not required. Note that $S(p)$ might be negative. If the firm prices high enough above marginal cost, the quantity subtracted [namely, $(p-c)K$] could exceed the fixed costs (F) such that the "subsidy" is negative. In this case, the regulator takes money away from the firm; that is, S(p) is actually a subsidy if positive and a tax on the firm if negative.[7]

The firm's profit is the sum of its profit, including subsidy, in the peak and its profit, including subsidy, in the off-peak:

$$\pi = (p_p - c)q_p - F + S(p_p) + (p_o - c)q_o - F + S(p_o), \tag{8.1}$$

where q_p and q_o are the quantities sold in the peak and off-peak, respectively. Note that fixed costs F are defined on a per-period basis rather than per day, such that F is incurred in both the peak and off-peak. This approach is not a restriction: if fixed costs are actually incurred on a daily basis, then our F is simple one-half of the daily fixed costs.

The firm cannot sell more than its capacity K in each period. Therefore, q_p is equal to capacity if quantity demanded in the peak exceeds capacity and is equal to quantity demanded if quantity demanded in the peak is less than capacity; and similarly for q^o and quantity de-

---

6. Note that the difference between price and marginal cost is multiplied by capacity, not output, which may be less than capacity.

7. The regulator need not actually subsidize or tax the firm directly. If access demand is fixed, the regulator can implement the subsidy/tax by raising or lowering the access fee. An access fee would be required to cover the firm's fixed costs at the first-best prices anyway; Riordan's scheme simply adjusts the level of the fee in a way that depends on the price that the firm charges in each period.

manded in the off-peak.[8] The question is: what price will the firm charge in each period and what quantity will it sell in each period to maximize profits?

The firm will clearly never choose to price below marginal cost in either period. With $p < c$, the firm does not cover its variable costs [that is, $(p - c)q$ is negative] and it receives no subsidy. It therefore loses its entire fixed costs plus a portion of its variable costs. It would clearly be better off raising price at least to marginal cost, at which point it would cover its variable costs and receive a subsidy for its fixed costs, thereby earning zero profits.

With price at least as high as marginal cost in each period, the subsidy in each period is $S(p) = F - (p - c)K$. Substituting this into equation 8.1, the total profits of the firm are:

$$\pi = (p_p - c)q_p - F + F - (p_p - c)K + (p_o - c)q_o - F + F - (p_o - c)K$$
$$= (p_p - c)(q_p - K) + (p_o - c)(q_o - K).$$

Consider the profits made in the peak, namely $(p_p - c)(q_p - K)$; the arguments regarding the off-peak are analogous. Because the firm does not price below marginal cost, the term $(p_p - c)$ is either zero or positive. However, since output cannot exceed capacity, the term $(q_p - K)$ is either zero or negative. There are four possibilities for the magnitudes of these two terms:

	Output is below capacity $(q_o - K) < 0$	Output equals capacity $(q_p - K) = 0$
Price equals marginal cost $(P_p - c) = 0$	A: profit = 0	B: profit = 0
Price exceeds marginal cost $(P_p - c) > 0$	C: profit < 0	D: profit = 0

8. We are implicitly assuming that the firm must meet demand in each period. The possibility that the firm leaves some demand unmet is discussed in the next footnote. We also assume, following Riordan, that demand in each period is not affected by the price in the other period. In reality, demand in each period usually depends on the prices in both periods. For example, if price in the peak is raised, some customers might shift their consumption to off-peak times, such that off-peak demand increases with the peak price. The specification can be generalized to allow for this possibility; however, the demonstration that the firm charges optimal prices becomes less transparent.

The most profit the firm can earn under this subsidy scheme is zero, which occurs in cases *A*, *B*, and *D*. The firm will clearly not choose to price above marginal cost and sell less than capacity because doing so will result in negative profits (case *C*). The firm will price at marginal cost if the quantity demanded at that price is less than or equal to capacity (cases *A* and *B*, respectively). Or, the firm will raise price above marginal cost and sell an amount equal to capacity (case *D*). This last case is possible only if the quantity demanded when price equals marginal cost exceeds capacity (such that raising the price results in demand equaling capacity).[9]

Stated succinctly: The firm will price at marginal cost in the peak as long as doing so results in demand less than or equal to capacity. If demand exceeds capacity at marginal-cost pricing, the firm will raise price until demand equals capacity. As described in section 8.2, this pricing rule is optimal.

The decision process of the firm under this subsidy can also be shown graphically. Figure 8.5 depicts the two possibilities: demand is less than capacity when price is set at marginal cost (panel a) or demand exceeds capacity at marginal cost pricing (panel b). Consider panel (a) first. The first-best price is $p_p^* = c$. At this price, the firm covers the variable costs of producing q_p^* units of output and receives a subsidy for its fixed costs, such that its peak-period profit is zero. That is: $S(p_p^*) = F - (p_p^* - c)K = F$, such that profit in the peak is $(p_p^* - c)q_p^* - F + S(p_p^*) = -F + F = 0$.

Suppose the firm were to raise its price above marginal cost, to say *r*, in an attempt to earn more profit. Its profit from operations would

---

9. If the firm can choose not to meet some demand, the firm could price at marginal cost even though demand at that price exceeds capacity: the firm would simply sell as much output as its capacity allows and leave the excess demand unsatisfied. That is, the firm could choose to be in case *B* by not meeting demand, rather than case *D*. Because the firm earns zero profits whether it (1) charges marginal-cost price and leaves excess demand unmet, or (2) raises price above marginal cost until demand equals capacity, the firm is indifferent between these two courses of action. Consequently, there is no guarantee that the firm would choose the latter, which is optimal, instead of the former, which is not. This problem can be solved by having the regulator levy a stiff penalty if the regulator obtains evidence that the firm is not meeting demand. Even if the chances are very low that the regulator would discover that demand is not being met, the firm will choose to raise price to choke off excess demand rather than risk the penalty. That is, zero profits without any risk is preferable to the firm to zero profits with the risk of a penalty, no matter how slight the possibility that this penalty would actually be levied.

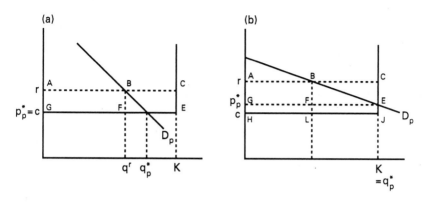

Figure 8.5
Firm's choices under Riordan's mechanism

increase by the area *ABFG*, namely, the amount by which price exceeds marginal cost times the quantity sold. However, the subsidy
the firm obtains from the regulator would be diminished by the area
ACEG, which is the amount by which price exceeds marginal cost
times the *capacity* of the firm's plant. Because the subsidy is reduced
by more than the firm's operating profits increase, the firm earns less
profit at r than at p_p^*. The driving factor in this comparison is that the
difference between price and marginal cost is multiplied by the quantity sold to obtain the increase in operating profits, and yet is multiplied by capacity to obtain the reduction in subsidy. Because the
quantity sold cannot exceed capacity, the firm cannot make more
money by raising price over marginal cost.

Consider now the possibility in panel (b) of demand exceeding capacity when price is set at marginal cost. The first-best price is $p_p^* > c$,
at which demand equals capacity. At this price, the firm earns operating profits equal to the area *GEJH*, minus its fixed costs. The subsidy consists of the fixed costs of the firm minus the area *GEJH*. Thus
the firm exactly breaks even. Suppose now that the firm were to raise
its price to r in an attempt to earn additional profits. Its operating
profits would increase by area *ABFG* minus *FEJL*. However, the firm's
subsidy would be reduced by the area *ACEG*. The net effect is a loss
for the firm. The basic reason again is the fact that operating profit is
calculated on the basis of quantity sold and the subsidy is calculated
on the basis of capacity. Because raising price above its optimal level
p_p^* necessarily reduces demand below capacity, the increase in operating profit is dominated by the reduction in subsidy.

The same arguments hold for the portion of profit that is derived from the off-peak. The product $(p_o - c)(q_o - K)$ is negative if the firm acts nonoptimally (by pricing above marginal cost while selling less than capacity) and is zero if the firm prices optimally (at marginal cost as long as demand does not exceed capacity and above marginal cost only if necessary to reduce demand to capacity). The firm therefore chooses to act optimally, earning zero instead of negative profit.

8.4 Optimal Capacity

Over time, capacity can often be adjusted; or, when a firm is being established, the capacity for the firm's plant(s) is chosen. The question is: Given demand in each period, what is the optimal capacity? Following our stylized cost specification, suppose that capacity can be constructed at a constant cost of b per unit. That is, we assume that it costs b dollars more to build a plant with capacity $K + 1$ than to build a plant with capacity K.[10] For reasons that become clear later, we represent capacity costs in terms of a flow of expenditures, such as the mortgage payments on a loan for the funds to build the capacity, or the lease payments for renting the capacity. The quantity b is therefore the extra payment per period for an extra unit of capacity.

As before, given capacity, the variable cost of producing output is assumed to be a constant c per unit. Long-run marginal cost is therefore $b + c$: the cost of expanding capacity by one unit plus the cost of producing an extra unit with the extra capacity. Short-run marginal cost, given capacity, is c for output up to the capacity and can be considered either undefined or infinite for higher levels of output.[11]

---

10. Alternatively, one can think of b as representing the cost of increasing capacity by one unit given an existing capacity. This way of considering b is appropriate for examining adjustments in capacity, while the concept in the text is appropriate when original capacity is being constructed.

11. By definition, long-run marginal cost is the cost of an extra unit of output when capital (in this case, capacity) is adjusted optimally for each level of output. Suppose the firm is producing output q and has a capacity that is exactly equal to this q; this capacity is optimal since no more or less capacity is available than needed for q units of output. To produce an extra unit, the firm must increase its capacity by one unit, which costs b; given this extra capacity, the firm must also pay the variable cost of the extra unit, which is c. Long-run cost is therefore $b + c$. Short-run cost, by definition, is the cost of an extra unit when capital (in this case, capacity) is fixed at a given level. If the firm is producing less than its capacity, the cost of producing an extra unit is c. If, however, the firm is producing at capacity, then an extra unit simply cannot be produced (in the short run, when capacity is fixed). Short-run marginal cost is therefore c up to capacity and then becomes undefined or infinite.

Consider first the optimal capacity when demand does not fluctuate over time. Figure 8.6 depicts the situation. Long-run marginal cost $(LRMC)$ is a constant $b + c$. The demand curve gives, at any quantity of output, the amount that consumers are willing to pay for an extra unit of output (or, stated alternatively, the demand curve gives the value that consumers obtain from an extra unit of output). For example, at output level q^1, consumers are willing to pay p^1 for an extra unit, which is the vertical distance XZ. This value to consumers can be decomposed into two parts to facilitate the analysis of optimal capacity. Part of this value is required to cover the variable costs of production given capacity; that is, cost c. The remaining portion, distance YZ, is therefore the amount that consumers are willing to contribute for additional capacity. In other words, YZ is the amount consumers would be willing to pay to have capacity expanded from q^1 to $q^1 + 1$, such that an extra unit of output could be produced.

Applying these ideas to all levels of output, the amount that consumers are willing to pay for additional capacity is the amount by which the demand curve is above c (that is, the vertical distance from c up to the demand curve). For high enough levels of output (beyond q^m in the graph), the demand curve is below c. This indicates that consumers are not willing to pay anything for additional capacity: they value an extra unit at less than even the variable cost of producing it and are therefore not willing to contribute anything to expanding capacity to allow more production. Stated completely: the amount that consumers are willing to pay for additional capacity is the differ-

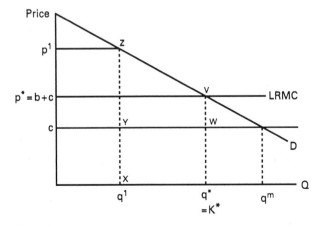

Figure 8.6
Optimal capacity with nonfluctuating demand

ence between the demand curve and c with a minimum of zero. Graphically, it is the the demand curve above c, with a kink, becoming flat (zero), at q^m.

As long as consumers are willing to pay more for additional capacity than the extra capacity costs, the capacity should, from a social perspective, be provided. Capacity costs b per unit; therefore, capacity should be expanded whenever consumers are willing to pay more than b for additional capacity. At q^{1} consumers are willing to pay distance YZ for extra capacity; since YZ exceeds b, extra capacity should be provided. As more capacity is provided, consumers' willingness to pay for additional capacity decreases, until, at q^*, the amount that consumers are willing to pay for extra capacity (distance WV) exactly equals the cost of extra capacity b. This is the optimal capacity: consumers are willing to pay no more or less than the cost of extra capacity. With capacity $K = q^*$, the optimal price is p^*, which equates quantity demanded with capacity.

This analysis could have been performed much more simply. From standard microeconomics, we know that the first-best price and output in the long run is where $LRMC$ intersects the demand curve: at p^* and q^*. The optimal level of capital (in this case, capacity) is that which is cost minimizing for the optimal level of output. The least-cost way of producing output q^* is with a capacity of exactly q^*: any less capacity would be insufficient and any more would be unnecessary.

While this latter method for determining optimal capacity is more straightforward in the case of fixed demand, it does not generalize as readily to the case of fluctuating demand. The explanation based on identifying consumers' willingness to pay for capacity provides the key for examining capacity choice when demand fluctuates.

Return now to the situation with peak and off-peak demand. With two periods, optimal capacity is determined by comparing the cost of extra capacity in both periods with the willingness to pay of customers in both periods. The cost of additional capacity in each period is b, such that the cost over the two periods, peak and off-peak, is $2b$. (Recall that costs of capacity are expressed in terms of a flow of expenditures, as under a lease or mortgage.) An extra unit of capacity should be provided if the amount that consumers in the peak are willing to pay for extra capacity, plus the amount that off-peak consumers are willing to pay, exceeds $2b$. Or, stated in per-period terms, an extra unit of capacity should be provided if consumers' willingness to pay for capacity, when averaged over the two periods, exceeds b, the cost per period. As these statements make evident, extra capacity could be desirable even though off-peak consumers are not willing to pay as much as b for extra capacity, as long as the peak consumers are willing to pay sufficiently more than b to make up the difference.

We apply these concepts to the demand curves in figure 8.7. Consumers in the off-peak are willing to pay the distance between their demand curve and c for an extra unit of capacity, up to q_o^m; they are not willing to pay anything for extra capacity in excess of q_o^m. Peak consumers are willing to pay the vertical distance between their demand curve and c, up to q_p^m, and nothing beyond. Each of these two groups of customers pays in their periods only (the peak period consumers paying in the peak and the off-peak consumers paying in the off-peak). The average willingness to pay per period is therefore the willingness to pay of peak consumers averaged with that of off-peak consumers. We can construct a new curve that represents this average willingness to pay. For example, at q^1, off-peak consumers are willing to pay AE for an extra unit of capacity, and peak consumers are willing to pay AG. The average of these two amounts is AF, which becomes the point on the new curve associated with q^1. That is, at q^1, the average amount that consumers in the two periods are willing to pay for capacity is AF. This concept is applied to all levels of capacity up to q_o^m. Beyond this point, consumers in the off-peak are not willing to pay anything for additional capacity. At q^2, for example, consumers in the off-peak are willing to pay nothing; however, peak consumers

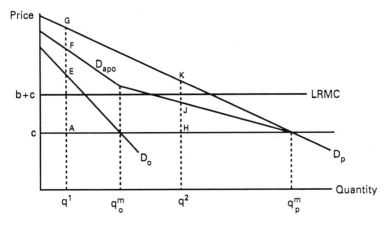

Figure 8.7
Average willingness to pay for capacity

are willing to pay HK. The average amount consumers are willing to pay is therefore half of HK; this is HJ and constitutes another point on the new curve. Stated succinctly, the new curve D_{apo} (where the subscript refers to the average of peak and off-peak) is the vertical average of D_o and D_p, each truncated at c. The vertical distance between this curve and c gives the average amount that consumers are willing to pay per period for extra capacity.

The optimal capacity is identified by comparing the average willingness to pay for extra capacity with its cost per period. Figure 8.8 contains the same demand and cost curves as figure 8.7 and also identifies the optimal capacity, prices, and outputs. At K^*, the amount that consumers are willing to pay for extra capacity, averaged over the peak and off-peak periods, is the distance NM. This amount exactly equals the cost of extra capacity per period, such that K^* is the optimal capacity. Given this capacity, the (short-run) marginal cost of output is c up to output K^*, after which no more output can be produced in the period. The rules derived in section 8.2 are used to determine optimal prices given this capacity. In the off-peak, the optimal price is $p_o^* = c$: with price set at the cost of producing an extra unit with the given capacity, the quantity demanded is less than capacity; hence that price is optimal. In the peak, pricing at c results in demand exceeding capacity. The optimal price is attained by raising price until demand equals capacity. This occurs are p_p^*.

Note that in this case, peak consumers pay the entire cost of the

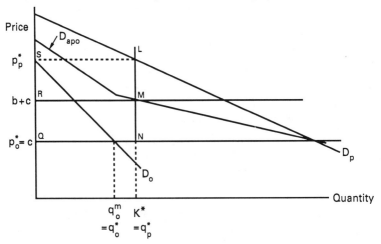

Figure 8.8
Optimal capacity with peak and off-peak demands

capacity. The total cost of capacity per period is b times K^* (the cost per unit times the number of units of capacity), which constitutes the area $NMRQ$. Over the two periods, peak and off-peak, the cost of capacity is twice this amount. Peak consumers pay a price p_p^*, which exceeds the variable cost of production c by the distance NL. With consumption at $q_p^* = K^*$, the peak consumers pay a total of the area $NLSQ$ in excess of the variable costs of their consumption. By construction, the area NLSQ is twice as large as the area $NMRQ$: the distance NM (the average that consumers are willing to pay for extra capacity) is the average of NL (the amount peak consumers are willing to pay) and zero (the amount off-peak consumers are willing to pay at this level of capacity); hence NM is half of NL such that $NMRQ$ is half of $NLSQ$. Peak consumers are, in this case, paying the entire cost of capacity over both periods. Off-peak consumers face a price that equals c and hence pay only the variable costs associated with their own consumption without contributing to the costs of capacity.

This outcome reflects the relative levels of the demand curves in the two periods. After capacity is sufficient to meet off-peak demand (that is, after a capacity of q_o^* has been provided), any additional capacity sits idle in the off-peak. For extra capacity to be warranted, the peak customers must value the extra capacity in the peak sufficiently to pay not only for the cost of the extra capacity in the peak but also for the cost of having the extra capacity in the off-peak, where it sits idle and provides no benefits.

If the difference between demand in the two periods is not as great as in figure 8.8, the optimal price can exceed c in both periods, such that off-peak consumers contribute along with peak consumers to the cost of capacity. Figure 8.9 illustrates such a case. D_o does not drop below c until after D_{apo} exceeds c by exactly b (i.e., intersects $LRMC$). The amount by which D_{apo} exceeds c is the average willingness to pay for extra capacity; this amount exactly equals b, the cost of extra capacity, at capacity K^*. At this capacity, pricing at c in the off-peak would result in demand exceeding capacity, such that the optimal off-peak price is above c; specifically, at p_o^*. Similarly, the optimal peak price is p_p^*. At the optimal capacity and prices, consumers in each period are willing to pay a positive amount for extra capacity (unlike the situation in figure 8.8 in which peak consumers were willing to pay for extra capacity but off-peak consumers are not). Consumers in each period pay a price in excess of the variable cost of production c and hence contribute to the cost of capacity.

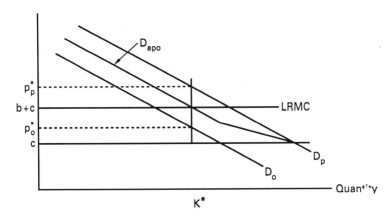

Figure 8.9
Optimal capacity with peak and off-peak demands: case 2

8.5   Riordan's Mechanism Applied to Capacity Choice

Riordan suggests two ways in which his subsidy mechanism can relate to the task of inducing the firm to choose the optimal capacity. Neither of the suggestions is a complete solution to the problem, as Riordan points out. We describe below each of the suggestions and discuss their potential and limitations.

First, suppose that the subsidy mechanism described in section 8.3 is applied with the firm choosing its own capacity. Recall the formula for the subsidy:

$$S(p) = \begin{cases} F - (p-c)K & \text{if } p \geq c \\ 0 & \text{if } p < c. \end{cases}$$

When capacity is fixed, as assumed in section 8.3, the firm can affect the amount of subsidy it receives only through its choice of prices. However, if the same subsidy formula is used and capacity is not fixed, the firm can affect its subsidy through its choice of capacity as well as its choice of prices. The firm's capacity choice determines K in the subsidy formula. It also determines F, because F is the cost of the capacity. In particular, given our specification that each extra unit of capacity costs b per period, F is actually bK per period.

Under this subsidy scheme, the firm earns at most zero profits at any level of capacity. Suppose the firm chooses some capacity, say, K^1. Once this capacity is given, the firm chooses the prices that maximize its profit, including the subsidy, with this capacity. As demonstrated in section 8.3, the firm earns zero profit if it chooses the prices that are optimal for its level of capacity and earns negative profit if it chooses any other prices. The firm of course chooses the optimal prices so as to avoid losses. Hence, if the firm chooses K^1 capacity, it earns zero profit.

The same argument applies for any level of capacity: the firm earns zero profit by choosing the prices that are optimal for that level of capacity. In particular, the argument holds for the optimal capacity: the firm earns zero profit if it charges the optimal prices given the optimal capacity.

Because the firm earns zero profit at *any* level of capacity, it has no reason *not* to choose the optimal capacity. In this sense, the subsidy mechanism can be considered consistent with the firm choosing the optimal capacity.

While the firm has no reason not to choose the optimal capacity, it also has no reason to choose it. The mechanism therefore is consistent with optimal capacity choice, but does not necessarily induce it. This lack of a positive incentive is, of course, the difficulty of the mechanism in situations with variable capacity.

Riordan's second suggestion relies on the notion that if the regulator knows the optimal capacity, this information can be used to induce the firm to choose it. In essence, the indifference of the firm among capacities (all of which result in zero profit under the subsidy mechanism) can be broken by assessing the firm a penalty for not choosing the optimal capacity. The firm then chooses to earn zero profit with the optimal capacity rather than negative profit (zero profit minus the penalty) at any other capacity level.

Riordan suggests a revised formula for the subsidy that incorporates the regulator's knowledge of the optimal capacity. The revised formula implicitly levies a penalty on the firm if it chooses a nonoptimal capacity.

The revised subsidy formula is the following:

$$RS(p) = \begin{cases} F^* - (p-c)K^* & \text{if } p \geq c \\ 0 & \text{if } p < c. \end{cases}$$

This is the same formula as earlier, but with the optimal capacity K^* replacing the firm's actual or chosen capacity (and the cost of the optimal capacity F^* replacing the cost of the firm's chosen capacity). The firm is allowed to choose any capacity it wants, but its subsidy is calculated on the basis of the optimal capacity. That is, the subsidy is calculated as if the firm chose the optimal capacity, even if the firm chooses some other capacity.

Under this revised subsidy, the firm earns zero profit if it chooses the optimal capacity, just as under the original subsidy. However, if the firm chooses any other capacity, its profit under the revised subsidy is negative. This fact is demonstrated in figure 8.10. At the optimal capacity and prices (K^*, p_o^*, and p_p^*), the firm earns zero profits after the subsidy. Suppose the firm were to reduce its capacity below the optimal level, to say K^1. We can show that the firm will earn negative profits at this nonoptimal capacity under the revised subsidy formula. With K^1, the firm prices at p_p^1 in the peak, at which demand equals capacity. Given the way the curves are drawn in this illustration, the chosen off-peak price is not affected by the reduction in capacity. Consider now the firm's profits over the peak and off-peak periods. The cost of capacity in each period is bK^1, which is the area $AEKL$. Over both periods, the cost is twice this amount: area $AFJL$. Revenues in the off-peak exactly cover variable costs. Revenues in the peak cover variable costs plus the amount $AGHL$. The firm, before the subsidy, therefore earns a profit of $AGHL$ minus $AFJL$, which is area $FGHJ$. Consider, however, the subsidy. In the off-peak, the firm obtains subsidy equal to the cost of the optimal capacity, which is area $AENM$ for the one period. Because price equals variable cost in the off-peak, nothing is subtracted from this amount. In the peak period the subsidy includes the cost of optimal capacity, $EFRN$ (which is the same size as $AENM$). However, because the firm is pricing above

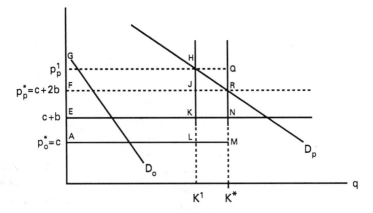

Figure 8.10
Choice of optimal capacity under revised subsidy

variable cost, the subsidy is reduced by the amount by which price exceeds variable cost times the *optimal* capacity, namely, area $AGQM$. The sum of the subsidy over both periods is therefore $AFRM$ (the cost of the optimal capacity over both periods) minus $AGQM$ (the excess of price over variable cost times optimal capacity), which is negative by the amount $FGQR$. That is, the subsidy becomes a tax in the amount of $FGQR$. The firm earns profits before the subsidy of $FGHJ$, but then loses more than this amount through the tax (negative subsidy), which is $FGQR$ in size. On net, the firm loses $JHQR$. Clearly, the firm is better off choosing the optimal capacity and earning zero profits. Similar arguments can be made with other demand curves and with the firm increasing instead of decreasing capacity from the optimal level.

The revised subsidy mechanism indeed induces the firm to choose both the optimal capacity and the optimal prices. However, to implement the mechanism, the regulator must know the optimal capacity. This informational requirement is stringent, and, more fundamentally, conflicts with the purpose of establishing incentive structures for regulated firms. Regulatory mechanisms are established to induce the firm to act optimally when the regulator does not know exactly what the optimal outcome is. The revised subsidy mechanism assumes that the regulator knows the variable that the mechanism is supposed to induce the firm to choose, namely the optimal level of capacity. The regulator knows this not in conceptual terms only (as in knowing that price should equal marginal cost), but knows the exact number. If the regulator knows the optimal capacity, the regulator can simply mandate that the firm provide that capacity. A regulatory mechanism is not required.

Riordan's suggestions regarding optimal capacity are valuable, however, at a more fundamental level. The revised formula reflects the important concept that the regulator can use information on the optimal capacity to penalize the firm for not choosing it. While the formula as specified requires that the regulator have complete knowledge of the optimal capacity, the concept introduces the possibility of developing mechanisms that utilize partial knowledge. That is, the regulator might have some evidence of whether the firm's chosen capacity is optimal, without knowing the actual level of optimal capacity. Regulatory mechanisms can perhaps be devised that use this information to push the firm, if not to, then at least close to, the optimal capacity. This issue of inducing optimal capacity in the context of fluctuating demand is an important area for further research.

9   Self-Selecting Tariffs and Sibley's Mechanism

9.1 Introduction

In recent years, utilities have begun to offer their customers a choice among tariffs. For example, many electric utilities offer both time-of-use and standard (non-time-differentiated) rates and allow each customer to choose the rates under which its bill will be calculated. Local phone companies often offer both flat-rate and measured service: the customer can choose to be billed either a fixed amount per month without additional charge for local calls (flat-rate service) or a lower fixed amount per month with an additional charge for each local call (measured service). Each long distance carrier offers a variety of tariffs, including WATS and WATS-like services and plans like AT&T's "Reach Out America" program, under which the customer obtains an hour of off-peak calling each month for a fixed cost and then pays a reduced rate for additional calling.

When a customer has a choice among two or more tariffs, the tariffs are called "optional," "voluntary," or "self-selecting." The last term is probably most accurate, because it incorporates the fact that the customer necessarily pays for the service and only chooses the schedule under which its bill is calculated. The term "optional" or "voluntary" tariff seems to mistakenly suggest that paying is optional, like the voluntary admission fee of some museums and performing arts.

Self-selecting tariffs have recently become popular for a variety of reasons. It is usually easier for a regulated firm to obtain permission from its regulator to offer a new rate schedule as an option to customers, rather than as a substitute for the existing schedule. For most new tariffs, some customers would be hurt by being charged under the new schedule; for example, customers who consume a relatively large share of electricity in the peak would be hurt if their consumption were charged under time-of-use rates instead of standard rates. If a new schedule is offered as an option, customers who would be hurt under the new schedule can choose to stay on the existing schedule. This possibility prevents these customers from opposing the introduction of the new schedule. It also avoids the ethical problem of needing to trade off the benefits to some customers against the harm to others in determining whether the new schedule constitutes a social improvement.[1]

Under traditional assumptions about customer behavior, self-selecting tariffs provide utilities and their regulators with a mechanism for increasing surplus. As shown in section 9.4, if prices under an existing tariff are not equal to marginal cost, then it is possible to design a new tariff that, when offered on a self-selecting basis in addition to the existing schedule, increases surplus. It is even possible to attain Pareto dominance, that is, to make every party better off without hurting anyone.

Not all self-selecting tariff offerings allow for Pareto dominance or even increase surplus. When not appropriately designed, the introduction of a new self-selecting tariff can decrease surplus. As described in section 9.4, the appropriate design of self-selecting tariffs requires information on the demand of customers, which the regulator generally does not possess. The basic question therefore arises: how can the regulator induce the firm to design and introduce self-selecting tariffs that increase surplus without the regulator knowing beforehand what tariffs are appropriate?

Sibley (1989) has proposed a regulatory mechanism that, under certain conditions, does just this. In particular, Sibley's mechanism induces the firm to offer a self-selecting tariff in each time period that increases surplus in that period; in equilibrium, first-best optimality is attained. The conditions under which this mechanism can be shown to operate effectively are fairly restrictive: (1) demand for access to the service is assumed to be fixed independent of price (at least within the range of prices considered) and (2) either all customers have the same demand, or the firm knows the demand of each individual customer and is able to offer a separate tariff to each customer. The analysis is valuable, however, even for settings in which these restrictions do

---

1. The offering of a new tariff on an self-selecting basis is not necessarily Pareto dominating, because it could decrease the profits of the firm if the tariff is not appropriately designed. This issue is discussed in section 9.4.

not apply and constitutes a seminal contribution on optimal regulation with self-selecting tariffs.

The chapter is organized as follows. Section 9.2 describes customers' choice among self-selecting tariffs under the traditional assumptions about customer behavior. Section 9.3 shows, under the standard assumptions, that a set of self-selecting tariffs is equivalent to one multipart tariff. This equivalence allows us in section 9.4 to show that self-selecting tariffs can be designed that increase surplus and Pareto dominate, using concepts developed in chapter 7 for multipart tariffs. In section 9.5, an application of self-selecting tariffs in the real world is examined. The evidence indicates that Pareto dominance was achieved, which shows that the theoretical results regarding self-selecting tariffs can indeed occur in the real world. Section 9.6 describes Sibley's mechanism and shows that it induces the regulated firm to design and offer self-selecting tariffs that increase surplus, reaching first-best optimality in equilibrium. The chapter concludes with a cautionary section on how the surplus implications of self-selecting tariffs may differ if, as empirical work has consistently found, customers do not behave in accordance with the standard assumptions.

The findings of the chapter can be summarized as follows:

• Under standard assumptions, each customer chooses the self-selecting tariff that provides it with the greatest surplus for its known demand.

• For any set of self-selecting tariffs, an equivalent multipart tariff can be designed. This equivalent tariff, offered without selection, results in the same consumption level and bill for each customer as would occur with the self-selecting tariffs.

• Suppose the firm offers a new tariff without changing its original tariff offerings. No customer is hurt, because each customer can choose to stay on its existing tariff. Any customer that switches to the new tariff necessarily benefits; otherwise, it would not choose the new tariff. Depending on the design of the new tariff and the distribution of customers' demands, the firm's profit could either rise or fall.

• Given any set of self-selecting tariffs with usage prices in excess of marginal cost, a new tariff can always be designed that, when offered in addition to the original tariffs, increases surplus and even Pareto dominates the offering of the original tariffs alone. Because no customer is hurt by a new tariff offering, this fact implies that, when prices exceed marginal cost under existing tariffs, a new tariff offering can always be designed that increases (or does not decrease) the profit of the firm.

• Given a non-time-differentiated (non-TOU) price that is below marginal cost in the peak and above marginal cost in the off-peak, a time-of-use tariff can be designed that, when offered in addition to the non-TOU price, increases surplus and Pareto dominates the offering of the non-TOU price alone.

• Sibley proposes a mechanism under which the firm offers two self-selecting access/usage tariffs in each period. The firm is free to design one of the tariffs. The regulator designs the other. The regulator designs its tariff in such a way that the firm can make strictly positive profit only if the firm designs and offers a tariff that increases total surplus. In the first period after this mechanism is imposed, the firm offers a tariff with usage price equal to marginal cost. With access demand fixed (as Sibley assumes), first-best optimality is therefore attained in the first period. By the second period, profits are zero. This mechanism requires that either (1) all customers have the same demand, or (2) the firm knows each customer's separate demand and can offer separate tariffs to each customer.

• Empirical work indicates that customers do not choose tariffs in accordance with the traditional assumptions. The implications of this finding depend on how customers' behavior is interpreted. If customers are thought to make mistakes in their choice of tariff, then multipart tariffs are probably better than self-selecting tariffs. Under the traditional assumptions, a multi-part tariff can be designed that is equivalent to self-selecting tariffs, such that any function served by self-selecting tariffs can also be served by multipart tariffs. However, when the traditional assumptions do not hold, multipart tariffs protect customers from their own mistakes. It might be the case, on the other hand, that customers do not make mistakes but rather choose among tariffs on the basis of factors other than surplus under known demand, considering, for example, issues of uncertainty, risk, the effort of optimization, information costs, and so on. The implications of self-selecting tariffs for surplus have not been derived when customers' decision making is rational but more complex than traditionally assumed. It is possible that in these cases self-selecting tariffs could offer benefits that cannot be obtained with the multipart tariff.

9.2   Customer Choice among Tariffs under Traditional Assumptions

Under the traditional analysis, the customer is assumed to know, at the time of choosing among tariffs, its demand curve for the good. The customer calculates the consumer surplus that it would obtain under each tariff and chooses the tariff that provides the greatest surplus.

Consider, for example, a customer whose local phone company offers two tariffs. Under tariff I, the customer is charged $8 per month plus 10 cents for each local call. Under tariff II, the customer is charged $10 month and 6 cents for each call. The customer knows that its demand for local calls is that depicted in figure 9.1. Using this demand curve, the customer calculates its surplus under each tariff. Under tariff I, the consumer's surplus is the area A minus $8. (Area A is the surplus the customer obtains from local calls given a price of 10 cents per call and ignoring the fixed charge; subtracting the $8 fixed charge from this amount gives the actual surplus incorporating the fixed charge.) Surplus from tariff II is areas A and B, minus the $10 fixed fee.

The customer in this example chooses tariff I if area A minus $8 exceeds area A and B minus $10; otherwise the customer chooses tariff II. Given the demand curve in figure 9.1, area A is $12 and area B

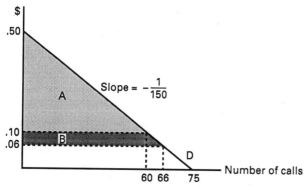

Tariff I: $8 per month plus 10¢ per call
Tariff II: $10 per month plus 6¢ per call

Figure 9.1
Customer choice between two access/usage tariffs

is $2.52. Surplus under tariff I is therefore $4, while surplus under tariff II is $4.52. The customer chooses tariff II.

The comparison of the two tariffs can be seen in an another way. Tariff II costs more than tariff I on a monthly basis, but levies a lower price per call. The customer's question is: are the benefits from having a lower per-call price sufficiently large to warrant the higher fixed charge? More specifically, the customer chooses tariff II over tariff I if the extra surplus the customer obtains at the lower per-call price exceeds the extra fixed charge. The extra surplus is area B, which is $2.52: the extra fixed charge is $2. The customer chooses tariff II.

Two other graphs are sometimes useful in examining a customer's choice among tariffs: the outlay schedule and the mapping of indifference curves against budget constraints. An outlay schedule gives the bill the customer would receive as a function of the quantity consumed, under the tariff situation the customer is facing. For the tariffs in our example, the outlay schedules are shown in figure 9.2. Under tariff I, the customer would face line I-I as its outlay schedule; and, under tariff II, line II-II. The customer has a choice between these two tariffs. For any given number of calls, the customer necessarily chooses the cheaper tariff. The outlay schedule that the customer faces in the presence of these self-selecting tariffs is, therefore, the bold, kinked line, that is, the lower of the two individual tariff schedules at each number of calls. The location of the kink, at fifty calls, can be easily calculated. If the customer makes fifty calls, its bill would be the same

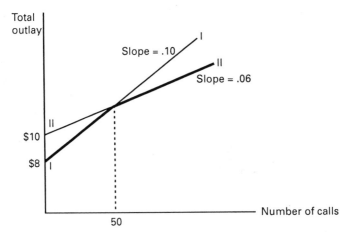

Figure 9.2
Outlay schedule

under both schedules (under tariff I: $8 + (50) · .10 = 13$; under tariff II: $10 + (50) · .06 = 13$). For fewer than fifty calls, tariff I is cheaper; whereas tariff II is cheaper for more than fifty calls.

Note that the outlay schedule provides only partial information on the customer's choice. In particular, it provides information on which tariff is cheaper and hence chosen, *given* the number of calls made. However, the number of calls the customer makes is *not* given, but is determined simultaneously with the choice of tariff. As indicated in figure 9.1, the customer would make sixty calls under tariff I and sixty-six calls under tariff II; it chooses tariff II and makes sixty-six calls. The outlay schedule can be used to determine the cost to the customer of making sixty-six calls and to verify that the customer must be choosing tariff II if it is making sixty-six calls (because tariff II is cheaper for that number of calls). However, it cannot be used (directly at least) to determine that sixty-six calls will be made.

The mapping of indifference curves and budget constraints allows the customer's choice of tariff and its choice of quantity to be presented on the same graph. For our example, consider two goods: local calls and all other goods, with the price of all other goods set at $1 and the customer's income being $70. The budget constraint associated with tariff I is the line I-I in figure 9.3: it starts at sixty-two because $8 of the customer's income must be foregone in paying the fixed charge under this tariff; the slope is -0.10 because for each additional call, .10 units of other goods must be foregone. Similarly, the budget constraint for tariff II is the line II-II with y-intercept of sixty and a slope of -.06. The customer has a choice between the two tariffs. The budget constraint the customer actually faces is therefore the bold, kinked line, which is the "farther out" portions of the budget constraints for each of the two individual tariffs.[2] The customer maximizes utility subject to its budget constraint; that is, the customer moves out as far as possible on its indifference mapping while staying on the bold, kinked budget constraint. The customer chooses point

---

2. Consider, for example, point M. Under tariff II, the customer cannot increase its consumption of other goods without decreasing the number of calls it makes: by definition, M is on the budget constraint for tariff II. However, because the customer has a choice of tariff, the customer can switch to tariff I and consume more other goods without making fewer calls (moving from M to N). Point M is therefore *not* on the customer's budget constraint when the customer faces a choice between tariffs. At point N, the customer cannot increase consumption of other goods without making fewer calls, even if the customer were to switch tariffs. Point N *is* therefore on the customer's budget constraint for the self-selecting tariff situation.

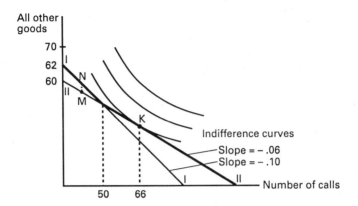

Figure 9.3
Budget constraint and indifference mapping

K, which represents sixty-six calls. Because *K* is on the line II-II, the customer in choosing point *K* necessarily chooses tariff II.

For situations with more than two tariffs, or more complex tariffs, the concepts developed in our example are applied analogously. In each case, the customer calculates its surplus under each tariff and chooses the tariff that provides the greatest surplus. The outlay schedule it faces is comprised of the lowest portions of the outlay schedules for each of the tariffs offered. The budget constraint the customer faces consists of the "farthest out" (that is, least constraining) portions of the budget constraints for the individual tariffs; the customer chooses the point that attains the highest indifference curve, thereby choosing both a tariff and a consumption level.

9.3   Equivalence to Multipart Tariffs

Given that the customer knows its demand curve for the good, a set of self-selecting tariffs is equivalent to one tariff that embodies elements of each of the self-selecting tariffs. "Equivalent" in this context means that the behavior of the customer is the same: that the customer would consume the same quantity of the good, pay the same total bill, and face the same marginal price.

Consider the example of self-selecting tariffs in the previous section: tariff I consisting of an $8 fixed charge and a 10 cents usage price, and tariff II with a $10 fixed charge and 6 cents per call. The outlay schedule and the budget constraint that the customer faces under these self-selecting tariffs is given by the bold, kinked lines in figures 9.2 and 9.3. A three-part tariff can be constructed that has the same outlay schedule and budget constraint and hence results in the same customer behavior. Specifically, consider a tariff, called tariff M, that levies a fixed fee of $8 plus a per-call charge of 10 cents for up to fifty calls and then a charge of 6 cents for each call over fifty. The outlay schedule for tariff M is the bold, kinked line in figure 9.2: the customer's bill is $8 for no calls, increases by 10 cents for each call up to fifty, and then increases by 6 cents for each call over fifty. For any given number of calls, the customer would pay the same total bill if it faced tariff M without choice of tariff as it would if it faced tariffs I and II with selection.

The budget constraint is also the same, namely, the bold, kinked line in figure 9.3. With no calls, the customer under tariff M pays a fixed charge of $8, leaving $70 − $8 = $62 for other goods. The y-intercept of the budget constraint is therefore sixty-two. For each call up to fifty calls, the customer must pay 10 cents and hence forego consumption of .10 units of other goods. For each call over fifty, the customer must forego only .06 units of other goods. The budget constraint therefore has a slope of −.10 from zero to fifty calls and a slope of −.06 beyond fifty calls. Because the budget constraint is the same whether the customer faces tariff M without selection or tariffs I and II with selection, the behavior of the customer is the same: the customer makes sixty-six calls and consumes 56.04 units of other goods ($70 minus a bill of $13.96 for the calls, divided by the $1 price for other goods).

The customer also faces the same marginal price. Under tariff M, the customer, at its chosen consumption level of sixty-six calls, faces a price of 6 cents for an extra call. Under tariffs I and II with self-selection, the customer, at its chosen consumption level of sixty-six calls, chooses tariff II under which a price of 6 cents is charged for an extra call.

These concepts can obviously be generalized. It is possible, for any set of self-selecting tariffs, to design one tariff that, if implemented without customers having any choice among tariffs, would result in the same behavior, total bill, and marginal price for each customer. The design of this equivalent tariff is most easily accomplished with reference to the outlay schedule for the self-selecting tariffs. Figure 9.4, for example, illustrates a situation that is increasingly common for local phone service. The phone company offers three options to

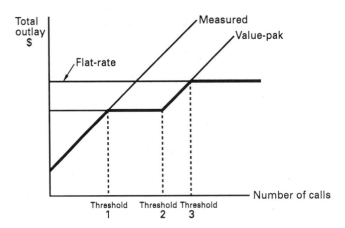

Figure 9.4
Outlay schedule for flat-rate, measured, and value-pak options, plus an equivalent tariff without selection

its customers: *flat-rate service*, which, for a fixed monthly fee, allows unlimited local calling without extra charge; *measured service*, which levies a lower monthly fee but charges for each call; and a hybrid that is often called "*value pak*," which, for a midlevel fixed fee, allows a certain number of local calls to be made without additional charge (this is referred to as the "calling allowance") and then charges for calls beyond this allowance at the same rate as under measured service. The non-self-selecting tariff that is equivalent to this set of options consists of a fixed charge and four per-call prices, each charged in a different range of calls. The fixed charge is the same as that for measured service. For low levels of calling, the per-call charge is the same as under measured service. After the first threshold (which occurs at the number of calls at which measured service and value pak would cost the same), the per-call charge becomes zero. After the second threshold (the calling allowance under value pak), the per-call charge becomes that charged under measured service (because calls under value pak are charged the same as under measured service in this range of calls). Finally, after the third threshold (at which value-pak and flat-rate service cost the same), the usage charge becomes zero again. For customers who know their demand curves, being charged under this one tariff without any choice would be the same as being offered a choice among flat-rate, measured, and value-pak services. And because the number of calls made by each customer and the bill paid by each customer would be the same, the costs, revenues, and profits of the phone company would also be the same.

9.4 Welfare Implications of Self-Selecting Tariffs

In chapter 7 it was shown that, in many circumstances, surplus can be improved and Pareto dominance even achieved through the judicious use of multipart tariffs. We have just shown that self-selecting tariffs are equivalent to appropriately designed multipart tariffs without selection. It follows therefore that, in many situations, surplus can be improved and Pareto dominance achieved by the judicious use of self-selecting tariffs. This fact is amplified below, using methods that are analogous to those in chapter 7.

Self-selecting tariffs possess a unique feature that is important in itself and also facilitates the analysis of surplus. Specifically, the introduction of a new self-selecting tariff in addition to existing tariffs can only benefit customers. Consider a firm that is initially offering a set of tariffs. If the firm, at some point in time, adds a new tariff without changing the original ones, then no customer is made worse off by this addition and some customers might be made better off. No customer is hurt because each customer can choose to remain on its original tariff, with no change in its behavior or surplus. Any customer that would obtain more surplus from the new tariff than it does from its originally chosen tariff can, and will, switch to the new tariff, becoming better off. Consequently, some customers—namely those who switch to the new tariff—benefit, and no customer is hurt.

Although no customer is hurt, the firm might be. Depending on the design of the tariff, the firm's profits could either increase or decrease from the offering of a new tariff in addition to existing tariffs. Several examples will suffice to illustrate the fact. Consider an energy utility that originally provides electricity under standard, non-time-differentiated rates. If the utility offers time-of-use (TOU) rates as an option to its customers in addition to the standard rate, then customers only stand to gain: those who would benefit from the TOU rates switch to them while those who would not benefit remain on the standard rates. However, depending on the extent to which customers who switch to TOU rates change their consumption patterns, the firm could either gain or lose money. At one extreme, suppose that the customers are totally non-price-responsive in their TOU consumption of electricity. Those customers with sufficiently low peak-period consumption would receive a lower bill for the same consumption under the TOU rates compared to the standard rate. These customers would switch to the TOU rates; but because their consumption is not price responsive, they would consume the same amount of electricity in each period as under the standard rates. Because consumption levels are the same, the costs of the firm would be the same. However, the customers who switched to TOU rates would be paying lower bills, such that the revenues of the firm would be lower. With lower revenues and the same costs, the firm's profits decrease.

At the other extreme, customers might be highly price responsive. Suppose the customers who switch to TOU rates shift all of their peak-period consumption to the off-peak. The costs of the firm decrease substantially, because off-peak production is cheaper than peak production. Although the customer's bills, and the firm's revenues, are also lower, the reduced costs can easily dominate the reduced revenues, such that the firm's profits increase.

Another example arises in the context of local phone service. If a phone company that has traditionally provided only flat-rate service starts to offer measured service as an option, its profits could either increase or decrease. If customers are not price responsive and choose the service that offers the lower bill for their fixed number of calls, the phone company will lose money. However, if customers that switch to measured service reduce their calling in response to the higher price, the costs of the firm could decrease more than its revenues.

To summarize: if a new tariff is offered as an option in addition to existing tariffs: (1) no customer is hurt, and any customer that switches to the new tariff is benefited, and (2) the firm might obtain either more or less profit.

Although it is true that customers are not hurt when a new tariff is introduced as an option in addition to existing tariffs, the fact that the firm might be hurt can eventually have detrimental consequences for customers. In particular, if the firm loses money, it might be necessary for the firm to change the original tariffs, raising rates under these schedules. For example, if an energy utility introduces TOU rates and loses money from doing so, it might raise the standard rate in an effort to recoup the loss. In this case, the new tariff is not being offered in addition to the existing tariffs; rather, the existing tariffs are being changed. With higher rates under the original tariffs, customers who remain on their original tariffs would be hurt. This scenario—of the firm losing money and raising rates under the original tariffs—is especially likely if the form of regulation assures that the firm breaks even. Consequently, the issue of whether the firm losses or gains from the offering of a new tariff option is of concern to customers as well as shareholders.

If a tariff can be designed that, when offered in addition to existing tariffs, increases the firm's profits, then Pareto dominance can clearly be achieved. No customer is hurt, and the firm is better off. In fact, the extra profit can be returned to customers in the form of lower rates under all tariffs. Two results establish some conditions under which it is possible to design such a tariff.

Result 1: Given any set of N self-selecting tariffs with usage prices that exceed marginal cost and customers that are at least somewhat price responsive, a set of N + 1 self-selecting tariffs can be designed the offering of which Pareto dominates the offering of the original N tariffs.

If the new set of $N+1$ tariffs consists of the original N plus an additional tariff, we know that no customer will be hurt by the addition and some customers might benefit. The task in demonstrating the result is therefore to show that a new tariff can be designed that, when added to the original set of tariffs, increases the profits of the firm (or, alternatively, benefits at least one customer without decreasing the profits of the firm).

Consider the customer with the highest level of consumption under the original N tariffs. This customer has the largest bill (given, as will always be the case in practice, that the outlay schedule under these tariffs increases with consumption). Call this customer "the largest customer" and denote its consumption as Q_L, its bill as B_L, and the marginal price the customer faces as P_L, which, by assumption, exceeds marginal cost. The demand of this customer is depicted in figure 9.5.[3]

We can design a new tariff offering that this customer will choose and that will generate additional profit for the firm. Let the new tariff consist of: (1) an access fee of B_L (that is, an access fee equal to the largest customer's original bill), (2) a price of zero for the first Q_L units

---

3. The customer faces a price of P_L for units of consumption near Q_L; the line at P_L is dotted for lower units of consumption because a price other than P_L might be charged for other levels of consumption (that is, the inframarginal price might not equal the marginal price). All that is required for our analysis is a designation of the marginal price.

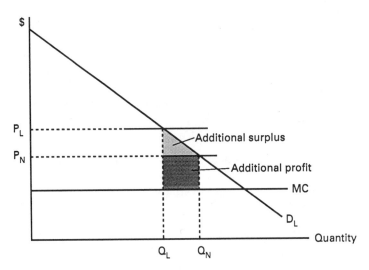

Figure 9.5
Pareto-dominating tariff

of consumption, and (3) a price of P_N for each unit of consumption over Q_L, where P_N is below P_L and above marginal cost. For its original level of consumption, Q_L, the customer is just as well off under the new tariff as under its original tariff: in either case it pays B_L. However, under the new tariff, the customer faces a lower marginal price for consumption beyond Q_L, which allows it to obtain greater surplus. In particular, the customer, if it chooses the new tariff, will increase consumption from Q_L to Q_N and obtain additional surplus equal to the shaded area in figure 9.5. Because the customer obtains greater surplus under the new tariff than under its original tariff, the customer will choose the new tariff.

Consider now the firm. Because the new marginal price is above marginal cost, the firm earns additional profit when the customer increases its consumption. For the original Q_L units of consumption, the firm obtains the same revenue from the customer as under the customer's originally chosen tariff and incurs the same costs; however, for the additional units of consumption (from Q_L to Q_N), the firm collects extra revenue in excess of its extra costs, such that its profits increase.

Consider, finally, all other customers. The access fee under the new tariff is higher than the bill that each other customer paid under the original tariffs (recall that the access fee is equal to the total bill of the customer with the highest bill under the original tariffs). Consequently, the bill that each of these customers would receive for its original level of consumption would be higher under the new tariff than under the original tariffs. It might be the case that none of these customers would choose the new tariff because of this. In this case, the new tariff benefits the largest customer and the firm, and does not affect any other customers: Pareto dominance is achieved.

It is possible, however, that some customers (in addition to the largest) will choose the new tariff. Recall that the new tariff offers a lower marginal cost. The extra surplus that a customer can obtain due to the lower marginal price may exceed the extra bill that it is charged for its original level of consumption. If this is the case, the customer will choose the new tariff, obtaining a net increase in surplus. The firm also benefits from any customer that chooses the new tariff. Each customer pays a higher bill for its original level of consumption such that the firm obtains more revenues, and any increase in consumption that the lower marginal price induces generates even more profit for the firm, because the revenue of these extra units exceeds the cost of producing them. Again, Pareto dominance is achieved.

The result can made even stronger. A portion of the extra profit that the firm obtains can be refunded to all customers in the form of lower prices under all tariffs. If all of the extra profits are refunded (as would be required if the firm were allowed to make no more than zero profit), all customers would benefit and the firm would not be hurt by the offering of the new tariff. If the firm were allowed to retain some of the additional profits, customers and shareholders would all benefit.

Note that, in the above argument, the marginal price under the new tariff is set above marginal cost. This feature of the new tariff is what allows the firm to increase its profits by offering the new tariff, which in turn allows the opportunity of reduced rates under all tariffs. If the marginal price under the new tariff is set *equal to* marginal cost, rather than above it, then the largest customer, and any other customer that chooses the new tariff, would benefit from the new tariff. The firm would not earn additional profit from additional units of consumption. However, if any customer aside from the largest chose the tariff, the firm would obtain extra revenue from these customers' original consumption. Pareto dominance is still achieved.

A corollary to result 1 is that, under the same conditions as stated in the result, a new tariff can always be designed that increases surplus when offered in addition to existing tariffs. Result 1 shows that Pareto dominance can be achieved. The offering of the new tariff that attains Pareto dominance necessarily increases surplus, because the surplus of some parties increases and no one's surplus decreases. Other tariffs might obtain an even greater increase in surplus.

The tariff that we designed to achieve Pareto dominance might provide only a small increase in surplus. It is possible that only the largest customer will choose the new tariff, such that the surplus gain is only the increased surplus to this one customer and the extra profits generated from this one customer. When averaged over a large number of customers, the benefits might be so small as to be negligible. The point of result 1 is, however, simply to show that a surplus improvement and Pareto dominance is possible. In particular situations, it may be possible to identify tariffs that increase surplus considerably. These may, and probably will, be quite different from the one designed for the purposes of the proof. The importance of the result is to indicate that a search for new tariff offerings that increase surplus is worth pursuing because we know that at least one such tariff can necessarily be found.

For result 1, we assumed that usage prices exceed marginal cost. When demand and/or costs vary over times of day or periods of the week, marginal cost may at certain times (e.g., the "rush hour" or "peak") exceed the price charged under existing tariffs. The next result indicates that Pareto-dominating tariff offerings can be designed for these situations as well (Train 1990).

Result 2: Given a non-time-differentiated rate that is below marginal cost in the peak and above marginal cost in the off-peak, and customers that are at least somewhat price responsive, a time-of-use tariff can be designed that, when offered as an option to customers in addition to the original non-time-differentiated rate, Pareto dominates the use of the non-time-differentiated rate alone.

Suppose there are two time periods, called "on-peak" and "off-peak," with the same usage rate, r, charged in both periods. Marginal cost in the on-peak, MC_{on}, exceeds r, while MC_{off} is below r. To construct a time-of-use (TOU) tariff, identify the customer with the largest ratio of off-peak to on-peak demand at the original non-TOU rate. Call this customer the "target customer" and its original consumption levels Q^0_{off} and Q^0_{on}. The TOU tariff is designed by raising price in the on-peak *toward*, but not beyond, the marginal cost in the on-peak, and by lowering the price in the off-peak toward, but not beyond, the marginal cost in the off-peak. Furthermore, the TOU prices are set such that the target customer's bill for its original consumption is the same under the TOU rates as the original non-TOU rate.

To be concrete, let us lower the price in the off-peak by Δp_{off}; that is, set the off-peak price at $p_{off} = r - \Delta p_{off}$. In the on-peak, raise price by exactly the target customer's ratio of off-peak to on-peak consumption times the amount of the price drop in the off-peak; that is, set the on-peak price at $p_{on} = r + (Q^0_{off}/Q^0_{on})\Delta p_{off}$. In making these changes, be sure that Δp_{off} is small enough that p_{off} is *above* MC_{off} and p_{on} is *below* MC_{on}. At these TOU rates, the target customer would receive the same bill for its original consumption as it does under the non-TOU rate:

$$
\begin{aligned}
\text{Bill under TOU rates} &= p_{off}Q^0_{off} + p_{on}Q^0_{on} \\
&= (r - \Delta p_{off})Q^0_{off} \\
&\quad + (r + (Q^0_{off}/Q^0_{on})\Delta p_{off})Q^0_{on} \\
&= rQ^0_{off} + rQ^0_{on} \\
&\quad - \Delta p_{off}Q^0_{off} \\
&\quad + ((Q^0_{off}/Q^0_{on})\Delta p_{off})Q^0_{on} \\
&= rQ^0_{off} + rQ^0_{on} \\
&\quad - \Delta p_{off}Q^0_{off} + Q^0_{off}\Delta p_{off} \\
&= rQ^0_{off} + rQ^0_{on} \\
&= \text{bill under non-TOU rate.}
\end{aligned}
$$

For all other customers, who have a lower ratio of off-peak to on-peak consumption, the bill for their original levels of consumption would be higher under these TOU rates than under the non-TOU rate.

The target customer will choose this TOU tariff. Figure 9.6 provides the relevant information. The shaded areas in the on-peak and off-peak graphs are equal in size, because the TOU rates are designed such that the increase in the target customer's bill for its original on-peak consumption is exactly offset by the reduction in its bill for its original off-peak consumption (such that its total bill is unchanged). Under the TOU rates, the target customer will adjust consumption in each period and obtain additional surplus. In the on-peak, the customer will decrease consumption from Q^0_{on} to Q^1_{on}, foregoing the units of consumption for which marginal benefit is below the new price. This reduction in consumption at the new higher price provides the customer with extra surplus equal to the area ABC. Similarly, in the off-peak, the customer increases consumption in response to the new,

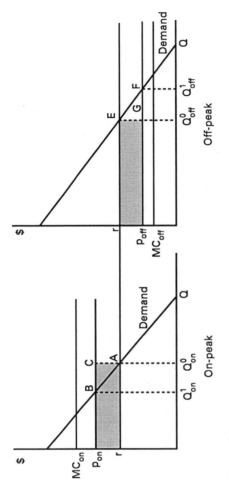

Figure 9.6
Pareto-dominating TOU rate option: target customer

lower price, obtaining additional surplus in the amount of area EFG.[4] If there is the possibility of shifting consumption across periods, the customer will do this also, obtaining further increases in surplus. Because the target customer obtains greater surplus under the TOU rates than under the original non-TOU rate, it will choose the TOU rates.

The firm will earn additional profit from the target customer under the TOU rates. Because $MC_{on} > p_{on}$, profits rise when the customer decreases its consumption in the on-peak: the lost revenues are more than made up by the cost savings to the firm of not producing those foregone units. And because $MC_{off} < p_{off}$, the extra consumption in the off-peak generates additional profit for the firm.

Consider now all the other customers. The bill that each of these customers would receive for their original consumption would increase under the TOU rates. Nevertheless, some of these customers may choose the TOU rates if they are able to respond sufficiently to the TOU rates such that their surplus increases. The firm will earn additional profits from these customers, because their bills for their original consumption are higher and their response to the TOU rates consists of decreasing on-peak consumption and increasing off-peak consumption.

The peripheral statements that were made about result 1 also apply to result 2. If profits are refunded to customers in the form of lower rates under both the non-TOU and TOU tariffs, all customers can benefit. The TOU tariff designed for the purpose of the result may increase total surplus by only a small amount. Other tariffs may produce a far greater surplus gain. The result simply indicates that, under the specified conditions, the search for a surplus-increasing, and even a Pareto-dominating, optional TOU tariff will necessarily be successful.

---

4. It might seem peculiar that the customer obtains additional surplus by decreasing consumption in the on-peak and increasing consumption in the off-peak: it seems that the customer gets more surplus no matter what it does. Actually, the customer obtains extra surplus only when it adjusts its consumption in the opposite direction of the change in price. In the on-peak, the price rises under the TOU rates compared to the non-TOU rate, such that the customer obtains extra surplus by decreasing consumption. In the off-peak, price drops, and the customer obtains more surplus by increasing consumption. In a sense, both adjustments are in the same direction, namely, opposite that of the price change.

9.5   An Application of Self-Selecting Tariffs

This section presents the results of an empirical investigation of a real-world application of self-selecting tariffs. Train and Toyama (1989) examined the optional time-of-use (TOU) rates for electricity that were offered to agricultural customers of the energy utility in northern California. They found that the offering of TOU rates in addition to the standard, non-TOU rate under which the customers had traditionally been charged Pareto dominated the offering of the non-TOU rate alone. Specifically, many customers chose the TOU rates and the firm's profits were estimated to have risen due to the TOU tariff offering. This result indicates that surplus-increasing and even Pareto-dominating self-selecting tariffs are possible in practice as well as in theory.[5]

Farms and other agricultural firms (such as nurseries) use electricity to pump water for irrigation. Under mandate from the California Public Utilities Commission, the northern California energy utility introduced optional TOU rates in the agricultural sector, first in 1981 for selected firms and starting in 1983 for all eligible firms. The tariff was available for any agricultural pumping installation that draws a maximum load of a least thirty-five kilowatts and is used at least 300 hours a year (i.e., all but the smallest installations). Farms with several pumping installations had the option of TOU rates for each installation. Commercial and industrial firms were also eligible for the rates for their agricultural pumping installations (e.g., for watering lawns) though not for electricity used in their commercial and industrial activities.

Under the standard, non-TOU tariff, installations were billed at a rate of $0.07877 per kilowatt-hour (kWh) as of January 1, 1985. Under the TOU rates, the kWh charge was differentiated by three times of day (called on-peak, partial-peak, and off-peak) in each of two times of year (called summer and winter). The definitions of these periods and the rates charged in each period are given in table 9.1.

Of the 33,382 eligible pumping installations, 7,675 (23%) chose the TOU rate. Using the traditional concepts, Train and Toyama assumed that these customers benefited from the TOU rates, because otherwise they would have remained on the non-TOU rate. The customers

---

5. As further support, Heyman, Lazorchak, Sibley, and Taylor (1987) have designed self-selecting tariffs for NYNEX's telecommunications services and shown that these tariffs Pareto dominate the existing offering.

Table 9.1
TOU rate schedule

	Times	
	Summer (May 1–Sept. 30)	Winter (Oct. 1–April 30)
On-peak	12:30 p.m.–6:30 p.m. Mon.–Fri.	4:30 p.m.–8:30 p.m. Mon.–Fri.
Partial-peak	8:30 a.m.–12:30 p.m. and 6:30 p.m.–10:30 p.m. Mon.–Fri.	8:30 a.m..–4:30 p.m. and 8:30 p.m.–10:30 p.m. Mon.–Fri.
Off-peak	10:30 p.m.–8:30 a.m. Mon.–Fri. All day Sat. and Sun.	10:30 p.m.–8:30 a.m. Mon.–Fri. All day Sat. and Sun.
	kWh Rates as of January 1, 1985	
	Summer	Winter
On-peak	0.13114	0.10689
Partial-peak	0.07945	0.08222
Off-peak	0.06780	0.06780

who remained on the non-TOU rate were not affected by the offering of TOU rates, because the non-TOU rate was not changed. The only issue therefore was whether the firm's profit rose or fell.

Using data on the energy consumption of eligible installations, Train and Toyama estimated a model of the demand for electricity by time of use. This model predicts the total electricity consumption of the customer and the share of consumption in the on-peak, partial-peak, and off-peak, respectively, taking as input the price for electricity in each period.

The demand model was used, along with cost information, to approximate the impact of the TOU tariff offering on the profits of the utility. In particular, the profits of the firm were determined twice. First, the profits the utility earned under the self-selecting tariffs were calculated. The demand model was used to estimate each customer's consumption under the tariff they actually chose. The revenues from this estimated consumption were calculated. Using the cost information, the cost of meeting this demand was estimated. Subtracting the costs from the revenues provided an estimate of the utility's profit under the TOU rate offering.

Second, the profit the utility *would have* earned had it not offered the TOU rates was calculated. The demand model was used to estimate each customer's consumption in each period under the standard, non-TOU rates. Revenues, costs, and profit from this consumption were then calculated.

Train and Toyama found that the customers who chose the TOU rates reduced their consumption in the on-peak, increased in the off-peak, and remained about the same in the partial-peak. Furthermore, the magnitudes of these shifts were such that the utility's profits *increased* as a result of the TOU tariff offering. The extra profit was small (about $360,000, a tiny percentage of the utility's total profit). The firm cannot therefore be considered to have obtained a windfall. However, because profits did not fall, there was no need for the non-TOU rates to be raised to recoup any losses.

In summary, the TOU tariff offering benefited 23% of the eligible agricultural customers (as evidenced by the fact that they chose it), did not hurt any other customers, and provided a small amount of extra profit for the firm. In this case at least, surplus was raised and Pareto dominance achieved by the judicious use of self-selecting tariffs.

9.6   Sibley's Mechanism

Sibley (1989) has proposed a mechanism under which the regulator uses self-selecting tariffs, given certain conditions, to induce the firm to move to first-best optimality. In fact, first-best optimality is achieved in the first period after the regulatory mechanism is imposed. To implement the mechanism, the regulator does not need to know the demand curve or the cost function of the firm. The regulator need only observe for each period the price the firm charges and the profit the firm earns.

The conditions under which the mechanism can be shown to operate effectively are fairly restrictive. The number of customers is assumed to be fixed; that is, access demand is assumed not to be price responsive, at least within the relevant range of prices. Regarding usage demand, either of two conditions is required: (1) each customer has the same demand, or (2) the firm knows the demand curves of each individual customer and can design a different tariff for each customer. While these conditions are unlikely to occur in the real world, the mechanism provides insight that is valuable in more general situations. In particular, the mechanism shows that by requiring the firm to offer one or more self-selecting tariffs that in some sense maintain the status quo, the firm is only able to increase its own profits over time by introducing new tariff options that increase consumer surplus. Compatibility between the firm's profit drive and surplus maximization is thereby established.[6]

9.6.1 Identical Customers

Consider first the situation in which each customer has the same demand. The mechanism operates as follows. In each period, the firm is required to offer two self-selecting tariffs to its customers. Each of the tariffs is an access/usage tariff, consisting of a fixed charge and a usage price. The rates under the two tariffs are specified for each period. The regulator designs one of the tariffs for each period on the basis of the price and operating profits of the firm in the previous period. The firm is free to design the other tariff to consist of whatever access and usage charge it chooses. For convenience, we call the tariff the regulator designs "the regulator's tariff" and that designed by the firm "the firm's tariff," remembering of course that both tariffs are offered by the firm.

The regulator's tariff in each period is designed on the basis of the firm's tariff in the previous period. Let P_t be the usage price under the firm's tariff in period t. (How this price is established by the firm is discussed below; for the purposes of the regulator's tariff, it is simply taken as given.) At this price, the firm collects revenues $Q_t P_t$ and incurs costs C_t, earning an operating profit per customer of $R_t = (Q_t P_t - C_t)/N$, where N is the number of customers. Note that operating profit is the profit the firm earns from usage independent of the access fee. The operating profit may be either positive or negative; for example, if P_t is set at marginal cost, then, given that the firm is a natural monopolist, R_t is negative.

The regulator uses this information to design the tariff it will require the firm to offer in the next period. In particular, the regulator's tariff in period $t + 1$ has a usage price of P_t (the usage price under the firm's tariff in the previous period) and a fixed fee of $-R_t$ (the

---

6. In results 1 and 2, the same concept operates as in Sibley's mechanism, but the status quo maintained by the self-selecting tariffs is somewhat different. Under Sibley's mechanism, the regulator requires that a self-selecting tariff always be offered that maintains *total* surplus; while in the demonstration of results 1 and 2, the offering of the original tariffs without change maintains the surplus of *each individual customer*. This difference is appropriate, because Sibley's mechanism is concerned with attaining first-best optimality, which relates to total surplus, whereas results 1 and 2 are concerned with attaining Pareto optimality, which requires maintenance of each individual's surplus.

negative of the firm's operating profit per customer in the previous period). If the firm earned a positive operating profit in the previous period, each customer is provided with a *negative* fixed charge—that is, a refund—equal to the amount of profit per customer. If the firm's operating profit was negative (e.g., if it charged marginal-cost prices), the fixed charge under the regulator's tariff is positive. Essentially, the regulator's tariff allows customers to face the same usage price that the firm offered in the previous period under its own tariff while refunding the excess profit or subsidizing the losses from the previous period.

The firm is required to offer the regulator's tariff. However, the firm is also allowed to offer a tariff of its own design. Note, however, that for the firm to get any customers to choose its own tariff, its tariff must provide greater surplus to customers than the regulator's tariff. That is: if the firm wants to make more profit than it would under the regulator's tariff, it must design a tariff that benefits customers as well as itself. This, as we see below, is the crux of why Sibley's mechanism works.

Let us start the analysis in a period, called period 0, before this form of regulation is imposed. Either the firm is unregulated in this original period, or some other form of regulation is operating.[7] The firm charges a price of P_0 and earns an operating profit of R_0 per customer. This profit may be either negative or positive, depending on whether the firm was losing or earning money before Sibley's mechanism is imposed.

In the first period after the mechanism is imposed, the regulator requires that the firm offer a tariff that consists of a fixed charge of $-R_0$ and a usage price of P_0. That is, the regulator designs a tariff that consists of the same usage price as the firm had been charging and a fixed charge that refunds to customers the profit the firm had been earning (or, if the firm had been losing money, charges customers an amount sufficient for the firm to recoup its losses). The regulator requires that the firm offer this tariff. However, the regulator also allows the firm to offer another tariff with whatever fixed charge and usage price the firm chooses. Customers will have a choice between the tariff that the regulator designs and the one designed by the firm.

The question is: what fixed charge and usage price will the firm

---

7. To avoid the possibility of strategic behavior, the firm is assumed not to know in period 0 that Sibley's mechanism will be imposed in the upcoming period.

choose for the tariff it is allowed to design? Because all customers have the same demand, all customers will choose either the tariff designed by the regulator or that designed by the firm, whichever provides the greater surplus. If all customers choose the tariff designed by the regulator, the firm will make zero profit. This fact is shown as follows.

Consider first the usage fee only. At P_0, the firm earns profit on usage of R_0 per customer, the same operating profit the firm earned before regulation was imposed. However, the regulator's tariff imposes a fixed charge of $-R_0$. Therefore, considering both the fixed charge and profit from usage, the firm ends up earning zero profit: $R_0 - R_0$.

If the firm wants to make positive profit, it must design a tariff that attracts customers away from the tariff the regulator designed. Suppose the firm sets the usage price under the tariff it designs at P_1. We can show that the maximum profit the firm can earn from offering a tariff with a usage price of P_1 is the change in total surplus (consumer surplus plus profit) that this price generates compared to the price P_0 under the regulator's tariff.

First, we must determine: What is the highest fixed fee that the firm can charge under its tariff and still have customers choose its tariff over the regulator's tariff? With this information, we can then determine the profit the firm would earn with its tariff. Customers would obtain a different level of surplus at price P_1 than at the P_0 they would face under the regulator's tariff. Label this difference in surplus (surplus at P_1 minus surplus at P_0) as ΔCS_1. For example, in figure 9.7, P_1 is below P_0 (the firm designs a tariff with a lower price), and consumer surplus is greater by the shaded area. In the discussion below, we assume for convenience that P_1 is below P_0; however, the arguments and results are the same if P_1 is above P_0 such that ΔCS_1 is negative.

Because the usage price is lower, the firm can charge a higher fixed charge on its own tariff than under the regulator's tariff and still have customers choose its tariff. In particular, the firm can charge a fixed fee that is higher by just about as much as the increase in surplus that the lower usage fee provides. Because the fixed fee under the regulator's tariffs is $-R_0$, the firm can charge a fixed fee of *nearly* $-R_0 + \Delta CS_1$ and still induce all customers to choose its own tariff. (If the firm sets the fee at exactly this amount, customers will be indifferent between the two tariffs, because both would provide the same total

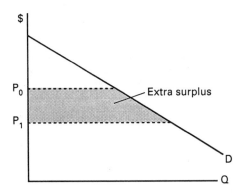

Figure 9.7
Change in consumer surplus for a price decrease

surplus. The firm can raise the fee to just slightly less than this amount and have all customers choose it.) The firm will therefore offer a tariff with a usage fee of P_1 and a fixed fee of (nearly) $-R_0 + \Delta CS_1$. All customers will choose this tariff over the one designed by the regulator. Under this tariff, the operating profits of the firm in the first period of regulation, labeled R_1, are $(P_1 Q_1 - C_1)/N$, where Q_1 is the quantity demanded at P_1, and C_1 is the cost of producing Q_1. The total profits of the firm, including the customers' fixed fee, are these operating profits plus the fixed fee of (nearly) $-R_0 + \Delta CS_1$:

$$\pi_1 \simeq R_1 - R_0 + \Delta CS_1.$$

This profit is simply the change in total surplus:

$$\pi_1 \simeq \Delta R_1 + \Delta CS_1 = \Delta TS_1,$$

where $\Delta R_1 = R_1 - R_0$ is the change in operating profits from before regulation to the first period of regulation, and ΔTS_1 is the change in total surplus (profits plus consumer surplus) over the same periods. That is, the firm earns profits in the first period that are (nearly) equal to the change in total surplus that its own tariff generates.

So far, we have said that the firm charges a usage price of P_1, but we have not determined the level of this price. We have shown that the firm will earn profit equal to the change in surplus generated by the tariff the firm designs. The firm therefore obtains the greatest profit by designing a tariff that increases total surplus as much as possible. This is accomplished by inducing all customers to face a price equal to marginal cost, since total surplus is highest when price equals marginal cost. The firm will therefore, in the first period under this mechanism, offer a tariff whose usage price equals marginal cost. The firm will set the fixed fee under this tariff at a level that induces all customers to choose it over the tariff designed by the regulator, generating profits for itself by doing so. Because all customers will choose the firm's tariff, all customers will face a usage price equal to marginal cost.

As well as attaining the first-best output level, the firm uses the cost-minimizing inputs to produce this output. The firm is allowed to keep whatever profit it earns in the first period under the self-selecting tariffs. By minimizing costs, the firm's profits are larger.

In this first period after the mechanism is imposed, the firm makes positive profit. In fact, as stated, its profit is equal to the increase in total surplus that its move to first-best optimality generates, which can be quite large. While this excess profit is not inconsistent with first-best optimality,[8] equity considerations might suggest that profit should be zero. It turns out that Sibley's mechanism reduces profits to zero in the second period, while maintaining marginal-cost pricing and cost minimization. In the second period, the regulator requires that the firm offer a tariff that has a fixed charge of $-R_1$ (the operating profit/loss of the firm, per customer, in the first period) and a usage price of P_1 (the usage price in the first period). The firm is allowed to offer another tariff with whatever fixed and usage charges it chooses. Using the logic above, the firm earns zero profit if customers choose the tariff the regulator designed. If the firm designs a tariff that customers choose, the most profit the firm can earn is the change in total surplus generated by that tariff. However, because the firm is already at first-best optimality, total surplus cannot increase. Therefore the firm can do no better than to allow all customers to consume under the tariff designed by the regulator. Under this tariff, customers face a usage price equal to marginal cost (because P_1 was set in the first period to equal marginal cost), and the firm obtains through the fixed fee exactly enough revenue to break even (because R_1 is the operating profit/loss per customer of the firm when charging P_1, and $-R_1$ is the fixed charge). Note that because P_1 equals marginal cost, operating profits are negative for a natural monopolist; the fixed charge is therefore positive, equal to exactly the loss per customer that the firm in-

---

8. Because the tariff includes a fixed charge and the number of customers is not affected by this charge, the profits represent only a transfer from customers to the firm, with no consumption implications.

curs under marginal-cost pricing. In all subsequent periods, the situation remains the same: first-best optimality with zero profit for the firm.

9.6.2 Heterogeneous Customers

In the analysis above, the firm designs a tariff in the first period that extracts as profit all the potential surplus gain. The firm, by maximizing profit, thereby maximizes surplus. After the first period, there are no further potential surplus gains available, because first-best optimality has been achieved, and so the firm's profits become zero.

If different customers have different demands, the firm cannot design *one* tariff that captures the increase in surplus for all customers. If the firm offers a tariff with a lower usage price than the regulator's tariff, it can attract all customers to this tariff only if it raises the fixed fee by no more than the *smallest* increase in surplus that any customer obtains from the lower usage price. In this case, the firm is not extracting the entire gain in surplus for customers whose surplus gain is higher. If the firm instead charges a higher fixed fee, some customers will not choose the firms's tariff. Again, the firm is not extracting the potential surplus gain for all customers.

To enable the firm to extract all the potential surplus gains, Sibley proposes that the mechanism be applied separately to each customer in situations in which customers' demands differ. In each period the firm is allowed to design a tariff for each customer and offer that tariff only to that customer. The regulator also designs a tariff for each customer that the firm is required to offer the customer. The regulator's tariff consists of the usage charge that the firm charged under its own tariff for the customer in the previous period; the fixed charge is the average operating profit per customer that the firm made in the previous period.

The mechanism operates the same as described above, only on a customer-by-customer basis. The logic is exactly the same for each customer as when all customers have the same demand. In the first period, the regulator requires that the firm offer each customer a tariff consisting of a usage price that is the same as charged by the firm prior to the implementation of the mechanism, and a fixed fee that is the negative of the operating profit per customer that the firm had been earning. The firm designs for each customer a tariff that consists of a usage price equal to marginal cost and a fixed fee that is different from the fixed fee under the regulator's tariff by (nearly) the amount of change in surplus that the customer obtains by moving to marginal-cost price. Because this change in surplus is different for customers with different demands, the fixed charge is different for customers with different demands. First-best optimality is attained in the first period, with the firm earning as profit the entire surplus gain of each customer. In the second period, profit is zero, because no further surplus gains are possible.

Essentially, Sibley's mechanism for customers with different demands works by combining the advantages of price discrimination with those of self-selecting tariffs. By itself, primary price discrimination allows the firm to extract all surplus; first-best optimality is achieved because the profits of the firm are the same as total surplus. However, the firm earns positive profits indefinitely. Self-selecting tariffs, judiciously used by the regulator, can reduce the firm's profits to be the *increase* in surplus from one period to the next, rather than the total surplus in any period. In particular, if the regulator requires the firm to offer tariff options that maintain the current level of total surplus and provide zero profit, the firm can earn more than zero profit only if it introduces other tariff options that benefit customers as well as itself, that is, that increase total surplus. When no further surplus gains are possible, the firm does not offer any new tariffs and earns zero profit under the tariffs required by the regulator. With self-selecting tariffs and price discrimination combined, first-best optimality is achieved along with zero profit.

9.7 Welfare Implications When Standard Assumptions Are Inappropriate

The analysis in this chapter has proceeded under the standard assumptions regarding customer behavior. In particular, customers are assumed to know their demand for the good at the time of choosing among tariffs and to choose the tariff that provides the most surplus. Empirical research repeatedly indicates, however, that customers do not choose in this fashion.[9] In particular, a significant share of customers are found to have chosen tariffs that do not provide the lowest bill for their observed level of consumption. In the context of phone

---

9. See for example, Kling 1985, Hobson and Spady 1987, Train, McFadden, and Ben-Akiva 1987, Kling and van der Ploeg 1989, and Train 1989.

service, for example, many customers choose flat-rate service over measured service, even though their bill would be lower under measured. Customers often do not enlist in calling plans offered by their long-distance carriers, even though the plans would reduce their bills for their current levels of calling; and, conversely, other customers are observed to join plans that actually cost them more money than under the carrier's standard rates for the same number of calls. Optional time-of-use (TOU) rates have been offered by energy utilities in many areas, and yet many customers do not switch to these rates even though they would receive a smaller bill for their current consumption levels under the TOU rates.

The implications of self-selecting tariffs are different when customers behave differently than assumed. Depending on how the observed behavior of customers is interpreted, the implications for surplus maximization can be either diminished or strengthened. Two interpretations with opposite implications are possible.

First, we might think that customers who choose tariffs that are not least costly for their observed consumption levels are simply making mistakes. If this is the case, one of the primary advantages of self-selecting tariffs is lost. Recall that under the standard assumptions, no customer is hurt if a firm offers a new tariff option without changing the original options. If, however, customers make mistakes in their choice of tariff, customers *could* be hurt in such a situation. In particular, a customer might mistakenly choose the new tariff, even though the new tariff actually decreases the customer's surplus.

The results on Pareto dominance (i.e., results 1 and 2) rely on the concept that offering a new tariff without changing the original ones does not hurt any customer. These results do not hold if customers make mistakes in their choice of tariff. It is not necessarily possible to design a tariff option that Pareto dominates, or even increases surplus, relative to an original set of options, if some customers whose surplus would decrease under the new tariff would mistakenly choose it.

A regulator who thinks that a significant portion of customers might make mistakes in their choices among tariffs is well advised to mandate multipart tariffs rather than self-selecting tariffs. As shown in section 9.3, a set of self-selecting tariffs can be represented equivalently as one multipart tariff when customers behave in accordance with the standard assumptions. Therefore, multipart tariffs serve the regulator as well as self-selecting tariffs when customers behave as assumed: any objective that self-selecting tariffs can achieve can also be achieved by multipart tariffs. Unlike self-selecting tariffs, however, multipart tariffs protect customers from making mistakes. Consider a multipart tariff that has the same outlay schedule as a set of self-selecting tariffs. If all customers choose among the tariffs correctly, their bill would be the same under the self-selecting tariffs as under the multipart tariff. However, if a customer mistakenly chooses the wrong tariff, its bill under the self-selecting tariffs would be higher than under the multipart tariff. For example, in figure 9.4, a customer who chooses flat-rate service and then makes fewer calls than the threshold at which flat-rate becomes advantageous ("threshold 3" in the figure) would pay more under the self-selecting tariffs than under the "equivalent" multipart tariff. Because multipart tariffs without selection can perform all the functions of self-selecting tariffs when customers behave as traditionally assumed, and can also protect customers from making mistakes, any regulator who thinks that customers are likely to make mistakes would be better served by multipart tariffs.

This argument would suggest that the recent proliferation of self-selecting tariffs is misguided. If, however, the behavior of customers is seen in a different light, the use of self-selecting tariffs is perhaps justified. In particular, customers may choose tariffs that are not least costly for their consumption—that is, choose the seemingly "wrong" tariff—because there is some other feature of the tariff that appeals to them, beyond the surplus obtained under observed demand.

For example, customers may realize that their demand fluctuates over time, or customers may be uncertain of their future demand at the time of choosing a tariff. In the face of fluctuating or uncertain demand, different tariffs subject the customer to different levels of risk. Under flat-rate service, the customer's bill is fixed, with no variation or uncertainty. Under measured service, the customer's bill fluctuates from month to month, depending on the demand that the customer ends up having in the month. Which tariff is better for the customer depends on the customer's risk preferences. In particular, it is quite possible that a rational customer would choose flat-rate over measured service even though, for the number of calls that end up being made, the customer's bill is higher under flat-rate than measured service. That is, what might appear as a mistake under the (false) assumption that customer's demand is known and fixed can actually be the outcome of a more complex, but rational, choice process that incorporates issues of risk.

It is important to note that risk aversion does not necessarily induce customers to prefer flat-rate service. Depending on the nature of the risk faced by the customer, a risk-averse customer might prefer measured service over flat-rate, all else equal. Consider for example a customer of a local phone service who does not know the amount of income he/she will receive in the upcoming months. With flat-rate service, the customer's phone bill is fixed, and the amount of money remaining for consumption of other goods varies as the customer's income varies. With measured service, the customer has the option to adjust its phone bill as its income fluctuates. In particular, when the customer's income is low (e.g., when between jobs), the customer can make fewer calls, saving money on its phone bill that can be used for consumption of other goods, such as food. Flat-rate service does not offer this type of protection against the possibility of low income. Risk-averse customers whose risk centers on income uncertainty might rationally choose measured service in this case, even if the customer's bill in months of normal income is higher.

The effort of optimization can also be a concern of customers. Under flat-rate service, for example, the customer does not have to worry about whether an extra unit of consumption is worth the price that must be paid for it. The convenience of not having to make such evaluations might in itself be worth something to the customer, such that a customer would be willing to pay more for flat-rate than measured service. Similarly, in choosing between time-of-use and non-time-differentiated rates, customers might compare the informational requirements of optimization under the two tariffs. To optimize under TOU rates, the customer must know the timing of its consumption, while this information is not necessary under non-time-differentiated rates.

In short: different tariffs are not simply different billing algorithms under known demand. They possess other features, such as the degree of risk, or the effort required for optimization. Customers have preferences over these features, and these preferences affect customers' decisions.

The implications of self-selecting tariffs (e.g., when they increase surplus, whether Pareto dominance is possible) have not been derived under behavioral assumptions that include these various factors. As a result, it is currently unknown whether self-selecting tariffs offer advantages that cannot be attained with multipart tariffs. It seems likely that they do. If tariffs are considered to possess features other than the surplus under known demand (e.g., degree of risk, effort of optimization) and different customers have different preferences over these features, then offering various tariffs allows customers' preferences to be matched more closely than with only one tariff. In a sense, self-selecting tariffs might possess the advantages of product differentiation, by which surplus is increased by providing different kinds of products (in our case, tariffs) to customers with different tastes. This analogy is by no means clear, however. If a multipart tariff is designed that combines the least-cost components of a set of self-selecting tariffs, can customers ever be strictly better off with the self-selecting tariffs than the multipart tariff? Answering this question is an important task for future research.

We can now summarize the concepts relating to the use of self-selecting tariffs in situations in which customers do not behave in accordance with the standard assumptions. If customers are thought to make mistakes in their choice among tariffs, self-selecting tariffs are probably inadvisable. The regulator's goals could be better served with multipart tariffs. If, on the other hand, customers are thought to choose tariffs that best satisfy their preferences—in a context that includes risk, uncertainty, information costs, the effort of optimization, and other issues that are not included in the standard assumptions—then self-selecting tariffs might offer advantages over multipart tariffs.

10

Optimality without Regulation

10.1 Introduction

Regulation in the real world is far from optimal, and it is perhaps unrealistic to believe that it ever will be. Posner (1969, 1970) has catalogued the inefficiencies of regulation in convincing (and depressing) detail. However, academic articles are not really needed as proof: any observer of regulatory processes in the real world can easily identify areas of extensive waste, mismanagement, missed opportunities, and other social ills.

The thrust of this book so far has been to explore mechanisms of regulation that can, it is hoped, reduce these inefficiencies, or, more accurately, provide insight that will allow some of these inefficiencies to be avoided. This approach presupposes that regulation is actually needed in natural monopoly situations and that the issue is simply how to devise the best regulation.

Several authors (most prominently Demsetz 1968; Posner 1972; Baumol, Bailey, and Willig 1977; Sharkey 1982; and Baumol 1982) have argued that, contrary to standard concepts, the existence of natural monopoly is not, in itself, grounds for regulation. Under assumptions that are similar to those maintained in standard theories of regulation, these authors have shown that optimality (or at least some major aspects of optimality) can be attained without regulation, even with only one producer.

Competition among numerous firms is shown by these authors to bring about optimality even in natural monopoly situations. However, the competition arises *not* among firms that *actually* produce in the industry, but rather among firms that *could* produce. Even though, in a natural monopoly situation, only one firm actually produces the good, numerous firms *could* produce the good. Pressure from these potential producers, exerted in somewhat different ways in the theories of different authors, forces the monopolist to produce with least-cost inputs and price as low as possible.

These theories suggest that perhaps regulation, with all its concomitant inefficiencies, is unnecessary and that market forces can be relied upon to attain optimality. This suggestion is certainly appealing. However, as with all theories of regulation, it is necessary to recognize that the abstract world of the theories is indeed just that: an abstraction. Direct application of the concepts in the real world raises numerous complications and could foster outcomes that differ substantially from those derived in theory. Williamson (1976), Schwartz and Reynolds (1983), and others have discussed these limitations. The value of the theories is that they describe important forces that operate toward optimality, forces whose power had not been recognized, or emphasized, in earlier concepts of natural monopoly. The regulator, understanding these forces, can use them along with the others to foster greater efficiency.

In the following sections, we describe the manner, power, and limitations of competition among potential producers. Section 10.2 describes the suggestion of Demsetz and Posner that the monopoly franchise (that is, the right to be the monopolist) can be auctioned off to the firm that offers to charge the lowest per-unit price to consumers. With enough noncolluding bidders, such an auction can be shown to result in efficient production and zero (economic) profits for the winning firm, at least in a world that does not change much over time. Section 10.3 introduces "contestability" as it applies to natural monopoly, a concept proposed in various forums by Bailey, Baumol, Panzar, and Willig. The notion of contestability rests on the existence of sufficiently free entry and exit of new firms into an industry. If a new firm can enter a monopolized industry without incurring costs that cannot be recouped if the firm later exits, the monopolist producing in the industry must produce efficiently and earn zero profit in order to avoid having its market taken over by an entrant.

The theory of contestability and the concept of auctions when applied in a world that changes over time, suggest that regulators should encourage, rather than prevent, entry into the market of a natural monopolist. However, while allowing entry can perhaps induce optimality in some situations, it can also actually destroy it in others. Depending on the cost structure faced by a natural monopolist, new firms might be able to enter and make a profit even if the monopolist is acting optimally. Faulhaber (1975) and Sharkey (1981) show that if a natural monopolist charges Ramsey prices, new firms might be able to enter profitably and supply a portion of the monopolist's market at a lower price. Allowing entry in these cases would prevent the attainment of Ramsey prices in equilibrium. In fact, Panzar and Willig (1977) and Sharkey (1981, 1982) show that, under some cost structures, new firms will be able to enter and make a profit no matter what prices the natural monopolist charges. Clearly, equilibrium with one firm, which is best from a cost perspective, would be unattainable if entry were allowed in these situations. Section 10.4 discusses these ideas. The findings are derived from the definition of "sustainable prices," namely, prices that prevent entry in a contestable market.

Section 10.5 concludes with a discussion of the basic question: To what extent should the regulator rely on market forces such as entry to achieve optimality, versus direct regulation? Following Williamson, we show that the two ways of handling natural monopoly are not as different, when applied in the real world, as might appear in theory. Furthermore, the appropriate approach cannot meaningfully be determined in general. Rather, the particular circumstances of each individual situation must be considered in choosing between the approaches, or, more accurately, in determining the most effective blend of approaches for each situation.

10.2 Auctioning the Monopoly Franchise

The concept is simple. Suppose increasing returns exist in the production of a good such that having one firm produce the good is desirable from a cost perspective. Though only one firm will produce the good, assume that many firms are capable of producing it. The regulator is assumed to have the power to decide which firm will be allowed to produce the good; that is, the regulator is able to award the monopoly franchise. The regulator auctions off the franchise in the following way. The regulator announces that it will accept bids from all firms that are willing and able to produce the good. The bid from each firm will consist of the price that the firm agrees to charge customers if awarded the franchise. The regulator will choose the firm that offers the lowest price. The winning firm becomes the monopolist and is required to charge customers the price it bid in the auction.

If numerous firms face the same technology and production costs, and these firms do not collude when bidding, the price of the product will be bid down to the point at which the winning firm makes (essentially) zero profits with least-cost production. This fact can be discerned by following the course of such an auction. Suppose that, at one point in the auction, the lowest price offered allows the firm presenting this bid to earn strictly positive profit. Another firm that can produce at the same costs as this first firm could offer a lower price and still make a positive (though smaller) profit. Given the choice of zero profit (which a firm earns if it does not win the franchise) and a small but positive profit, this other firm will choose the latter, bidding below the previously lowest bid. Similarly, suppose the lowest bid is made by a firm that would make zero profit, but would engage in some form of inefficiency in production. Another firm would see that it could produce without waste. With lower costs, its profits would be positive at the same price offered by the wasteful firm; it could therefore offer a slightly lower price and still make a positive profit. Again, given a choice between zero profit from not winning the franchise and a small but positive profit, this other firm would choose the latter and bid below the previously lowest bid. This process will continue until, for the winning price, profits are essentially zero with least-cost production.

It is useful pedagogically to describe the auction proceeding sequentially, as above, with firms bidding successively lower prices until profits are squeezed to zero. However, the process could actually occur all at once. If each firm knew that other firms faced the same technology and production costs, each firm would realize that it could only win the auction if it bids a price that provides zero profit with least-cost production. Each firm would make this bid, and the regulator would be faced with a multitude of identical bids, each of which consists of the lowest possible price to consumers. Which bid the regulator chooses at this point is immaterial from a welfare perspective. The point is simply that profits would be zero and production would be efficient without any direct intervention by the regulator (other than holding the auction).

It is important to note the type or extent of optimality achieved. First-best optimality is not attained. Pricing at marginal cost would, due to the presence of scale economies, require negative profits, and no firm would be willing to bid price down that far. As usual, second-best optimality is the best one can hope for. In a one-good situation, all aspects of second-best optimality are attained: price is at average cost because profits are zero, and least-cost production methods are utilized. In a multigood situation, the auction as described need not result in the Ramsey prices, and so this aspect of second-best optimality is not necessarily attained. The auction assures that profits are zero with least-cost production, but does not determine which of the various price combinations that result in zero profit will be offered.

The intriguing aspect of this analysis is that having a monopoly producer does not result in a monopoly price. Market forces, in the form of competition among potential producers, pushes price toward cost. In principle, there is no need for regulation of the monopolist, because there is no distortion of price from cost that would require regulation.

The limitation of this approach to natural monopoly arises when it is recognized that costs and demand change over time such that a price that was optimal at one point in time might not be optimal later (Williamson 1976). In a traditionally competitive market, equilibrium price adjusts to changes in costs and demand, reaching the new optimum after each change. However, in the auctioning of a natural monopoly franchise, adjustment to changes does not occur automatically. Recall that the regulator holds the auction, awards the franchise to the firm that offers to sell at the lowest price, and then requires that the firm charge that price when it becomes the monopolist. In a static world, the regulator and the winning firm could enter a long-term contract that specified the price that the firm would charge, essentially locking the firm into the price it offered at the time of the auction. With no changes in demand or costs, this contract would insure that the optimal price is maintained.

In a changing world, however, the optimal price changes. A long-term contract that locks the firm into a price that was appropriate at one point in time might later, when circumstances change, force the firm into bankruptcy or provide windfall profits. In the face of this fact, the regulator might attempt to write a contract that contains contingency clauses for possible future events. These contingency clauses could take either of two forms. The contract might (1) specify how the price will change if certain events occur, or (2) establish a procedure by which prices are revised periodically. The first approach attempts to list all possible future events and the price that would be charged if the events came to pass. Given the vast number of possibilities, this approach would be incomplete at best. Furthermore, the regulator might not be able to observe directly whether an event occurred; for example, the regulator might not know whether a new technology had allowed costs to drop. In an effort to increase its profits, the firm would not necessarily report events truthfully to the regulator. For example, the firm would have a clear incentive to report smaller cost savings from a new technology than actually occurred. This asymmetry of information places the regulator in the same situation as under direct regulation: needing a mechanism that would induce the firm to act optimally when the regulator does not have sufficient information to identify the optimal behavior beforehand. Hence, a contract with contingency clauses that relate price to certain events ends up being essentially the same as direct regulation.

The second contracting approach recognizes that all future events cannot be foreseen and, instead of trying to list all possible events, establishes a procedure by which price is reviewed periodically. In these reviews, the events that have actually transpired are examined, and the price is adjusted to take account of these changes. However, these reviews become, just as under the first contracting approach, the same as direct regulation. The firm has more information than the regulator on the changes in demand and cost that have occurred and cannot be relied upon to report this information truthfully. The contract therefore needs to establish a procedure that induces optimal behavior when the regulator lacks sufficient information to identify this behavior directly, which is exactly the task of direct regulation. In a changing world, the distinction between direct regulation and reliance on market forces fades, at least when the market forces are harnessed though an auction with a long-term contact.

Given the problems with a long-term contract, it has been suggested (e.g., Posner 1972) that the regulator instead write a short-term contract with the winning firm. When the contract expires, a new auction is held, and the monopoly franchise is given to the winner of the new auction, again with a short-term contract. The bids in the new auction will necessarily reflect any changes in cost and demand. If all firms have access to the same technology and costs for inputs, and possess the same information, the winning bid will be a price that provides zero profit under least-cost production. The firm that won the first auction and hence has been producing in the industry need not be the winner of the second or later auctions. However, because the incumbent knows that it can win and continue its operation only if it bids as low a price as possible, the incumbent can be expected to bid to win.

Repeated auctions with short-term contacts can be expected to result in the lowest possible price only if the incumbent has no cost or other advantage with respect to other firms that might bid for the franchise. Otherwise the incumbent can win each auction by pricing above its own costs but below the costs of other bidders, thereby earning monopoly profits and/or engaging in waste indefinitely.

The conditions under which repeated auctions can be used to attain the lowest possible price are actually the same as those required for a contestable market, which is the topic of the next section. In fact, the theory of contestability, although it operates in a different way than repeated auctions, is actually, at its most fundamental level, a formalization and generalization of the idea that motivates repeated auctions. The power and limitations of repeated auctions are therefore best understood as an aspect of contestability.

10.3   Contestability

A contestable market is defined as one in which entry is "free" and exit is "costless," with both of these terms having a particular meaning. Free entry does *not* mean that a new firm need not incur any costs to enter an industry. Rather, free entry means that a new firm does not have to incur any costs that are not also incurred by a firm that is already producing in the industry; that is, the entrant is not at a cost disadvantage with respect to an incumbent. Free entry therefore requires that the entrant have access to the same technology and input sources as the incumbent, and that consumers perceive the entrant's product to be the same as the incumbent's.

Costless exit means that any firm can leave an industry (that is, stop producing) and recoup all the costs it incurred when entering. For example, if a firm had to purchase equipment to produce in the industry, costless exit means that the firm can sell the equipment at the same price (minus depreciation) it paid to purchase the equipment.

Under these conditions, a monopolist will be forced to produce efficiently and price so as to earn zero profit. If the incumbent monopolist earned strictly positive profit, a new firm could enter, charge a slightly lower price that results in a smaller but still positive profit, and capture the incumbent's entire market, thereby becoming the new monopolist. If the original monopolist retaliated by lowering its own price, the new firm could simply leave the industry, recouping all entry costs. In either case, price is reduced. Similarly, if the incumbent monopolist is earning zero profit but is engaging in some form of inefficiency in the production process, a new firm could enter with a lower price, produce without this waste, and earn positive profit. Either the original monopolist would lose its market or it would eliminate the inefficiency in its production so as to meet the new firm's price. In either case, the inefficiency is removed.

With free entry and costless exit, the monopolist is not able to earn positive profit or produce at higher than minimum costs even for a short period. Entry will occur, because a new firm can enter at a lower price and earn a profit for the period of time (however short) before the original monopolist adjusts, and then the new firm can exit, recouping its costs of entry. Baumol (1982) describes this process as follows: "The crucial feature of a contestable market is its vulnerability to hit-and-run entry. Even a very transient profit opportunity need not be neglected by a potential entrant, for he can go in, and, before prices change, collect his gains and then depart without cost, should the climate grow hostile." Actually, entry will never have to occur, because the *threat* of entry would keep the incumbent monopolist at zero profit with efficient production.[1]

As with the auctioning of the monopoly franchise, contestability in a natural monopoly situation guarantees only that profits are zero and production is cost minimizing. First-best optimality is not achieved, because price equaling marginal cost requires negative profit.[2] Second-best optimality is fully attained in a one-good situation. In a multigood situation, prices need not be Ramsey, such that this aspect of second-best is not necessarily achieved.

---

1. Costless exit is key to the argument for "hit-and-run" entry. If a potential entrant could *not* recoup all its entrance costs when exiting, it would not necessarily enter even though it could make a profit at the incumbent's current prices. The potential entrant would realize that the incumbent would probably retaliate and that it (the entrant) would lose some of the costs it incurred when entering if it were eventually forced to exit. In this case, the potential entrant would only enter if the profit it expected to earn before retaliation exceeded the unrecoupable costs of entry. With costless exit, on the other hand, a potential entrant would not fear retaliation because, even if it lost the competition for the market, it would not lose any money. A new firm would enter whenever it saw an opportunity for profit, no matter how short-lived.

2. Baumol (1982) shows that, if the least costly number of firms is more than one (e.g., a natural duopoly), price will equal marginal cost in equilibrium, such that first-best optimality is attained. An equilibrium will not necessarily exist, however, because marginal-cost pricing need not result in zero profit, and zero profit is also required for equilibrium. In a natural monopoly situation, equilibrium occurs with zero profit without marginal-cost pricing.

The reader has probably already identified a major limitation of contestability theory. As Schwartz and Reynolds (1983) point out, the power of hit-and-run entry (or, more accurately, the power of the *threat* of such entry) rests on the notion that an entrant can enter a market and earn an profit *before* the incumbent can reduce its price. In most situations, it is much easier and quicker for an existing firm to reduce its price than for a new firm to purchase necessary equipment and other production facilities, hire employees, and notify customers of its existence. In these situations, the incumbent can maintain indefinitely a price in excess of the zero-profit level. When the incumbent observes that a new firm is starting to establish operations, it lowers its price before the new firm can actually offer service. After the new firm is run out of the market, the incumbent simply raises its price again. In fact, because the potential entrant knows that the incumbent will do this, the potential entrant will not enter even though the incumbent is earning positive profit and/or producing inefficiently.

There are two ways that contestability theory can confront this argument. First, the entrant can sign long-term contracts with customers before it establishes its operations. These contracts would bind customers to buy from the entrant after the entrant established its operations and would not allow customers to switch back to the incumbent (at least until the expiration of the contract). If the entrant offers a lower price than the incumbent, customers will be willing to sign with the entrant even if they know that the incumbent will lower its price when the new firm enters. They will sign because they also know that, if they do not sign with the entrant, the incumbent will raise its prices again after the entrant is run out. Their only hope of a long-term price reduction is to sign with the entrant.

The incumbent, on observing that a potential entrant is signing up customers, could also attempt to sign up customers on terms equal to or better than those offered by the entrant. However, if the incumbent is successful in preventing customers from signing with the entrant, price is still lower in the long term, because the incumbent succeeds by offering a lower price in a long-term contract. Furthermore, because the potential entrant can start to sign up customers before it establishes its operations, it need not expend any costs on entry until it knows that it can enter profitably.

The second way that contestability theory can be maintained is essentially through mandate of the regulator. In particular, the regulator can require that the incumbent not lower its price in response to entry. If the incumbent knows that whatever price it sets must be maintained even in the face of entry, it will choose a low price that prevents entry.[3]

10.4 Sustainable Prices in a Contestable Market

The theory of contestability and the notion of repeated auctions over time suggest that the regulator should allow entry, even in a natural monopoly situation. In fact, the theory suggests that the task of the regulator is not to oversee the incumbent's price and input decisions per se, but rather to establish policies that assure that the conditions for contestability—free entry, costless exit, and slow price response by the incumbent—are met as closely as possible.[4] When these conditions are met, the correct price and inputs will result automatically.

Allowing entry can, however, cause problems in many situations, even (in fact, especially) if the conditions for contestability are fully met. In particular, allowing entry can, depending on the cost structure of the natural monopolist, prevent equilibrium at the optimal prices. To demonstrate this possibility, and delineate the conditions under which it occurs, we introduce a new term: "sustainable prices."

The prices an incumbent firm charges are called sustainable if, under the conditions for contestability (free entry and costless exit), the incumbent earns at least zero profit and no new firm chooses to enter. "Sustainable" in this context means that the prices could be sustained over an extended period with no change in the number of firms in the industry, that is, without the existing firm leaving or new firms entering. The requirement that the incumbent earn at least zero profit reflects the fact that, if the firm loses money indefinitely, it will not be able to stay in business. Sustainability also requires, however, that potential entrants are *not* able to make a profit.

---

3. This approach requires that the regulator be able to distinguish price reductions in response to entry from those due to changes in costs or demand—a distinction that is often difficult in practice. The approach is also difficult politically, because the regulator must somehow explain to its constituency the seeming paradox that low prices are attained by preventing price reductions.

4. For example, the regulator might require that the incumbent share its technology with any new firm and purchase any equipment and facilities that a failed firm might need to dispose of when exiting. Of course, if the incumbent priced sufficiently low, no new firms would enter and none would hence fail. These obligations on the incumbent would therefore never be activated.

Several important results can be derived from the definition of sustainable prices.

Result 1: A firm's prices are sustainable only if its profits are exactly zero and it produces at least cost.

Profits must be at least zero for the firm to stay in business. However, for reasons given in section 10.3 on contestability, the prices that a firm charges must also result in no *more* than zero profit with cost-minimizing production in order to be sustainable. Otherwise, a new firm could enter, price below the original firm, capture the original firm's market, and earn a positive profit.

While zero profits and least-cost production are necessary, they are are not, in themselves, sufficient for sustainability. That is, the prices the firm charges might not be sustainable even if its profits are zero and it cost minimizes in production.

Suppose, for example, there are economies of scope in the production of two goods such that one firm can produce the two goods more cheaply than two firms. Suppose that a monopolist produces the two goods with least-cost inputs and prices them in a way that results in zero profit. It is possible, depending on the prices and the cost structure for production, that a new firm will be able to enter the market for *one* of the goods, undercut the monopolist's price for that one good, and earn a positive profit. In such a case, the monopolist is vulnerable to entry even though it produces efficiently and earns zero profit.

An example will suffice to demonstrate this possibility. Suppose that demand is fixed at 1,000 for each good. (The assumption of fixed demand is not essential; it simply makes the example more transparent.) Suppose the cost of producing the quantity demanded of both goods is $50,000 when the two goods are produced together by one firm. Suppose further that if either of the two goods is produced by itself (that is, by a separate firm that produces only that one good), the cost of production is $30,000. Economies of scope exist because the cost of producing the two goods separately ($30,000 + $30,000) exceeds the cost of producing them together ($50,000). Suppose now that the firm prices good A at $35 and good B at $15. The firm earns zero profit because its revenues ($35 \cdot 1000 + $15 \cdot 1000$) equal its costs ($50,000). Note, however, that a new firm could enter, produce only good A, charge a lower price than the original monopolist, and make a positive profit. If the new firm charges $34 for good A, it would obtain revenues of $34,000 (because all customers will buy from the new firm with the lower price). These revenues exceed the firm's costs of $30,000, such that the new firm makes a positive profit. In short, even though the incumbent monopolist is earning zero profits, the prices charged by the monopolist would induce a new firm to enter.

The problem is that the monopolist's prices are not sustainable. The monopolist could (in this specific case) revise its prices so that it obtained revenues of no more than $30,000 in each market. For example, the firm could charge $28 for good A and $22 for good B. These prices would still result in zero profit but would be sustainable: no firm could produce either good at a lower price and earn sufficient revenues to cover its costs.

The question arises: are there always prices that a natural monopolist can charge that will prevent entry, that is, are sustainable? If not, then allowing entry will prevent the attainment of an optimal equilibrium. The answer has been given by Baumol, Bailey, and Willig (1977), Sharkey (1981, 1982), and others. It constitutes our next result.

Result 2: It is possible that no sustainable prices exist for a natural monopolist.

Consider first a one-output situation. If economies of scale do not exist throughout the entire range of output, pricing at average cost will not be sustainable. Suppose, for example, that economies of scale exist up to 90% of market demand and then diseconomies set in. The average cost curve for this situation is depicted in figure 10.1. Diseconomies are not sufficient to warrant two firms producing in the industry: one firm is still cheaper than two. The only price that results in zero profit for the monopolist is p_m, which equals average cost for the entire market demand. However, a new firm could enter, charge a lower price (between p_m and p_e), sell 90% of market demand, and leave the remaining 10% to the original monopolist. Because the average cost of producing ninety percent of market demand is p_e, the new firm would make a profit at any price between p_e and p_m. Essentially, because the average cost of supplying a *portion* of the market is less than that of supplying the *entire* market, a new firm could earn a positive profit at a price below the average cost of the original monopolist.

In a multigood situation, the same type of problem could occur. A

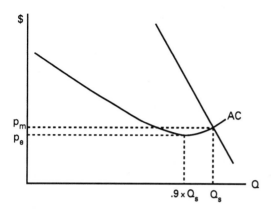

Figure 10.1
No sustainable prices for a one-good natural monopolist

convenient example is given by Zajac (1978). Suppose three services are provided and demand is fixed at 1,000 for each service. Suppose that each service could be provided by one firm at a cost of $30,000 apiece, for a total cost of $90,000 for all three services supplied by three separate firms. Suppose that economies of scope exist such that providing the services jointly is less expensive than separately. For example, suppose that any two of the services could be provided by one firm at a cost of $48,000, and all three services could be provided by one firm at a cost of $75,000. With three firms, total cost is $90,000; with two firms (one firm providing two services and the other firm providing the third), total cost is $78,000 ($48,000 + $30,000); and with one firm, total cost is $75,000. A natural monopoly exists because it is cheaper to meet market demand for these three services with only one firm than with more than one. However, there are no sustainable prices that a monopolist can charge.

To see this fact, suppose the monopolist prices each service at $25, earning $25,000 revenues on each service for a total revenue of $75,000. The monopolist's profit is zero because its costs are also $75,000. At these prices, however, a new firm could enter and provide *two* of the services at a lower price and make a profit. The new firm could charge, say, $24.50 for each of two services, which we can call services *A* and *B*. Because this price is below that charged by the monopolist, customers would buy services *A* and *B* from the new firm, providing it with $49,000 in revenue. Because the cost of providing two services is $48,000, the new firm would earn a profit of $1,000. The original monopolist would be left with only service *C*.

Consider the possibility of the monopolist lowering the price of services A and B to prevent the new firm from entering. Because the cost of providing two services is $48,000, the monopolist must price each of the two services at $24 to prevent the entrant from being able to make a profit on these two services. However, if the monopolist charges $24 for services A and B, it must price the third service at $27 to break even overall. (Revenue from services A and B is $48,000, and revenue from service C is $27,000, which just covers the firm's costs of $75,000.) At these prices, however, a new firm could enter and provide services A and C at a profit. The new firm could charge $23.50 for service A and $26.50 for service C, earning revenues of $50,000 (i.e., $23,500 from service A and $26,500 from service C). With costs of $48,000, the new firm would make a profit of $2,000.

Any other price combination that the monopolist tried would encounter the same problem: a new firm would be able to provide two of the services at a lower price and make a profit. Even though a natural monopoly exists and the incumbent monopolist is earning zero profit without waste, a new firm will be able to enter at whatever prices the incumbent charges. Clearly, in this situation, an equilibrium with one firm, which is optimal from a cost perspective, is not possible if entry is allowed.

Result 2 states that there *may* be no sustainable prices for a natural monopolist. It does not state that sustainable prices do not exist in *all* natural monopoly situations. Depending on the cost structure of the firm, sustainable prices may or may not exist. We have seen, in figure 10.1, a situation in which there is no sustainable price for a one-good natural monopolist: the average cost curve is such that an entrant can supply a portion of the market at a price that is lower than the monopolist can possibly charge for the entire market. If, on the other hand, the average cost curve is continuously downward sloping (that is, economies of scale exist throughout the entire range of output), then a sustainable price exists in a one-good situation. The situation is depicted in figure 10.2. The incumbent can price at p_m, which is the second-best optimum. Because average cost is continuously decreasing, an entrant cannot price below p_m and make a profit from selling a portion of market demand.

The important implication of result 2 is that the regulator, without knowing the cost and demand of the firm, cannot be assured that the desire for entry by another firm necessarily means that the incumbent is pricing too high. The incumbent may be operating efficiently and

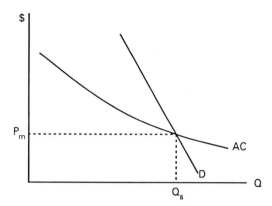

Figure 10.2
Sustainable price for one-good natural monopolist

pricing as low as possible, and yet the cost structure may be such that no sustainable prices exist. This in turn implies that a regulator, without knowing cost and demand, cannot necessarily rely on entry and the threat of entry to induce optimality.

Result 3: Ramsey prices may not be sustainable, even if sustainable prices exist for a multi-output natural monopolist.

Consider first the meaning of this result in relation to previous findings. Result 2 states that, in some situations, a natural monopolist may find that there are no prices that it can charge to prevent entry. If the regulator allows entry in these cases, then an equilibrium with one firm, which is optimal from a cost perspective, would not be possible. The question arises: What about situations in which sustainable prices *do* exist? Will allowing entry in these situations induce optimality? Result 3 implies that allowing entry could actually prevent optimal pricing by the incumbent. In particular, result 3 states that, even in situations in which sustainable prices exist, the Ramsey prices may not be sustainable. If the regulator allowed entry in these cases, equilibrium would occur with one firm, but with the firm charging some prices other than Ramsey.

Faulhaber (1975) and Sharkey (1981) demonstrate the result. An example of nonsustainable Ramsey prices is sufficient proof. Consider two goods, labeled A and B. Assume that demand for good A is fixed at 1,000, whereas demand for good B is price sensitive with demand being $Q = 1,280 - 10P$. If good A is produced by a firm on its own (that is, without producing good B), the firm incurs a fixed cost of

$20,000 and a marginal cost of $2 per unit. Similarly, good B can be produced on its own for a fixed cost of $30,000 and a marginal cost of $3. If the two goods are produced by one firm, certain equipment can be shared, such that economies of scope exist. In particular, the fixed cost of joint production is $40,000 as opposed to the combined fixed costs of $50,000 ($20,000 for good A and $30,000 for good B). With joint production, marginal costs are still $2 per unit of good A and $3 for good B.

Sustainable prices clearly exist for one firm that produces both goods. The monopolist could, for example, set the price of good A at $17 and the price of good B at $28. It would obtain revenues of $17,000 for good A and $28,000 for good B (i.e., $Q = 1,280 - 10(28) = 1,000$ times $P = 28$), for a total revenue of $45,000. The costs of the firm are the $40,000 fixed costs plus variable costs of $2,000 for good A and $3,000 for good B, such that total costs are $45,000. The monopolist breaks even. And, because revenue from each good is less than the fixed cost of producing that good alone,[5] no firm can produce either of the two goods at a lower price and make a profit. The prices are therefore sustainable.

The prices are *not*, however, the Ramsey prices. The demand for good A is fixed, while that for good B is price sensitive. The Ramsey rule requires, therefore, that the price of good B (the good with price-sensitive demand) be set at its marginal cost, while the price of good A (with fixed demand) be set sufficiently high for the firm to break even. That is, all fixed costs for both goods are to be loaded onto good A. The Ramsey prices are $42 for good A and $3 for good B.

At these Ramsey prices, a new firm could provide only good A, charge a lower price than the original monopolist, and make a profit. The new firm could charge, say, $40. Its revenues would be $40,000, and its costs would be $22,000 (fixed costs of $20,000 plus variable costs of $2,000), providing the new firm with a profit of $18,000. In short, while sustainable prices exist, the Ramsey prices are not sustainable. In this situation, the monopolist would not choose the Ramsey prices if the regulator allowed entry. To achieve Ramsey prices in this situation, the regulator must not allow new firms to enter the monopolist's markets.

Result 3 states that Ramsey prices *might* not be sustainable. It does not state the Ramsey prices are never sustainable. Whether Ramsey

---

5. Also, the elasticity of demand for each good is below one (in magnitude) in the relevant range of prices, such that decreasing price does not increase revenue.

prices are sustainable depends on costs and demand for the particular situation. Baumol, Bailey, and Willig (1977) provide conditions under which Ramsey prices are sustainable. In a one-good situation, we have already observed in figure 10.2 the conditions that are sufficient for the second-best optimum to be sustainable: when economies of scale exist for all levels of output up to market demand, the second-best price (i.e., p_m in the figure) is sustainable. For multigood situations, the conditions are more complex, involving a certain type of economies of scope in addition to economies of scale. We do not describe these conditions here: as well as being complex, it would be hard to ever determine whether the conditions are actually met in a given situation. The important point is simply that there *are* situations in which Ramsey prices are definitely sustainable.

When Ramsey prices are sustainable, the monopolist in a contestable market might charge Ramsey prices to prevent entry. Baumol, Bailey, and Willig call this tendency for Ramsey pricing a "weak invisible hand." An "invisible hand" is operating because market forces in the form of potential entry could induce a monopolist to attain second-best optimality. The invisible hand is "weak" because the firm will not *necessarily* charge the Ramsey prices. Although Ramsey prices are sustainable, other prices might also be sustainable, and the firm might choose these other prices instead.

A summary of the discussion can now be made. If certain conditions are met (such as economies of scale throughout the relevant range for a one-good monopolist), Ramsey prices are sustainable. The regulator can perhaps, in these situations, rely on the threat of entry as a way of inducing the monopolist to charge Ramsey prices. It must be remembered, however, that this inducement is weak, because the firm may charge other sustainable prices instead. If the conditions are *not* met, Ramsey prices may not be sustainable, and the regulator, by allowing entry, could be preventing the attainment of Ramsey prices. Furthermore, there is no guarantee than *any* sustainable prices exist. Allowing entry could therefore prevent the attainment of equilibrium with one firm, which is optimal from a cost perspective.

If the regulator knew the costs and demand faced by a natural monopolist, the regulator could determine whether sustainable prices exist and whether the Ramsey prices are sustainable. However, without knowing demand and cost, the regulator cannot know whether allowing entry will secure or prevent optimality. The power of potential entry, while indeed strong, needs to be used guardedly.

10.5   Market Forces versus Regulation for a Natural Monopoly

The basic question is: Should the regulator institute direct regulation or rely on market forces in a natural monopoly situation? The answer is of course less clear-cut than the question might suggest. First, as Williamson has pointed out and as we discussed in section 10.2, direct regulation and reliance on market forces, when applied over time in a changing world, are not as different as they might seem. If market forces are harnessed through an auction of the monopoly franchise with a long-term contract for the winning firm, the contract must somehow account for the fact that costs and demand change over time. The regulator will usually have less information than the firm on the way in which costs and demand have actually changed over time and cannot necessarily rely on the firm to report this information truthfully. The regulator therefore will want to establish in the contract some procedure that results in prices being adjusted optimally over time in the face of this informational asymmetry. Yet this is the task of direct regulation: the establishment of a regulatory mechanism that induces optimality when the regulator does not have sufficient information to know what prices are optimal.

The same convergence occurs if we consider the possibility of harnessing market forces through repeated auctions with short-term contracts or by allowing entry. Both of these procedures result in zero profit with cost-minimizing production under changes in costs and demand over time, provided the market is contestable at each point in time. To rely on these procedures, the regulator must assure itself that the market is indeed contestable and remains so over time. In particular, the regulator needs to know (among other things) whether the incumbent monopolist possesses a cost or demand advantage relative to potential entrants. This information allows the regulator to determine whether (or the extent to which) the incumbent can maintain prices above their optimal level while still preventing entry or winning the repeated auctions. Yet the regulator usually does not possess this information and must obtain it from the incumbent and potential entrants themselves, who cannot necessarily be relied upon to report truthfully. A mechanism is therefore needed that induces the firms to report information truthfully at each point in time, so the regulator can determine whether the repeated auctions or threat of entry are actually resulting in the lowest possible prices. Again, this is essentially the task of direct regulation.

The second point to be made about the question of direct regulation versus market forces is that the regulator would usually not want to choose one or the other of these approaches exclusively, but rather utilize some aspects of each. It is rare that a market will be sufficiently contestable for the regulator to be able to confidently rely on market forces exclusively. Some form of oversight of the incumbent's prices and costs would usually be desirable even if the market is considered to be fairly contestable. On the other hand, in markets that are clearly not contestable, the power of potential entry can still be utilized fruitfully, if only to guard against extremes. The regulator can always hold as an option—and make sure that the incumbent knows of this option—the possibility of negotiating with other producers to supply all or part of the incumbent's market. Even if potential entrants are at a cost or demand disadvantage, the threat posed by these firms still places a *limit* on the extent of waste and/or overpricing by the incumbent.

In light of these ideas, our original question regarding direct regulation versus reliance on market forces can be restated more meaningfully. As we have described, direct regulation and reliance on market forces are not so very different in practice, and the regulator will probably find it advantageous to use a mix of both approaches. The question becomes therefore: What is the appropriate combination of practices? The answer to this, as to all questions of how to regulate in the real world, is different in different settings. Even in one setting, no clear-cut answer is available. Judgment is essential. By understanding the power and limitations of market forces—knowing when the power is most effective and when limitations come into play—this judgment can perhaps be improved.

Appendix:
Price Caps

Recently, regulators in various settings have begun to utilize "price caps" as a means of regulating firms. Acton and Vogelsang (1989) specify four characteristics of price-cap regulation:

1. The regulator sets a price, called the price cap. The regulated firm can set a price below or equal to this cap, and it is allowed to retain whatever profits it earns at that price.

2. In multi-output situations, the regulator might define an aggregate cap for a basket of related products. This aggregate cap takes the form of a price index or a weighted average of prices. The firm is allowed to change prices for the goods (raising some and lowering others) as long as the index, or weighted average of prices, does not rise.

3. The regulator might specify that the price cap will be adjusted over time by a preannounced adjustment factor that is exogenous to the firm. For example, the cap may be tied to an index of input prices.

4. At longer intervals, the price cap is reviewed by the regulator and possibly changed. This review is expected to consider the cost, demand, and profit conditions of the firm.

This form of regulation has been adopted for AT&T's interstate service, for telecommunication services in California, and for natural gas and electricity in Great Britain. It is also being considered for many other settings.

The emergence of this new form of regulation provides an excellent opportunity to apply the concepts described in this book. To what extent and in what ways can we expect price-cap regulation to attain the optimal price, output, and input levels? Even if full optimality is not attained, can we expect price-cap regulation to be preferable to traditional rate-of-return regulation, which the analysis in chapters 1 and 3 indicates induces the firm to produce inefficiently?

We will address these questions within a sequence of increasingly complex settings. Starting with a fully static situation in which demand, costs, and the price cap do not change over time, we will then move to a situation in which costs and demand change and the regulator adjusts the price cap on the basis, at least partially, of the firm's profits in previous periods. This method of analysis allows a clear identification of the benefits and difficulties of price-cap regulation. The conclusions of this analysis can be summarized as follows.

1. If the price cap is fixed (or if it changes in a way that is exogenous to the firm), the firm will produce with the cost-minimizing input mix, invest in cost-effective innovation, and adjust optimally to changes in cost. The reason is clear: The firm is allowed to retain as profit any cost reductions that it achieves and, consequently, it will choose to produce efficiently. Total surplus therefore increases relative to a situation in which the firm does not cost-minimize (such as under rate-of-return regulation). However, unless the previous regulation resulted in higher prices than the firm would have charged without any regulation, the increased surplus accrues entirely to the firm: consumers do not benefit from the production efficiency.

2. If the firm produces more than one good and the price cap is expressed as an Laspeyres index of the prices for all the outputs, then the firm will adjust outputs and prices in a way that increases profit without decreasing consumer surplus. Total surplus will therefore rise. For marginal changes in prices, the entire gain will accrue to the firm with no gain for consumers. However, for larger-than-marginal changes, consumers will also benefit.

3. Over time, the regulator will review the price cap and adjust it up or down based on the profits of the firm under the existing cap and other factors. This periodic review is the heart of the issue regarding price caps. It provides the means by which consumers also benefit: the regulator can lower the price cap to require that at least some of the reduced costs be passed on to consumers. However, the existence of the review also introduces the possibility of strategic behavior by the firm, which could prevent the attainment of cost reductions. The form of the reviews has not been specified by regulators. Depending on what the firm expects the regulator to do in the review, the firm could be induced to incur higher costs than necessary as a strategic move, similar to that discussed in chapter 5 regarding the Vogelsang-Finsinger mechanism. Furthermore, if, as can perhaps be reasonably expected, the review of price caps is conducted like the price reviews under rate-of-return regulation, then the distinction blurs

between price-cap regulation and rate-of-return regulation. More work is needed on the form and timing of the price-cap reviews before an definitive statement can be made about whether, or the extent to which, price caps induce optimality or improve upon traditional rate-of-return regulation.

A.1   One-Output Firm in a Fully Static World

Suppose the demand and cost functions facing the firm are fixed and that the regulator has established a price cap, denoted P_{cap}. Under the terms of the regulation, the firm can choose any price equal to or below P_{cap} and can retain any profits it earns at that price. The behavior of the firm in this situation can be represented with the concepts developed in chapters 1 and 2. Figure A.1 gives, in the space of input combinations, the expansion path and the zero-profit contour of the firm. Point M is the top of the profit hill and as such is the point that the firm would choose if it were not regulated. Denote by Q_{cap} the level of output demanded at the price cap P_{cap}. The firm, by the terms of the regulation, can choose any price at or below P_{cap}, which means that it can choose any output at or above Q_{cap}. That is, the firm is constrained to choose an input combination on or above the isoquant for Q_{cap}.

There are two possibilities: the price cap is either below or above the price that the firm would charge if it were not regulated. Panel (a) depicts the more standard situation in which the price cap is below the unconstrained profit-maximizing price. Since P_{cap} is less than the price at M, Q_{cap} is above the output at M, meaning that the isoquant for Q_{cap} passes above M. The firm will choose point C, the point on

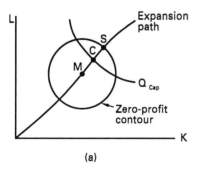 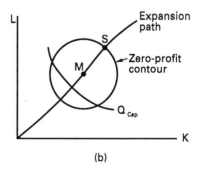

(a)   (b)

Figure A.1
Choice of firm under price caps

the expansion path associated with output level Q_{cap}. (The reason should be clear: at any output level, profits are higher on the expansion path than off, and profits decrease as the firm moves along the expansion path down the profit hill from M, the top.) The firm will charge the price cap, sell the output demanded at that price, and produce with the least-cost input combination. Essentially, the firm cost-minimizes because it is able to retain as profit any cost reductions that it attains. And the firm prices at the cap because this price allows it to be as close as possible to the unregulated profit-maximizing price.

Panel (b) depicts the other possibility: the price cap is above the price that the firm would choose if it were not regulated. The firm chooses point M, the top of the profit hill. The firm prices below the cap, sells more output than would be produced at P_{cap}, and uses the cost-minimizing inputs. In this case, price-cap regulation is equivalent to no regulation at all.

In both cases, the firm cost-minimizes but produces less output than is optimal. Recall that if the firm cannot be subsidized, then the optimal (second-best) output is that produced at point S, where the expansion path intersects the zero-profit contour. Ideally the regulator could set the cap at the optimal price (that is, set the cap such that the isoquant for Q_{cap} intersects the expansion path at S such that the firm chooses S). However, without knowing the cost and demand conditions facing the firm, the regulator cannot determine the optimal price. More fundamentally, if the regulator knew the optimal price, the regulator could simply mandate this price. If the cap is set so low that the firm loses money (that is, if the isoquant for Q_{cap} falls outside the zero-profit contour), the firm would go out of business eventually. Because the regulator cannot identify the optimal price, and a cap that allows only negative profits is infeasible, price will inevitably be higher than optimal and output will be lower than optimal. Stated succinctly: under price-cap regulation, the firm will choose the cost-minimizing inputs, but will produce less output than is optimal. The firm will price below the cap only if the cap is so high that price-cap regulation is equivalent to no regulation.

Consider now a comparison of ROR and price-cap regulation. In particular, suppose that ROR regulation has been applied in the past, and that the regulator decides to switch to price-cap regulation. It can be shown that total surplus will rise when ROR regulation is replaced with price caps. However, except in rare circumstances, all of the benefits of switching to price caps will accrue to the firm in the form of extra profits; consumers will not benefit from the change in regulation.

Under ROR regulation, price is presumably above the optimal level due to cost inefficiencies. Suppose the regulator sets the cap at the price the firm has charged under ROR regulation. Under price-cap regulation, the firm will eliminate the cost inefficiencies, retaining as profit the cost savings. The effect on price and output depends on the relation of the price under ROR regulation to the unconstrained profit-maximizing price. Two situations are possible, as depicted in the two panels of figure A.2. In both panels, the constraint curve is shown for the firm under ROR regulation with the fair rate of return exceeding the cost of capital. (For graphical simplicity, the zero-profit contour is not shown; however, the zero-profit contour is known to encircle the constraint curve because all points on the constraint curve result in positive profit.) As described in chapter 1, the firm under ROR regulation chooses point R. The firm produces output Q_r at this point and charges price P_r. When the regulator switches to price caps, the cap is set equal to P_r: the firm is constrained to produce at any point on or above the isoquant that goes through point R. The two panels differ in whether this isoquant passes above or below M.

In panel (a), the isoquant intersects the expansion path above M. The firm chooses point C under price-cap regulation. That is, when ROR Regulation is replaced with price-cap regulation, the firm moves from R to C. Output and hence price do not change. However, the firm reduces its costs, producing its output with the cost-minimizing inputs.

Note that only the firm benefits from the switch from ROR to price-

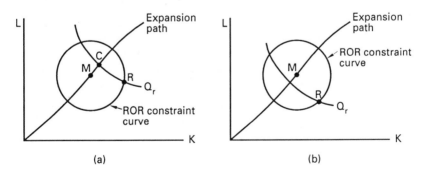

(a)   (b)

Figure A.2
Comparison of ROR regulation with price caps

cap regulation in this case. The firm reduces its costs, and yet none of these savings are passed on to consumers in the form of a lower price. Because price and output are unchanged, consumer surplus is constant. Profits rise by the amount by which the firm is able to reduce its costs (that is, by the amount of inefficiency it incurred under ROR regulation).

There is one circumstance in which consumers will benefit, depicted in panel (b). In this case, the price under ROR regulation exceeds the price that the firm would charge if it were unregulated. Recall from chapter 1 that this situation is possible: ROR regulation can, depending on the shape of the profit hill, induce the firm to produce less output and charge a higher price than if it were not regulated. In this case, the firm will choose point M, the unconstrained profit maximum, when ROR regulation is replaced with price-cap regulation. That is, the firm will lower its price from the level under ROR regulation to the unconstrained profit maximum. The firm earns more profit, but consumers also benefit because price is dropped.

Note that the situation in panel (b) arises only when ROR regulation is worse than no regulation (since it results in a price that is higher than the firm would charge without regulation) and price-cap regulation is equivalent to no regulation. The conclusions regarding a switch to price-cap regulation in a static world can therefore be summarized as follows. Total surplus necessarily rises when ROR regulation is replaced with price caps, because profits rise and consumer surplus does not fall. However, consumers benefit only if ROR regulation were worse than no regulation, in which case the switch to price-cap regulation is equivalent to eliminating regulation.

One might argue that the regulator could set the price cap below the price that the firm charged under ROR regulation, thereby assuring consumers some of the gains from the cost reductions. However, the regulator would only do this if it knew that the firm were engaged in some inefficiencies under ROR regulation. If the regulator knew that the firm's costs were too high, it would have disallowed these costs when the firm was under ROR regulation, thereby forcing the firm's price under ROR regulation to be lower. Since the regulator approved the firm's price under ROR regulation, the regulator must not know that the firm is not cost minimizing. (The regulator presumably suspects that the firm is not cost minimizing under ROR regulation—that is why the regulator shifts to price-cap regulation. However, the regulator does not know for sure whether, or the extent to which, costs can be reduced and therefore cannot require that the firm charge a lower price.)

A.2 Multi-Output Firm in a Fully Static World

If there is more than one output, the regulator has a choice of how to apply price-cap regulation. A separate cap could be established for each product. In this case, the analysis for each good is essentially the same as in the one-output case. In many settings, however, regulators have applied an aggregate price cap on a set of interrelated products. The aggregate cap takes the form of an index, or a weighted average of prices. The firm is allowed to raise the price for some goods as long as the prices for other goods are lowered sufficiently that the price index does not rise. As we show below, the use of an appropriately defined aggregate cap enables the firm to change prices in a way that increases its profits without decreasing, and perhaps even increasing, consumer surplus. Total surplus can therefore rise under price-cap regulation because of a more efficient output mix in addition to the cost reductions described in the one-output situation.

Our analysis is motivated by the concepts advanced by Brennan (1989). Consider a two-good situation; generalization to more goods is straightforward. Let P_1^0 and P_2^0, and Q_1^0 and Q_2^0 denote the prices and quantities of the two goods prior to the imposition of price-cap regulation. Suppose the regulator placed the following constraint on the firm. The firm is allowed to charge any prices P_1 and P_2 that satisfy the following inequality:

$$Q_1^0 P_1 + Q_2^0 P_2 \leq Q_1^0 P_1^0 + Q_2^0 P_2^0.$$

That is, the firm can charge any prices as long as the prices, when multiplied by the quantities of the goods sold prior to the price cap-regulation, do not exceed the revenues that the firm obtained before the price caps.

This constraint can be expressed as an index. Rearranging the inequality, we have

$$(Q_1^0 P_1 + Q_2^0 P_2) / (Q_1^0 P_1^0 + Q_2^0 P_2^0) \leq 1.$$

The left-hand side is a Laspeyres index of prices, with the prices in the period prior to price caps taken as the base. The firm is allowed to change prices as long as the price index does not rise above one—that is, above the base level.

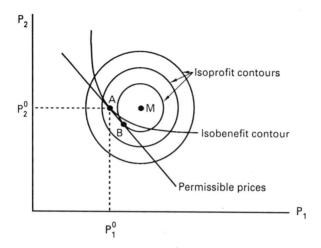

Figure A.3
Multi-output firm under price cap index

Using the concepts from chapter 5, we can represent this constraint graphically. Figure A.3 is a graph of price combinations. Originally prices are at A. The isobenefit contour through A gives the price combinations that result in the same consumer surplus as at A. Consumer surplus is higher for price combinations that are below this isobenefit contour (i.e., at lower prices). As discussed in chapter 5, the slope of the isobenefit contour at A is the ratio of outputs sold at those prices; i.e., $-(Q_1^0/Q_2^0)$. The tangency line is depicted in the graph; we can show that this tangency line is the set of permissible prices available to the firm.

Rearranging the inequality, we have

$$P_2 \leq k - (Q_1^0/Q_2^0)P_1,$$

where k equals $(Q_1^0 P_1^0 + Q_2^0 P_2^0/Q_2^0$. Considering the equality part only, we have an equation for a line. This line necessarily passes through A, since the firm can continue charging its original prices. The line has a slope of $-Q_1^0/Q_2^0$, which we have already stated is the slope of the isobenefit contour through A. The set of permissible prices therefore consists of the tangency line for the isobenefit contour through A, plus all price combinations below this line.

From the set of permissible prices, the firm chooses the price combination that provides the greatest profit. Note, however, that all the permissible prices provide at least as great consumer surplus as at A:

since the line of permissible prices is tangent to the original isobenefit contour, all permissible prices are on or below this contour. In the graph, the firm makes the most profit at B and hence choses these prices: the firm's profits increase, and consumer surplus also increases. In general, profits increase for any movement away from the original prices (that is, whenever the original prices do not provide more profit than any other permissible price). For marginal changes in prices (that is, infinitesimally small changes), consumer surplus does not increase: consumers stay on the same isobenefit contour at a point close to A. However, for larger changes, consumers, as well as the firm, benefit from the price changes.

The reason this form of multiproduct price cap operates to the benefit of consumers and the firm alike is essentially the same as the reason behind V-F regulation. The firm is required to trade off price increases and decreases at a rate that maintains or increases consumer surplus. In particular, the firm can raise the price of good 1 by one dollar only if it lowers the price of good two by at least Q_1^0/Q_2^0 dollars. Yet consumer surplus is unchanged for marginal price changes at this rate of trade-off (because the isobenefit contour has this slope) and increases for larger-than-marginal changes at this rate.

The results in this section are highly dependent on the particular form of the aggregate price cap placed on the firm. The use of other indexes for price-cap regulation with several products may allow profits to increase at the expense of consumer surplus. In fact, at an extreme, total surplus may decrease. The key to an appropriate index is to require price changes at the ratio of the original output levels.

A.3   Demand, Costs, and the Price-Cap Change over Time

Over time, costs and demand change. If the price cap does not change, the firm could end up either losing money or earning very large profits, neither of which can be feasibly or politically maintained. To account for these changes, the price cap must be revised. The crucial issue is how the cap changes over time.

In many settings the regulator has specified that the price cap will change in some predetermined way. For example, the price cap might be tied to a wholesale price index or an index of wages in the area, such that general increases in input prices translate into a higher cap. This procedure protects the firm from cost changes that are beyond its control.

If changes in the price cap are determined on the basis of factors that are outside the control of the firm, then the analysis of firm behavior is essentially the same as in a static situation. The firm will cost-minimize, because doing so increases its profits. As well as utilizing the efficient input mix and not wasting at each point in time, the firm will cost-minimize over time. In particular, the firm will adjust optimally to changes in input prices. The firm will also adopt cost-reducing new technologies and engage in research and development that can lead to such technologies whenever the present value of the expected cost savings to the firm exceeds the cost of the investment.[1] (Note, however, that the optimal amount of innovation will not necessarily be attained. First, the firm will not invest optimally in product innovations because the price cap prevents the firm from raising its price to capture the benefits to consumers of improved products. Second, the cost savings that result from new technologies depend on the output level of the firm. Because the firm produces less output than is optimal, technologies that would be cost-effective at the optimal output but not at the firm's output will not be adopted.)

The firm will price at the cap at each point in time unless the cap exceeds the unconstrained profit-maximizing price. Because the unconstrained profit-maximizing price changes over time when costs and demand change, the firm may charge at the cap in some periods and below the cap in others. As long as the firm earns positive profit, the firm's output is less than optimal. If costs and demand change in a way that preclude the firm from earning a positive profit at the prevailing cap, then the firm will request a formal review. In general, therefore, output will be lower than optimal and price higher than optimal.

It is expected, and usually specified by the regulator, that a review of the price cap will be conducted periodically, even without the request of the firm. In fact, Acton and Vogelsang (1989) include this review as their fourth aspect of price-cap regulation. The form of this review—that is, the way in which the cap will be revised—has not

---

1. Cabral and Riordan (1989) show that if the cap that is prespecified for future periods is too low from the firm's perspective, the firm will *not* invest in cost-saving technologies. The argument hinges on the fact that the firm can, at any time, request a formal review as under ROR regulation rather than submit to a cap. If the firm knows that the future cap will be so low that it will lose money even with the cost-saving technologies, it has no incentive to invest in these technologies. The firm is better off by simply waiting until the cap is too low and then requesting a rate review, which it knows will result in a price that will cover its (inefficiently high) costs.

been established in the settings in which price caps have been imposed. However, it is reasonable to assume that the regulator will consider the profits the firm has earned in the past when determining the new cap. More to the point, it is reasonable to assume that the firm expects the regulator to act in this way.

When the price cap is changed on the basis of the firm's profits rather than only on exogenous factors, the analysis of the firm's behavior becomes far more complex. The possibility of strategic behavior must be considered, and the outcome can differ drastically from that derived above in a static setting or with exogenously determined changes in the cap. In particular, it is possible that the firm will waste so as to convince the regulator to allow a higher cap. Whether or not the firm engages in suboptimal strategic behavior depends on how the new cap is determined—or more precisely, on how the firm thinks the regulator will determine the new cap.

Numerous situations can be identified in which the firm has an incentive, for strategic reasons, not to cost-minimize. An incentive such as that identified in chapter 5 on V-F regulation might operate. For example, suppose the firm is currently under rate-of-return regulation and knows that the regulator will be switching to price-cap regulation. Under ROR regulation, the firm is allowed to recover its costs through higher prices. The firm would have an incentive to waste while under ROR regulation as a means of obtaining a higher cap when price-cap regulation is imposed. The waste would not reduce the firm's profits under ROR regulation because, by the terms of ROR regulation, its costs can be recouped. However, its profits would be higher after the switch to price caps. Total surplus would be reduced in two ways: (i) the waste of the firm in anticipation of the caps and (ii) the loss of consumer surplus (or more precisely, the deadweight loss) due to the higher price after price-cap regulation is imposed.

Consider another possibility, which could occur even after price-cap regulation has been imposed for a while. Suppose the regulator reviews the cap every three years and changes the cap on the basis of the firm's profits in the year immediately prior to the review (reflecting, perhaps, the idea that the most recent year is the most relevant). The firm would cost-minimize in the first and second years between reviews, but would have an incentive to waste in the third year. The reduced profit in this third year would translate into a higher cap than if the firm had not wasted. And this higher cap allows the firm to earn higher profit for the next *three* years. Unless the firm's discount rate is very high, the present value of current and future profits will be higher if the firm wastes in the year before a review. This result can be obtained, though to a lesser extent, if the regulator considers all three years' profits but places more importance on the most recent year.

The review might be conducted like the price review under rate-of-return regulation. In this case, the distinction between price-cap and ROR regulation blurs. If reviews under price-cap regulation are conducted with the same frequency as under ROR regulation, the two forms of regulation become the same and the observed inefficiencies that have arisen under ROR regulation can be expected to carry over to price-cap regulation. The issue reduces therefore to the timing of the reviews. The more frequent the review, the more price-cap regulation will induce the inefficiencies of rate-of-return regulation. The less frequent the review, the greater the incentive of the firm to cost-minimize between reviews (absent any strategic behavior of the type described above).

These examples are not meant to imply that the firm will necessarily engage in suboptimal strategic behavior. It is possible that the form of the periodic reviews is such that the firm behaves the same as if the price caps were fixed or determined exogenously. The form that the review takes (or, more precisely, that the firm expects the review to take) is crucial to the behavior of the firm and hence to the advisability of price-cap regulation. Yet the review process has not been specified. And even if the regulator specified the procedure, the firm would not necessarily trust the regulator to adhere to the stated procedure when the time came. The issue of price caps rests, therefore, on what the firm believes the regulator will consider when adjusting the cap. Much more work is needed on this important area of investigation before a definitive statement can be made about whether, or the extent to which, price-cap regulation induces optimality or improves upon traditional ROR regulation.

References

Acton, J. and I. Vogelsang, 1989, "Introduction," Symposium on Price Cap Regulation, *Rand Journal of Economics*, Vol. 20, No. 3, pp. 369–372.

Averch, H., and L. Johnson, 1962, "Behavior of the Firm Under Regulatory Constraint," *American Economic Review*, Vol. 52, No. 5, pp. 1053–1069.

Bailey, E., 1973, *Economic Theory of Regulatory Constraint*, Lexington Books, Lexington, MA.

Bailey, E., and R. Coleman, 1971, "The Effect of Lagged Regulation in the Averch-Johnson Model," *Bell Journal of Economics and Management Science*, Vol. 2, No. 1, pp. 278–292.

Bailey, E., and J. Malone, 1970, "Resource Allocation and the Regulated Firm," *Bell Journal of Economics and Management Science*, Vol. 1, No. 1, pp. 129–142.

Baron, D., and D. Besanko, 1984, "Regulation, Asymmetric Information, and Auditing," *Rand Journal of Economics*, Vol. 15, No. 4, pp. 447–470.

Baron, D., and R. Myerson, 1982, "Regulating a Monopolist with Unknown Costs," *Econometrica*, Vol. 50, No. 4, pp. 911–930.

Baumol, W., 1982, "Contestable Markets: An Uprising in the Theory of Industry Structure," *American Economic Review*, Vol. 72, No. 1, pp. 1–15.

Baumol, W., E. Bailey, and R. Willig, 1977, "Weak Invisible Hand Theorems on the Sustainability of Multiproduct Natural Monopoly," *American Economic Review*, Vol. 67, No. 3, pp. 350–365.

Baumol, W., and D. Bradford, 1970, "Optimal Departures from Marginal Cost Pricing," *American Economic Review*, Vol. 60, No. 3, pp. 265–283.

Baumol, W., and A. Klevorick, 1970, "Input Choices and Rate-of-Return Regulation: An Overview of the Discussion," *Bell Journal of Economics and Management Science*, Vol. 1, No. 1, pp. 162–190.

Baumol, W., J. Panzar, and R. Willig, 1982, *Contestable Markets and the Theory of Industry Structure*, Harcourt Brace Jovanovich, San Diego.

Bawa, V., and D. Sibley, 1980, "Dynamic Behavior of A Firm Subject to Stochastic Regulatory Review," *International Economic Review*, Vol. 21, No. 3, pp. 627–642.

Boiteux, M., 1960, "Peak-Load Pricing," *Journal of Business*, Vol. 33, No. 2, pp. 157–179.

Brennan, T., 1989, "Regulating by Capping Prices," *Journal of Regulatory Economics*, Vol. 1, No. 2, pp. 133–147.

Cabral, L., and M. Riordan, 1989, "Incentives for Cost Reduction Under Price Cap Regulation," *Journal of Regulatory Economics*, Vol. 1, No. 2, pp. 93–102.

Coase, R., 1946, "The Marginal Cost Controversy," *Economica*, Vol. 13, pp. 169–189.

Courville, L., 1974, "Regulation and Efficiency in the Electric Utility Industry," *Bell Journal of Economics and Management Science*, Vol. 5, No. 1, pp. 53–74.

Das, S., 1980, "On the Effect of Rate of Return Regulation under Uncertainty," *American Economic Review*, Vol. 70, No. 3, pp. 456–460.

Davis, E., 1973, "A Dynamic Model of the Regulated Firm with a Price Adjustment Mechanism," *Bell Journal of Economics and Management Science*, Vol. 4, No. 1, pp. 270–282.

Demsetz, H., 1968, "Why Regulate Utilities?" *Journal of Law and Economics*, Vol. 11, No. 1, pp. 55–65.

Dreze, J., 1964, "Some Postwar Contributions of French Economists to Theory and Public Policy, with Special Emphasis on Problems of Resource Allocation," *American Economic Review*, June, Vol. LIV, No. 4, Supplement, Part 2.

Faulhaber, G., 1975, "Cross-Subsidization: Pricing in Public Enterprises," *American Economic Review*, Vol. 65, No. 5, pp. 966–977.

Finsinger, J., and I. Vogelsang, 1981, "Alternative Institutional Frameworks for Price Incentive Mechanisms," *Kyklos*, Vol. 34, pp. 388–404.

Finsinger, J., and I. Vogelsang, 1982, "Performance Indices for Public Enterprises," in L. P. Jones et al., eds., *Public Enterprise in Less-Developed Countries*, Cambridge University Press, Cambridge.

Finsinger, J., and I. Vogelsang, 1985, "Strategic Management Behavior under Reward Structures in a Planned Economy," *Quarterly Journal of Economics*, Vol. C, No. 1, pp. 263–269.

Heyman, D., J. Lazorchak, D. Sibley, and W. Taylor, 1987, "An Analysis of Tapered Access Charges for End Users," Bell Communications Research, Economics Discussion Paper #31.

Hobson, M., and R. Spady, 1987, "Demand for Local Telephone Service under Optional Local Measured Service," Technical Memorandum, Bell Communications Research.

Houthakker, H., 1958, "Electricity Tariffs in Theory and Practice," *Economic Journal*, Vol. 61, No. 1, pp. 1–25.

Kafoglis, M., 1969, "Output of the Restrained Firm," *American Economic Review*, Vol. 59, No. 4, pp. 553–559.

Keeler, T., and K. Small, 1977, "Optimal Peak-Load Pricing, Investment, and Service Levels on Urban Expressways," *Journal of Political Economy*, Vol. 85, No. 1, pp. 1–25.

Klevorick, A., 1973, "The Behavior of A Firm Subject to Stochastic Regulatory Review," *Bell Journal of Economics and Management Science*, Vol. 4, No. 1, pp. 57–88.

Kling, J., 1985, "Estimation of Local Exchange Elasticities," Report, Michigan Bell Telephone Service.

Kling, J., and S. van der Ploeg, 1989, "Estimating Local Telephone Call Elasticities with a Stochastic Model of Class of Service and Usage Choice," paper presented at the Seventh International Conference of the International Telecommunications Society, MIT.

Laffont, J.-J., and J. Tirole, 1986, "Using Cost Observation to Regulate Firms," *Journal of Political Economy*, Vol. 94, No. 3, pp. 614–641.

Lee, D., 1974, "Cost Components for Selected Public Transportation Modes in the San Francisco Bay Area," Institute of Urban and Regional Development, University of California, Berkeley.

Loeb, M., and W. Magat, 1979, "A Decentralized Method for Utility Regulation," *Journal of Law and Economics*, Vol. 22, pp. 399–404.

Logan, J., R. Masson, and R. Reynolds, 1989, "Efficient Regulation with Little Information: Reality in the Limit?" *International Economic Review*, Vol. 30, No. 4, pp. 851–862.

McFadden, D., 1975, "The Measurement of Urban Travel Demand," *Journal of Public Economics*, Vol. 3, pp. 303–328.

Merewitz, L., and R. Pozdena, 1974, "A Long-Run Cost Function for Rail Rapid Transit Properties," Working Paper Number 240, Institute of Urban and Regional Development, University of California, Berkeley.

Mohring, H., 1970, "The Peak Load Problem with Increasing Returns and Pricing Constraints," *American Economic Review*, Vol. 60, No. 4, pp. 693–705.

Panzar, J., 1977, "The Pareto Dominance of Usage Insensitive Pricing," in H. Dorick, ed., *Proceedings of the Sixth Annual Telecommunications Policy Research Conference*, Lexington Books, Lexington, MA.

Panzar, J. and R. Willig, 1977, "Free Entry and the Sustainability of Natural Monopoly," *Bell Journal of Economics*, Vol. 8, No. 1, pp. 1–22.

Peles, Y., and J. Stein, 1976, "The Effect of Rate of Return Regulation is Highly Sensitive to the Nature of Uncertainty," *American Economic Review*, Vol. 66, No. 3, pp. 278–289.

Peterson, H., 1975, "An Empirical Test of Regulatory Effects," *The Bell Journal of Economics*, Vol. 6, No. 1, pp. 111–126.

Posner, R., 1969, "Natural Monopoly and Its Regulation," *Stanford Law Review*, Vol. 21, No. 3, pp. 548–643.

Posner, R., 1970, "Natural Monopoly and Its Regulation: A Reply," *Stanford Law Review*, Vol. 22, No. 3, pp. 540–546.

Posner, R., 1972, "The Appropriate Scope of Regulation in the Cable Television Industry," *Bell Journal of Economics and Management Science*, Vol. 3, No. 1, pp. 98–129.

Posner, R., 1974, "Theories of Economic Regulation," *Bell Journal of Economics and Management Science*, Vol. 5, No. 2, pp. 335–358.

Ramsey, F., 1927, "A Contribution to the Theory of Taxation," *Economic Journal*, Vol. 37, No. 1, pp. 47–61.

Riordan, M., 1984, "On Delegating Price Authority to a Regulated Firm," *Rand Journal of Economics*, Vol. 15, No. 1, pp. 108–115.

Riordan, M., and D. Sappington, "Awarding Monopoly Franchises," *American Economic Review*, Vol. 77, No. 3, pp. 375–387.

Robinson, J., 1933, *Economics of Imperfect Competition*, Macmillan, London.

Sappington, D., 1980, "Strategic Firm Behavior Under a Dynamic Regulatory Adjustment Process," *Bell Journal of Economics*, Vol. 11, No. 1, pp. 360–372.

Sappington, D., 1983, "Optimal Regulation of a Multiproduct Monopoly with Unknown Technological Capabilities," *Bell Journal of Economics*, Vol. 14, No. 3, pp. 453–463.

Sappington, D., and D. Sibley, 1988, "Regulating without Cost Information: The Incremental Surplus Subsidy Scheme," *International Economic Review*, Vol. 29, No. 2, pp. 297–306.

Schmalensee, R., 1981, "Output and Welfare Implications of Monopolistic Third-Degree Price Discrimination," *American Economic Review*, Vol. 71, No. 1, pp. 242–247.

Schwartz, M., and R. Reynolds, 1983, "Contestable Markets: An Uprising in the Theory of Industry Structure: Comment," *American Economic Review*, Vol. 73, No. 3, pp. 488–490.

Sharkey, W., 1981, "Existence of Sustainable Prices for Natural Monopoly Outputs," *Bell Journal of Economics*, Vol. 12, No. 1, pp. 144–154.

Sharkey, W., 1982, *The Theory of Natural Monopoly*, Cambridge University Press.

Sibley, D., 1989, "Asymmetric Information, Incentives, and Price-Cap Regulation," *Rand Journal of Economics*, Vol. 20, No. 3, pp. 392–404.

Spann, R., 1974, "Rate of Return Regulation and Efficiency in Production: An Empirical Test of the Averch-Johnson Thesis," *The Bell Journal of Economics and Management Science,* Vol. 5, No. 1, pp. 38–52.

Steiner, P., 1957, "Peak Loads and Efficient Pricing," *Quarterly Journal of Economics,* Vol. 71, No. 4, pp. 585–610.

Takayama, A., 1969, "Behavior of the Firm under Regulatory Constraint," *American Economic Review,* Vol. 59, No. 3, pp. 255–260.

Taylor, L., 1980, *Telecommunication Demand: A Survey and Critique,* Ballinger, Cambridge, MA.

Townsend, R., 1979, "Optimal Contracts and Competitive Markets with Costly State Verification," *Journal of Economic Theory,* Vol. 21, pp. 265–293.

Train, K., 1977, "Optimal Transit Prices under Increasing Returns to Scale and a Loss Constraint," *Journal of Transport Economics and Policy,* Vol. 11, No. 2, pp. 185–194.

Train, K., 1989, "Self-Selecting Tariffs under Pure Preferences Among Tariffs," Working Paper, Department of Economics, University of California, Berkeley.

Train, K., 1990, "Pareto Dominating Optional Time-of-Use Prices," Working Paper, Department of Economics, University of California, Berkeley.

Train, K., D. McFadden, and M. Ben-Akiva, 1987, "The Demand for Local Telephone Service: A Fully Discrete Model of Residential Calling Patterns and Service Choices," *Rand Journal of Economics,* Vol. 18, No. 1, pp. 109–123.

Train, K., and N. Toyama, 1989, "Pareto Dominance through Self-Selecting Tariffs: The Case of TOU Electricity Rates for Agricultural Customers," *Energy Journal,* Vol. 10, No. 1, pp. 91–109.

Varian, H. R., 1985, "Price Discrimination and Social Welfare," *American Economic Review,* Vol. 75, No. 4, pp. 870–875.

Vogelsang, I., and J. Finsinger, 1979, "A Regulatory Adjustment Process for Optimal Pricing by Multiproduct Monopoly Firms," *Bell Journal of Economics,* Vol. 10, No. 1, pp. 157–171.

Williamson, O., 1966, "Peak-Load Pricing and Optimal Capacity under Indivisibility Constraints," *American Economic Review,* Vol. 56, No. 4, pp. 810–827.

Williamson, O., 1976, "Franchise Bidding for Natural Monopolies—In General and With Respect to CATV," *Bell Journal of Economics,* Vol. 7, No. 1, pp. 73–104.

Willig, R., 1978, "Pareto Superior Non-linear Outlay Schedules," *Bell Journal of Economics,* Vol. 9, pp. 56–69.

Zajac, E., 1970, "A Geometric Treatment of Averch-Johnson's Behavior of the Firm Model," *American Economic Review,* Vol. 60, No. 1, pp. 117–125.

Zajac, E., 1978, *Fairness or Efficiency,* Ch. 7, Ballinger, Cambridge, MA.

Index

This index is intended primarily as a guide to locating definitions of terms and references to authors' work.

Access charge, 191
Acton and Vogelsang, 317, 326
AISS. *See* Approximate incremental surplus subsidy scheme
A-J. *See* Averch and Johnson
Allowance under access/usage tariff, 194
Allowed profit, 37
Approximate incremental surplus subsidy scheme, 187–188
Asymmetry
  informational, xi, 147
  in treatment of uncertainty, 96
Auction of monopoly franchise, 298, 299
  repeated, 302
Averch and Johnson, xi, 19
  effect, 40

Bad luck, 98
Bad-luck profit hill, 99
Bailey, xi, 2n, 20, 65, 69, 298. *See also* Bailey and Coleman; Bailey and Malone; Baumol, Bailey, and Willig
Bailey and Coleman, 19n
Bailey and Malone, 2n
Baron and Besanko, xii, 167, 168n
Baron and Myerson, 180n
Baumol, 297, 298, 304, 304n. *See also* Baumol and Bradford; Baumol and Klevorick; Baumol, Bailey, and Willig; Baumol, Panzar, and Willig
Baumol and Bradford, xii, 116
Baumol and Klevorick, xi, 2n, 19n, 20
Baumol, Bailey, and Willig, 297, 308
Baumol, Panzar, and Willig, xiii
Bawa and Sibley, 19n
Ben-Akiva. *See* Train, McFadden, and Ben-Akiva
Besanko. *See* Baron and Besanko

Block rates tariff, 192
  declining, 192, 213
  inverted, 192, 221
Boiteux, xiii, 241n
Bradford. *See* Baumol and Bradford
Brennan, 323
Budget constraint
  under block rates tariffs, 214, 221
  under self-selecting tariffs, 269

Capacity, 241
  optimal, 252
Capital, nonproductive, 53
Capture theory, 4
Coase, 196, 197
Coleman. *See* Bailey and Coleman
Collection point, 224
Competition, 1, 8, 16n, 297
Congestion, 246
Constant returns to scale, 47n
Constraint plane, 36
Consumer surplus, 13
Contestability, xiii, 1n, 298, 303
Costless exit, 303
Costs
  fixed, 6
  transaction, 195
Courville, 61

Das, xi, 96
Davis, 19n
Deadweight loss, 185
Declining block rates tariff, 192, 213
Demand, elastic/inelastic portion of, 32
Demand elasticity, 122
  relation to marginal revenue, 31
Demand function, 26, 26n
Demsetz, xiii, 297, 298

Dependent risk, 100
Discount rate, 171
Discrimination, price, 72
Diseconomies of scale, 6
Duopoly, natural, 8

Economic profits, 34
Economies of scale, 5, 5n
  pecuniary/nonpecuniary, 5n
Economies of scope, 8
Elasticity of demand, 122
  net, 139
  relation to marginal revenue, 31
Elastic portion of demand, 32
Entry
  free, 303
  hit-and-run, 304
Erikson, 4
Excess profits, 34
Exit, costless, 303
Expansion path, 24
Expected profit, 98
Expected profit hill, 99, 100

Fair rate of return, 20, 34n
Faulhaber, 299, 311
Feasible profit, 37
Finsinger and Vogelsang, xii, 178, 178n,
  187–190. See also Vogelsang and Fin-
  singer
First-best outcome, 16, 69
Fixed costs, 6
Fixed proportions production, 55n
Flat-rate bias, 211
Flat-rate service, 192
Franchise, monopoly, xiii, 298
Free entry, 303

Goldplating, 53
Good luck, 98
Good-luck profit hill, 99

Hit-and-run entry, 304
Homothetic production function, 47, 47n
Houthakker, 241n

ISS. See Incremental subsidy surplus
  scheme
Incentive compatible, 3n
Incremental subsidy surplus scheme, xii,
  182–183
Independent risk, 100
Inelastic portion of demand, 32
Informational asymmetry, xi, 147
Inframarginal price, 193
Inverted block rates tariff, 192
Invisible hand, 1. See also Visible hand

Isobenefit contour, 129
Isocost-isoquant mapping, 22
Isocost line, 23
Isoprofit contour, 29
Isoquant, 23, 23n

Johnson. See Averch and Johnson
Joskow, 19n

Kafoglis, 2n
Keeler and Small, 241n
Klevorick, 19n. See also Baumol and Kle-
  vorick

Laffont and Tirole, 180n
Laspeyres index, 318, 323
Lee, 141
L-M. See Loeb and Magat
Loeb and Magat, 178–182, 203
Logan et al., 19n
Luck, good/bad, 98

McFadden, 141. See also Train, Mc-
  Fadden, and Ben-Akiva
Magat. See Loeb and Magat
Malone. See Bailey and Malone
Marginal price, 193
Marginal product of labor/capital, 62
Marginal rate of technical substitution,
  23, 61, 62
Marginal revenue, 30
  relation to demand elasticity, 31
Measured service, 192
Merewitz and Pozdena, 141
Mohring, 241n
Monopoly, natural, 1, 12
Monopoly franchise, xiii, 298
MRTS. See marginal rate of technical sub-
  stitution
Multipart tariff, xiii, 191
Myerson. See Baron and Myerson

Natural duopoly, 8
Natural monopoly, 1, 12
Nonpecuniary economies of scale, 5n
Nonproductive capital, 53

Off-peak period, 244
One-part tariff, 191, 191n
Optimal outcome, 13
  first-best/second-best, 16
Optional tariffs. See Self-selecting tariffs
Outlay schedule, 213

Panzar, xiii, 230, 298. See also Baumol,
  Panzar, and Willig; Panzar and Willig
Panzar and Willig, 299

Pareto improvement/dominance, 228
Peak period, 244
Pecuniary economies of scale, 5n
Peles and Stein, 96
Permissible prices under V-F, 149, 156
Peterson, 61n
Posner, xiii, 4, 297, 298, 302
Pozdena. *See* Merewitz and Pozdena
Present value, 171
Price caps, 317
Price discrimination, 72, 88
Prices
  marginal/inframarginal, 193
  permissible under V-F, 149, 156
  Ramsey, xii, 116
  sustainable, 306
  time-of-use, xii, 239
Price schedule, 213
Principal-agent problem, 3n
Production function, 26
  fixed-proportions, 55n
  homothetic, 47, 47n
Profit, 13
  allowed, 37
  economic, 34
  excess, 34
  feasible, 37
Profit hill, 28, 28n, 36
  expected, 99, 100
  good luck/bad luck, 99
  silhouette, 39
  sliced-off, 37
Pseudorevenue, 151
Public utilities, 3. *See also* Natural monopoly

Ramsey, xii, 116
Ramsey prices, xii, 116
Ramsey rule, 126
Rate of return, 33
  fair, 20, 34n
Rate-of-return regulation, 33
Resale markets, 91
Return-on-cost regulation, 71, 81–82, 82n
Return-on-output regulation, 70, 72, 72n
Return-on-sales regulation, 71, 80–81, 80n
Returns to scale, constant, 47n
Reynolds. *See* Schwartz and Reynolds
Riordan, xiii, 239, 240, 247–252, 258–261
Riordan and Sappington, 181n
Risk, independent/dependent, 100
ROC. *See* Return-on-cost regulation
ROO. *See* Return-on-output regulation
ROR. *See* Rate-of-return regulation
ROS. *See* Return-on-sales regulation

Sappington, xii, 148, 156n, 180n. *See also* Riordan and Sappington; Sappington and Sibley
Sappington and Sibley, xii, 178, 178n, 182–187, 187n, 203
Scale
  diseconomies of, 6
  economies of, 5, 5n
Schmalensee, 88
Schwartz and Reynolds, 298, 305
Scope, economies of, 5, 5n, 8
Second-best outcome, 16, 70
Self-selecting tariffs, xiii, 263
Sharkey, 297, 299, 308, 311
Sibley, xiii, 263–266, 284–291. *See also* Bawa and Sibley; Sappington and Sibley
Small. *See* Keeler and Small
Spann, 61n
S-S. *See* Sappington and Sibley
Stein. *See* Peles and Stein
Steiner, 241n
Strategic response, 164
Subadditivity, 11
Surplus
  consumer, 13
  improvement, 228
  total, 4, 12, 69
Surplus subsidy schemes, 177–178
  approximate incremental, 187
  incremental, xii, 182
Sustainable prices, 306

Takayama, 19n
Tariff, xii, 191
  block rates, 192, 214
  multipart, xiii, 191
  one-part, 191, 191n
  Pareto-dominating, 230
  self-selecting, xiii, 263
  time-of-use, xii, 239
  usage/access, 191, 197
Taylor, 198n
Threshold under block rates tariff, 217
  optimal, 227
Time-of-use prices, xii, 239
Tirole. *See* Laffont and Tirole
Townsend, xii, 166
Train, 141, 208, 278. *See also* Train, McFadden, and Ben-Akiva
Train, McFadden, and Ben-Akiva, 209, 211
Transaction costs, 195

Uncertainty, 15
Usage/access tariff, 191, 197
Usage charge, 192

Varian, 88
V-F. *See* Vogelsang and Finsinger
Visible hand, 2. *See also* Invisible hand
Vogelsang. *See* Acton and Vogelsang;
    Finsinger and Vogelsang; Vogelsang
    and Finsinger
Vogelsang and Finsinger, xii, 147–175,
    202
Voluntary tariffs. *See* Self-selecting tariffs

Waste, 169
  pure, 53
Williamson, xiii, 241n, 298, 301, 314
Willig, xiii, 230, 298. *See also* Baumol, Bai-
    ley, and Willig; Baumol, Panzar, and
    Willig; Panzar and Willig

Zajac, 2n, 20, 309
Zero-profit contour, 29, 128